In a Rebellious Spirit

John Phillip Reid

In a
Rebellious
Spirit

THE ARGUMENT OF FACTS, THE LIBERTY RIOT, AND THE COMING OF THE AMERICAN REVOLUTION

The Pennsylvania State University Press
University Park and London

Library of Congress Cataloging in Publication Data

Reid, John Phillip.
  In a rebellious spirit.
  Includes bibliographical references and index.
  1. Law—Massachusetts—History and criticism.
  2. Massachusetts—History—Prerevolutionary period, ca. 1766–
  1775. 3. Law—United States—History and criticism.
  I. Title.
  KFM2478.R43   340′.09744   78-50065
  ISBN 0-271-00202-6

For
Macdonald and Agnes Smith Budd
of Monroe Place

That in general, our opposition to the Stamp-Act
has been highly approved of in England,—except
the acts of violence,—the destruction and plunder
of private property; which tho' generally
disapproved among us, and executed by Men not all
concerned in our cause, who, taking occasion from
the tumults which oppression naturally produces,
to perpetuate their evil designs without discovery,
furnish the enemies of the colonies, (authors of
their oppression, and consequently of all the
tumults and disorders arising therefrom) with
arguments which they are glad to improve against
them, and endeavour to impute to the general body
of the inhabitants, whom they would represent as
actuated by a rebellious spirit, disaffected to the
legal government of their country.

—*A private letter quoted in the* Boston Evening
Post, *3 March 1766.*

Contents

1

An Appearance of Tranquility

INTRODUCTION

Law and history must be approached with caution. Although often mixed, they do not mix well. To employ history as legal precedent is to tempt the anger of Clio. To use legal briefs, litigation, or forensic confrontation as historical evidence of motivations is to run the risk of distortion and misinterpretation. The historian cannot treat the words of a lawyer speaking professionally as the words of a nonlawyer might be treated. All too often what an individual says while engaged in a forensic argument tells us not what that person thought, but what he wanted someone else to think. Historians cannot rely on an argument of facts as evidence of events that have occurred or explanations of why those events occurred. It may be—in truth it is most likely—that a forensic argument of facts is evidence only of what the arguer wanted someone to believe had occurred or why it had occurred.

During the stamp-act crisis of 1765, when mobs moved freely on the streets of Boston, Governor Francis Bernard of Massachusetts Bay was a man besieged. Then, as whigs anticipated repeal of the act, a period of good feelings and political calm reigned in the colony. "There is such an appearance of tranquility that I may remain here a cypher some time longer," the governor then wrote London.[1] When we read this statement our first reaction is to think that Bernard was fearful of events or had been fearful at the time of the stamp-act riots. Far more likely, the words do not reveal that the governor, in fact, was afraid of Boston's mob. He may have been but it is not certain. Rather, what the words reveal is that Bernard wanted his superiors in Great Britain to believe that he was afraid.

Francis Bernard, when he wrote of "an appearance of tranquility," was not so much reporting a fact as using a fact to make an argument. He had a case to win and that case was a forensic case. He was making an argument of law, not an argument of fact.

Other imperial officials representing Great Britain on the North American continent would argue the same case, although not all saw the need until the prerevolutionary crisis erupted. "I do not believe," Thomas Hutchinson, who was lieutenant governor and chief justice of Massachusetts, had written before the stamp-act riots occurred, "that the officers of the customs are better supported in the execution' of their trust in any government upon the continent than they are in this." Within less than a year, all would change. "In the capital towns of several of the colonies, & of this in particular, the authority is in the populace," Hutchinson was to write, "no law can be carried into execution against their mind. I am not sure that the Acts of Trade will not be considered as grievous as the stamp act. I doubt whether at present, any custom house office would venture to make a seizure."[2]

It is worth a moment to be certain that we do not misunderstand what Hutchinson said. It is not a matter of legal definitions or statutory implications that worries him, but of law enforcement. In May 1765, he was not claiming that Americans were reconciled to the novelty of imperial taxation, only that the local colonial government was capable of enforcing the customs laws. In March 1766, he says much more than that the government is helpless. Government, Hutchinson asserts, has slipped into the hands of the "populace." He exaggerates, of course, but foretells the future. It will be a decade before the imperial influence is erased. What has occurred during the ten months from the first to the second letter is the beginning of a stalemate between the institutions of local government and the institutions of imperial government, a struggle between whig and tory that will be marked by the slow growth of whig "law" on one hand, the steady erosion of imperial authority on the other.

Writing less than two weeks before Hutchinson's second letter, Governor Bernard described the current conditions of law with far more accuracy. The executive council, from which he had to obtain consent for any gubernatorial action, was elected by the house of representatives, whose members, in turn, were elected by those citizens qualified to vote at town meetings. "The people," Bernard explained, "have felt their strength, and flatter themselves that it is much greater than it is; and will not, of their own accord, submit readily to any thing they do not like; and there is no internal principle of policy which can by any means restore the power of Government, and enforce a due subordination. In this Province (which, though Royal in appointment of a Governor, is democratical in all its other parts, especially in, what is frequently regretted, the appointment of the Council) the springs of Government are so relaxed, that they can never recover their tone again by any power of their own."[3]

Much had happened in just two years. As late as 1764, Thomas Hutchinson believed, Americans would never have dreamed of denying the supremacy of parliament. Then came the sugar act of that year, raising for the first time the constitutional question of "how far the Parliament of right might impose taxes upon them." The stamp act of 1765 furnished London's answer to the question. The American crowds that rose up in most of the mainland colonies provided a different answer. They forced all the stamp agents to resign and saw to it that no stamps were ever issued. Parliament, they believed, had exceeded its constitutional authority—the constitution was to be their guide throughout a decade of controversy with the mother country—and when parliament disagreed, the "mobs" took to the streets, not to oppose the constitution, but to uphold it. They won their point, though not the principle. Parliament repealed the stamp act and at the same time reasserted its supremacy. Then, as if to prove its own point, parliament reduced the duty on molasses to one penny a gallon. It was a tax pure and simple, a revenue measure, not even disguised as an effort to protect the sugar islands of the British West Indies, marking a definite departure from the old mercantilism that had levied duties only for the purpose of regulating commerce. Once again the American crowd arose.[4]

On the eleventh of March 1766, William Jenkins, a customs officer at Newburyport, went to the neighboring town of Salisbury and there seized a schooner. Before he got the vessel back to Newburyport, as Bernard explained, "the same were beset by six Boats full of armed Men in Disguise, which took the Boat and Goods from the said Officer by Force, together with the Boat he went down in, leaving him and his Men on the Beach all Night in a Snow Storm." The quotation is from the governor's proclamation offering a reward for the "discovery" of the perpetrators. A futile gesture, according to Hutchinson. "A proclamation with promise of reward upon discovery," he lamented, "is nothing more than the shew of authority, no man will venture a discovery and I imagine a few more such instances will make it settled law that no act but those of our own legislature can bind us."[5]

Again it is well to mark the chief justice's words. He speaks of "settled law" not lawlessness or even public opinion. Once more Hutchinson exaggerates, though he is less in error than premature. It was not yet "settled law" that acts of parliament had no force in Massachusetts Bay. It was only in the area of taxation for the purpose of raising a revenue that the whigs asserted "that no act but those of our own legislatures can bind us." We may think of many explanations why the reward offered by Governor Bernard was never collected, but all lead to the principal reason: that too large a part of the population believed the sugar act unconstitutional and agreed that necessity made forcible resistance either lawful or, at least, not unlawful. "Upon this occasion," Bernard observed, "People do not wonder at the goods being rescued, but at an Officer's being so hardy & foolish as to seize them & think he would be able to retain them."[6]

There were other "rescues" that year. Indeed, for every seizure there was a rescue. From the standpoint of law, the most revealing occurred at Falmouth, the small colonial seaport that has since grown into the city of Portland in the state of Maine. Francis Waldo, collector of the port, and Arthur Savage, the comptroller, armed with a writ of assistance, searched the home of Enock Itsley. There they found contraband sugar and rum which the officers marked forfeited "and put a Lock upon the Door of the Store house." They had hoped to transport the property away as quickly as possible but no citizen would rent them a wagon. They had no alternative but to place the building under the guard of Joseph Noyes, deputy sheriff of Cumberland County, giving him a warrant they had obtained from a local justice of the peace and ordering him to take whatever steps were necessary to prevent a rescue. Again we may turn to the governor's proclamation for the remainder of the story. In the evening, just as it was growing dark,

> a Number of People assembled and beset the House of the said Comptroller, to which the Collector and Comptroller had retired, it being near the House of the said *Itsley,* and pelted it with Clubs and Stones with Intermissions, untill past ten o'Clock; during which time, as it is supposed, the Goods were removed; And at nine o'Clock the next Morning the Collector found that all the said Goods were missing from the said Store-house, and the said *Enoch Itsley* denied that he knew by whom they were taken; and the said Deputy-Sheriff declared that he was forcibly borne away by the Mob, and his Pockets rifled, and the Warrant taken from him.[7]

This time it was Bernard, not Hutchinson, who wrote London of the futility of proclamations and the growing acceptance by the local majority of the legitimacy of forcible resistance. "As often as any Seizures are made in this Province, in its present state," he explained, "so often shall I have a proclamation of this kind to issue, which is now become a meer farce of Government; since no one dares to discover or prosecute the Offenders, if they were so disposed." But, of course, the governor added, they were not "so disposed." After all, "the Offenders are some times, as in this Case, the greatest part of the Town," and in Massachusetts, law enforcement depended on public support.[8]

We are primarily interested in conditions that existed in Massachusetts, but it would not do to imply that rescues were unique to that province. Popular resistance to the customs service occurred in virtually every colony, in North Carolina, Rhode Island, New York, Pennsylvania, and Connecticut. And it was not merely the civil authorities, but the military as well who were beginning to feel helpless. Just four days before Bernard wrote of the uselessness of proclamations, the captain of the warship stationed at New Haven for enforcement of the customs law had let London know of his frustrations. There was, he claimed, a "Spirit of Opposition" in "direct contempt of all Government," and unless force was used to crush it, what revenue could be collected would soon be decided by "the caprice of every turbulent Association who fired with the Ideas of imaginary independency and followed by a Mob, [will be able] to plant Obstacles and show Difficulties to the Officer in his Legal Duty."[9]

The last two words contain the crux of the problem: "Legal Duty." Bernard, Hutchinson, and those of their persuasion would have said the same. "Formerly," Bernard wrote the lords of trade, "a rescue was an accidental or occasional Affair; now, it is the natural & certain Consequences of a seizure, & the Effect of a predetermined Resolution that the Laws of Trade shall not be executed." It was a matter of law, and yet even Bernard must have known that his definition of "law" was London's definition, not Boston's. Once it had been Boston's, and it would be again, but for the moment a sense of divided sovereignty reigned, with tories saying that law was the expression of parliament and whigs that law was conformity to the usages and conventions of the constitution.[10]

2

A Mutual Fear

THE AMERICAN BOARD

It was into this world of conflicting definitions of "law" and legal self-help that three of the five commissioners of the American customs stepped on the fifth of November 1767. Their offices had recently been created by act of parliament, and they had been sent to Massachusetts Bay to supervise—a more accurate word would be to "implement"—enforcement of the imperial revenue laws. Two of them had never before been in the colonies and, as they climbed ashore, it must have been a shock to discover one of Boston's famous mobs on hand to greet them.[1]

How unlucky, Commissioner Henry Hulton wrote a sister back in England, to encounter, on his very first day in Boston, a crowd, numbering perhaps a thousand, waiting by the seashore to escort him and his colleagues to their quarters. Even more disturbing, many had "Labels on their breasts" reading "Liberty & Property & no Commissioners." If the words were threats, the newcomers treated them lightly. At least Hulton reported laughing at "em with the rest."[2]

We may imagine that the only native American among the three customs commissioners who landed that day, Charles Paxton, was not amused. Boston-born, he had learned from experience the fury of the local crowd. Long active in the imperial revenue service, Paxton was one of the most unpopular customs officials anywhere in the colonies, and the most vicious mob in Massachusetts history—the stamp-act rioters who gutted the house of Thomas Hutchinson—had also gone after him. It might have done much damage to his property had it not been persuaded he had left Boston and removed his effects from the residence where he lived.[3]

The more militant whigs believed Charles Paxton had gone to London to lobby for creation of the new board, been rewarded with the spoils of office, and, while aboard ship returning to New England, took advantage of their isolation to poison the minds of other imperial officials against his fellow colonials. Bostonians had not cared for him earlier; now they bore him a grudge. They did not want the customs commissioners in their town and thought Boston had become the board's headquarters due to Paxton. Considering the geography of the continent, Samuel Adams would argue, it had been illogical to locate the commissioners "almost at one end of it." The explanation was Paxton. He had a house in town and "a large Field of revenge to satisfy."[4]

While we may smile at the idea that the ministry placed the commissioners in Boston to satisfy Paxton's thirst for personal vengeance, it would be unwise to laugh at Adams's assertion. Too many whigs thought it made sense. There were reasons to believe that Paxton had as strong a grudge against his native town as it had against him, and there were, as we shall see, even stronger grounds for suspecting that he wanted a regiment of regular troops stationed in the Bay colony to bolster the tory element of the population as well as support the revenue service. How better show London the need for bringing a military force to Massachusetts than by providing proof that important imperial officials could not function in its capital? After accepting the premises, it was not difficult—indeed it was logical—to conclude that the commissioners of the American customs had been placed in Boston, rather than in more centrally located Philadelphia or Charleston, to provoke a riot.[5]

There can be little doubt that there were whigs in Boston who worried that the mob might rise against the customs commissioners. It was fast becoming accepted legal theory that unconstitutional statutes required no obedience, and as Thomas Hutchinson noted less than a year after the commissioners arrived, "the people" believed that the customs board was an "unconstitutional" innovation. Disobedience, however, did not mean violence, at least until violence became necessary. The whig concern was that the crowd might act for the wrong reasons. On the very day that collection of the new duties prescribed by the Townshend Acts was to commence, three days after the commissioners had taken the oath of office, a town meeting was convened for apparently no other purpose than to calm public opinion. The moderator, James Otis, made a long, rambling speech in which he seemed to support the pretensions of the imperial government. Many months earlier he had been reported by Governor Bernard to have told another town meeting that "the Merchants were great Fools if they submitted any longer to the Laws restraining their Trade, which ought to be free." Now he surprised some listeners by arguing that the customs commissioners had been lawfully appointed and should be respected as representatives of the crown. Too many

7

people, he warned, were mistakenly confusing the new revenue measure with the new board, and there was talk "that we must get rid of the latter to avoid the former." The thought was absurd, just as "it was absurd to suppose that the commissioners had the least hand or influence in laying or procuring those duties."[6]

When a newspaper reported the speech, Otis claimed that he had been misunderstood. The point he had made, Otis asserted, was that the tax, not the commissioners, was the "Matter of Grievance, and this I think is a great One." Violence directed against the men sent to collect the new duties would not repeal those duties. If, Otis wrote, "to disapprove of all tumultuous and riotous Proceedings, and upon all proper Occasions to bear my most humble testimony against them is to be a *Tory* I am, and ever have been so far a *Tory*. On the other Hand if to *stand* like *Men* for the *Rights* of *Men* be a distinguishing Characteristic of the *Whigs,* I hope I am, and ever shall be, so far a *Whig*."[7]

Whatever Otis may have intended to say about the constitutionality of the customs board, and whether anyone understood or agreed with it, his call for restraint surely reflected the prevailing opinion that day. Taking "into Consideration the ill conduct of some evil-minded Persons, tending to excite Tumults and Disorders," the assembled people "unanimously voted their Abhorrence of any such Measures, and that they would use their utmost Endeavours to preserve Peace and good Order."[8]

Both the calling of the town meeting and the resolution itself are important. They show that many Bostonians were concerned that even if the commissioners had not come to provoke a riot, their presence was provocative. Just as significant was James Otis's fear that he had been misunderstood. His clarification may have enlightened some Boston whigs, but the distinction between legal opposition to parliament's laws and unnecessary violence was lost on most tories. When imperial officials such as the commissioners of the customs encountered American opposition to British statutes, they thought it a problem of law enforcement, not a question of constitutionality. Their reaction was not to try persuasion but to call for the army. Typical of tory attitudes were the predilections of customs Commissioner Henry Hulton, and it would be well to understand what he was thinking and why. If the vote of the Boston town meeting tells us that some whigs were fearful the board might provoke a riot, Hulton tells us what was on the worried minds of imperial officials.

From the moment he landed in Boston, Hulton knew he was surrounded by people who did not think of or define "law" in the same way as did he. It was, he would later write, a matter of regret that Americans had not been taught a lesson during the stamp-act crisis. Measures should have been taken to enforce the stamp tax as well as every statute of parliament. Outright repeal of the stamp act had been a mistake not only because it allowed Americans to think they had scored a political triumph but because it permitted them to assert a constitutional precedent based on their peculiar legal theory. At the very least the ministry should have retained a duty on "some articles of little consequence." Had that been done, "the authority [to tax] would have been supported, and there might have been a better plea for altering the mode of taxation from that to other articles." Thus the timing of the Townshend duties on paper, glass, painters' colors, and tea had proved a serious blunder. "[A]s the Stamp Act had been repealed the year before, it was very extraordinary that fresh duties shou[l]d be imposed, and no effectual measures taken to support the authority of government, or conciliate the minds of the people."[9]

A point must be repeated so that it may be emphasized. Hulton viewed the growing conflict between Great Britain and her North American colonies not as a constitutional controversy but as a failure of law enforcement. "We have an arduous task," he warned in 1769, "but the raising of a Revenue is only a secondary consideration until the authority of the Laws is restored." Years later, after the constitutional debate had grown into armed rebellion, Hulton still viewed matters in the same terms. "Most people of property," he recalled, "were averse to the new Laws of Parliament, and no Magistrate would stand forth to support the officer whose duty it was to carry them into execution." Indeed, any official who attempted to enforce the imperial revenue acts "was exposed to [the mob's] resentment, without the least probability of receiving any protection." An imperial police force, independent of local control, was needed to deal with people so unruly as Americans, a fact especially true for Bostonians whom, Hulton believed, had lost all respect for law. "Contention and broil seem necessary to the existence of a Bostonian," he once observed, and there were many, very many, in and out of government, who agreed.[10]

Governor Bernard was one of those concurring. Lack of imperial law enforcement was especially perilous in Boston, he believed, because the people were so easily swayed to violence by ambitious and unscrupulous leaders. An alarming instance had occurred after the speech in which James Otis warned that local merchants would be "Fools" to submit any longer to British trade laws. He did not report Otis's words to London until nine months after they were uttered, following the rescue of seized property from the customs service that had so alarmed Thomas Hutchinson. Bernard then implied there was a cause-and-effect relationship between the speech and the wave of violence against the revenue agents.

"It was observed by serious Men," he told the Earl of Shelburne, "that *Otis* had thereby made himself answerable for all the disturbances which should thereafter happen in the execution of the Laws of Trade." The "natural Consequence" of that speech, "& what immediately followed was, that a common talk prevailed among the People that there should be no more Seizures [by the customs service of contraband property] in this Town." Since that time, all seizures made in Massachusetts Bay had been "rescued with a high hand." This development was alarming, to be sure, yet another event occurred that, the governor implied, was even more troublesome. During a "rescue" staged in Boston, a merchant using force to prevent seizure by customs officers of goods he had imported illegally "sent for *Otis,* & he went thither as his Councillor."[11]

Francis Bernard had a marvelous talent for dramatizing his difficulties. When his letter arrived in London the lords of trade may well have imagined that affairs had reached a strange turn in Massachusetts Bay. Merchants were not only rescuing goods seized by revenue agents, they were acting on advice of their lawyers. Little wonder there had been no arrests and that Chief Justice Hutchinson was predicting none would be made. Those who read the letter probably thought Bernard was exaggerating, and he was—but not by much.

3

A House Besieged

THE MALCOM AFFAIR

Francis Bernard did not use the word "riot" when telling London about the affair in which James Otis served as "Councillor" to that Boston merchant opposing enforcement of British revenue laws. Other imperial officials, however, did call it a riot and a riot was what most observers in Great Britain understood had occurred. The English attorney general was asked to rule whether laws had been broken and the event was considered important enough to be raised in the house of commons. Moreover, the commissioners of the customs, even though the incident occurred before they came to America, cited it along with subsequent "rescues" as evidence proving the need for imperial law enforcement. Although we can never be certain, it seems a reasonable guess that Charles Paxton used it to persuade his two British-born colleagues that they would find the streets of Boston unsafe. We should, therefore, take a look at the Malcom affair, a prerevolutionary episode that imperial officials called a riot and American whigs described as a harmless gathering. It may well be that some of the most famous of Boston's prerevolutionary riots were not what we would call riotous.[1]

Captain Daniel Malcom had a home on Fleet Street in Boston that apparently doubled as his place of business and a storehouse for some of his goods. On 24 September 1766, Benjamin Hallowell, comptroller of the port of Boston, and William Sheaffe, deputy collector, accompanied by Benjamin Cudworth, deputy sheriff of Suffolk County, and two tide-waiters named Ambrose Vincent and Lewis Turner, arrived at Malcom's door, intent on inspecting the premises for "customable" products. The comptroller and collector were the ranking officials of the port, two men doing roughly the same job the whigs contended, a multiplicity of offices serving little purpose except to furnish lucrative incomes to Englishmen

11

possessing influence at home. They had a point, although London did not think so. The comptroller was supposed to keep an eye on the collector, who, if left unsupervised, might succumb to local influence and bribery. There was also a surveyor general with continental jurisdiction who was responsible for checking both the collector and comptroller in each seaport while they checked one another.[2]

Boston's collector was Charles Paxton, then in London lobbying for the reforms that would be enacted in 1767, and Sheaffe, along with Hallowell, was in charge of the port. The two men had information that Malcom had "run" goods ashore without entering them at the customshouse; information, the surveyor general, John Temple, wrote, "I believe was good."[3]

Between eight and nine o'clock in the morning according to the customs men, at "about eight" according to Malcom, the five officials arrived at Malcom's brick house. A whig newspaper would report that they tried to force their way in, but as they will remain scrupulously careful throughout the day to observe the law we may dismiss that accusation. They were too cautious to have committed so glaring a blunder at the very start of their investigation. Malcom did not accuse them of unlawful entry. He said he was upstairs and, hearing a noise, went down where he found Sheaffe and Hallowell "in my Parlour, which surprized me much to see those Gentlemen there as it was so early in the Morning."[4] They told him they wanted to search the house for uncustomed goods and Malcom showed them over the premises, permitting them to open chests and closet doors until they came to a room in the cellar that was locked. He could not let them in there, he told Hallowell, as it was used and occupied by Captain William Mackay who had the only key. Deputy Collector Sheaffe was sent to find Mackay, whom Hallowell called Malcom's "friend and partner."[5]

When Sheaffe returned with Mackay, the customs men demanded the door be opened. There was no key, Mackay announced, and Malcom refused to allow anyone to force the lock, stating emphatically that "if any Man attempted it he should blow his Brains out." Hallowell, probably wanting witnesses, called in the two tidewaiters and the deputy sheriff. Malcom did not back down. He "Repeated his Threats of Blowing any persons Brains out that should touch a Door of his and went and took a Pistol in his hand and soon after another and then put on a sword and swore by God that no Officer would touch anything in his House and that he Could have Assistance Enough." Such, at least, was the story told by Hallowell and Sheaffe. Later, Malcom did not deny the threat, but put it in a context that made it quite a different matter from the point of view of law. Hallowell, he claimed, voiced the first threat. When Captain

Mackay told him that he could not open the door as he had no key, the comptroller "swore" he would break it open and asked Malcom if he knew who he was. "I told him I did and that he was a dirty fellow," Malcom wrote. "I told him also that the first Man that would break open my House without having Legal Authority for the same, I would kill him on the Spot, then he said he would, and I said why dont you, who hinders you." It was only after Hallowell "threatened to have me tryed for my life," which "made my Passion rise," that Malcom seized his pistols, buckled on his sword, and ordered the officials "to be gone immediately out of my House." Neither of the pistols had "Flint nor anything else within them."[6]

We must believe Malcom rather than Hallowell. Throughout the day both he and Mackay would prove that they had been well tutored in the law. It served the customs men's purpose to report the threat of violence and omit the qualification that it would be used only against someone forcing the locked door "without having Legal Authority." To say that, and no more, made it appear that Malcom was prepared to resist under any circumstances and that they had no alternative but to back away from bloodshed. Actually, Malcom told them, as the town of Boston put it, they could enter the closed room "at their Peril," meaning at their legal peril. By saying he would use force if they acted without lawful authority, he was removing any possibility that they could argue he had not been emphatic enough or that they had misunderstood him. Malcom did not have to intend the use of force. He had reason to put the pistols in his hands even if they were unloaded.[7]

Each side knew precisely what it was doing. Both kept the situation within acceptable bounds though at times the atmosphere grew quite tense. Malcom and Hallowell disliked one another. Hallowell's house had been sacked on the night of the famous stamp-act riot, much as had the house of Chief Justice Thomas Hutchinson, and there was some suspicion Malcom had been a leader of the mob. According to the tidewaiters, Malcom threatened Hallowell with more of the same. If he invaded people's houses, Malcom warned, the comptroller might be revisited by the Boston crowd. "[I]t would be no Difficulty," Hallowell snapped back, "to fix on one, two, or three Persons that were Principally Concern[e]d in the mob, and that he [sic] the said Malcom had better be quiet on that Lead."[8]

The deputy sheriff apparently became uneasy that Hallowell would fall into Malcom's legal trap by losing his temper and acting rashly. He sought to protect himself by letting everyone know beforehand that he was not a party. He had, the deputy assured Mackay, "no Authority to break any Place open,"[9] and called out to Malcom, "I hope you are not angry with me, . . . I have nothing against you or yours, nor I don't know what the Officer brought me here for." Malcom seized the opportunity to restate his legal position. "No, Mr. Cudworth I am not, but if you have anything against me or my Property do your Duty, only mind to do nothing but according to Law."[10]

By noon the affair had reached an impasse, the customs officers withdrew, and Malcom walked down to the exchange where the merchants usually gathered at lunchtime. There he again was approached by Hallowell and Sheaffe, who offered "to give up our own parts of such goods as might be Seized." Malcom refused to compromise and once more challenged them to test the law. "I told them if they had a Right to break open my House they might, but if they persisted in breaking open my House I would take all Legal Methods to have myself righted." They would not get into that locked cellar room except "by breaking open my House."[11]

The officers might have abandoned the effort then and there, knowing they would never again be admitted through Malcom's front door, but if they were to submit a report to London that convincingly depicted the helplessness of their situation there were certain formalities to be pursued. First they went to the governor, who, luckily for them, was meeting with the council. Together the governor and council constituted the highest executive authority in Massachusetts, and if they either refused to aid the customs service or could not do so, Hallowell and Sheaffe would be able to lay a pretty tale indeed before their superiors in the mother country. We need not be surprised that the council, whose members were chosen by the popularly elected lower house of the general court, declined to furnish assistance, and the governor, appointed by the crown and in no respect answerable to the people of Massachusetts Bay, did what little he could.

Of course, the council claimed it was eager to enforce the law. It always said that much, but there was nothing it could do or even had to do. As the high sheriff of Suffolk "has it in his power to raise the *Posse Comitatus,* any aid from his Excellency and the Board does not appear at present to be needful."[12] The answer was typical of those Governor Bernard had come to expect from the council. Imperial law was not directly challenged. The customs officials had a job to do, but it was not the council's constitutional task to lend a hand. The high sheriff, not the members of the council, was empowered to enforce British statutes. The suggestion that he could always raise the *posse comitatus*—"the power of the county" or the people—might be ridiculous in whig Boston, but it was the law and not even the British ministry could fault the council for adhering to the law.

Bernard did not press the issue. The council would not change its mind. Sending for Stephen Greenleaf, high sheriff of Suffolk County, the governor ordered him to apply to several justices of the peace who lived in the vicinity of Malcom's house "for their Aid and Assistance" and "if needful to Raise his Posse Comitatus."[13]

The three men—Hallowell, Sheaffe, and Greenleaf—went first to Foster Hutchinson, brother of the lieutenant governor, who was both a justice of the peace and judge on the Suffolk inferior court. He gave Greenleaf a warrant "directed to the Civil Officers Commanding them to be Aiding and assisting us to Enter the House and Cellar of said Danl Malcom." A lawyer might have said the warrant was unnecessary—in fact both the chief justice and the attorney general had recently ruled that Massachusetts justices were not "impowered to grant Warrants to break open stores or other houses to search for customable goods"—but legal opinions were beside the point.[14] Officials enforcing imperial law in whig Boston moved cautiously and Sheriff Greenleaf was no exception. He probably was thinking less that the warrant gave him additional authority should Malcom oppose his entry into the cellar than that it provided additional justification to defend himself should Malcom sue him for trespass.

Armed with Foster Hutchinson's warrant, the three officials arrived at Malcom's house to find the place prepared to withstand a siege. The gate was bolted, the front door closed, and the shutters fastened across the windows. A crowd had gathered and Greenleaf persuaded two of Malcom's neighbors to call to him. No answer was returned and no one tried to open the gate. After standing around for half an hour, Greenleaf left to find John Ruddock, a justice of the peace whom the governor had ordered the sheriff to consult. Ruddock was a militia captain and the sheriff was told to tell him to "Raise his said Company and Put them under Arms if Necessary."[15]

We may well wonder what Sheriff Greenleaf hoped to accomplish when he went to the house of John Ruddock. The man was not only a justice of the peace but a militant whig. He had been elected a selectman the previous March, and received 83 votes in the balloting for Boston's representatives to the lower house during May, not enough to win one of the town's four seats but a good indication that the people knew where his principles lay. With such credentials he was not likely to cooperate with Greenleaf.

When the sheriff suggested that Ruddock call out his militia company the justice replied that he "had Dismissed all my people last Monday with an intent to Enlist them a New,"[16] and "had not then Authority to Command One single Man."[17] Greenleaf may have been amazed at the audacity of the answer, but having anticipated a direct refusal he could not quarrel with a man who gave him an excuse for not pursuing an impossible task.

Greenleaf tried another approach. Would Ruddock come anyway, as a justice of the peace, without his "battery" and do what he could to "Preserve the Peace," the sheriff asked. Ruddock replied "that he was a Very Heavy Man and Unable to Walk far that if he went at all he must be Carried in his Chaise and that he tho't that his going could be of very little Service." It was true he was fat—six years later when he died the justice was said to weigh "between 5 and 600 weight"—but that never stopped him from exerting himself when whig rather than imperial law had to be enforced. During March 1769, for example, he would engage in fisticuffs with British soldiers disturbing the whig peace and he was always available to fill the magistrate's chair when there were tories to be arraigned.[18]

Granting that John Ruddock had no intention of aiding the customs service, it must be conceded that he had been correct when he told the sheriff he "could be of very little Service." Had the crowd gathered at Malcom's house gotten out of hand, Greenleaf would have found the justice—any justice—useful as he needed a magistrate to proclaim a riot, but aside from that possibility Ruddock had no role to play. He possessed no more authority than the sheriff, the comptroller, or the deputy collector to force Malcom to open the cellar door.

Considering the odds against obtaining cooperation, we surely must ask what Greenleaf had in mind. Although he may have wanted Ruddock around to quiet the crowd—the man possessed great prestige among the whigs—it is also possible he was seeking to protect himself from the criticism of Bernard and Thomas Hutchinson by making every effort to enforce the law before giving up the task as hopeless. He seems, however, to have been ordered to visit Ruddock by the governor, perhaps going also at the urging of Hallowell and Sheaffe, and the most likely explanation why he was sent is that the imperial officials were gathering evidence. It was well known in America that justices and other local officials would not support the customs service, but that fact was not fully appreciated in London. Hallowell and Sheaffe would report Ruddock's refusal but not Ruddock's contention that it was not "my duty as a Justice to be an Assistant in Person to a Sheriff and Custom house Officers, and wou'd sooner resign my Commission than Disgrace the Dignity of a Justice So Much."[19]

John Ruddock may have wanted no part of the Malcom affair, but there were other magistrates in Boston and Sheriff Stephen Greenleaf was not completely rebuffed, as he was able to persuade Justice of the

Peace John Tudor to return with him to the house. The two agreed that Tudor would mix among the people, talk with them, and report their attitudes to the sheriff. Later, according to Greenleaf, the magistrate "told him and the Custom house Officers that he found that the People were determined to with stand them in every Attempt to force Capt[ai]n Malcom's house."[20] The sheriff then decided to play the last act in the drama. He had only one deputy in Boston. If he were to force his way into Malcom's house where, he was told, perhaps four men were hidden, Greenleaf needed the *posse comitatus*. Should the people refuse to join, he would be able to document their hostility without taking measures that might precipitate overt acts of opposition.

Greenleaf went over to the crowd. He had faced mobs before and would do so again for he was sheriff throughout the entire prerevolutionary period. He was also a tory, though at the moment a rather popular one, for just a few months earlier he had let it be known he would disobey the stamp act and serve unstamped writs. While perhaps not an act of political courage, it indicated that crown officials were not united, and Greenleaf's announcement had drawn a round of applause from the Boston town meeting. Now, in front of Malcom's house, the crowd, while hostile toward his intentions, was not unfriendly toward his person or his office, but it was about to give him a lesson in whig law.[21]

Sheriff Greenleaf said that he "expostulated" with the people for "sometime" and "was Civilly treated by them." He knew better than to demand assistance of the *posse comitatus,* so he asked if they would help if requested. A man answered that "he would but he would not Enter the House." That was one solution to the whig dilemma of showing respect for a local official without cooperating with the enforcement of imperial law: state for the record that you supported and did not oppose legal authority, but qualify your support to conform with whig notions of what was legal and what arbitrary. The bulk of the people, however, decided to take a firmer line and perhaps establish an important precedent. The sheriff was told "that no admission into Capt. Malcom's house would be suffered, except the Custom house Officers would go before a Justice and make Oath who their informer was." Greenleaf pointed out that Hallowell and Sheaffe had already made oath to Foster Hutchinson "and that he did not apprehend that the Laws obliged them to tell who their informer was." The crowd replied that it knew better. Officers of the customs had to swear to a warrant naming their informer "before they should go into the House."[22]

Daniel Malcom had said the same after he had locked his gate and shuttered the windows. One of the men waiting with him inside asked why if he and Mackay had no contraband "Effects that was seizable in that Cellar that he did not gratify the Officers." Malcom answered "that they refused bringing the informer which he thinks the law requires and also that Capt. Hallowell used him with great rudeness which had angered him."[23]

We may doubt if Malcom said precisely what is claimed. He was well versed in law, too well versed to have thought that Hallowell and Sheaffe had no authority to search his house unless their informer accompanied them. What may have been correct—a point in dispute, denied by the British, asserted by American whigs—was the legal point argued by those outside the house: that valid search warrants could be issued only on particular information, sworn to in court, revealing not only what was being looked for but why the officers thought it there.

The whigs probably held the sounder legal position, but whether they did or not is a question best postponed until another is resolved: what were Malcom and his supporters out to prove? Perhaps they were, as Hallowell and Sheaffe believed, protecting uncustomed goods from seizure; then again, it is possible they were seeking to do what Malcom said, to test the law and see where it led.

There are several considerations to take into account—considerations of fact and considerations of constitutional theory—that serve to establish that the whigs both outside and inside Malcom's house were seeking to create a legal precedent. The factual consideration is particularly striking and its significance must be stressed. The crowd gathered in front of Malcom's house did not want the customs officer to swear out a new warrant in order to learn the identity of the informer. It was no secret. He was Ebenezer Richardson and even small schoolboys were shouting his name, saying "that they knew where he lived and that they'd goe and give him three cheers for the great Prize he'd got."[24]

Greenleaf had had experience before with a crowd making "whig law." The day after the stamp-act mob gutted the houses of Comptroller Hallowell and Chief Justice Hutchinson, the governor sent him out to arrest Ebenezer Mackintosh, reputed to be the mob's leader. Quiet was then being maintained in Boston by a band of citizen volunteers patrolling the streets. When the sheriff seized Mackintosh he was not physically opposed. Instead he was told that if Mackintosh was taken to jail there would be no patrols that night. Greenleaf immediately freed his prisoner.[25]

The release of Mackintosh tells us a good deal concerning the sources of law in prerevolutionary Boston. It might be thought that the sheriff of Suffolk County was acknowledging the weakness of imperial law and that there was a point beyond which it could not be enforced. In fact, he was doing more. When he set Mackintosh free Greenleaf was admitting that to enforce any law remotely associated with the political controversy he would have to accept whig-ordained conditions. No whig rioter was again arrested in Boston.[26]

For Greenleaf and a few other officials not directly involved in the constitutional controversy it was a matter of adjustment and mutual tolerance. The people understood and accepted the fact that he had duties to perform. If Hallowell and Sheaffe insisted on forcing their way into Malcom's house and were opposed, he told the crowd, "they knew it was his Duty to command their Assistance, and he hoped that no man there would refuse it, to which the general Voice was, that they hoped no body would hurt him, they knew he was oblidged to do what he did, but they believed that he would have no Assistance except the Informer was discovered or delivered up."[27]

Leaving the crowd, Greenleaf went to consult with Hallowell and Sheaffe. To continue the siege, they told him, "might be attended with most Terrible Consequences." Better to pursue the effort no further—"to quiet the Minds of the Populace and preserve the Peace of the Town"— and so Greenleaf "returned with them to the Province House to inform the Governour of what had passed."[28] They would have had to leave anyway. It was almost evening and the writ of assistance would do them no good once night came on. Writs were valid only during daylight hours.

After it became dark and all was safe, Captain Malcom opened his door and sent a tap of wine—said to be well watered—to the crowd. "Good night to you, Gentlemen," he called out, "we thank you."[29]

A tame event perhaps—no gunplay, no violence, no broken bones. But then most arguments of law are unexciting and what had occurred may fairly be compared to the pretrial maneuvers of lawyers seeking to put their respective cases in the strongest possible position before the main contest begins. The day had ended with the representatives of imperial law in retreat and some of the more militant whigs of Boston drinking from an open tap. But as all participants understood, nothing had been settled. The main struggle was about to begin.

4

A Test of Law

THE USES OF LAW

The Malcom affair was a minor matter, a comedy of blundering revenue officers and barricaded colonials, but were we to dismiss it in haste we might run the risk of dismissing much of the story of the American Revolution. On the surface it seems to have been a riot in defiance of law, and even a lawyer describes it as lawlessness,[1] overlooking the possibility that it could tell much about the true state of law in rebellious Boston. It is law that reveals what the controversy was about, and when we test events by the law of the case we may discover that it was less of a riot than meets the eye.

Contemporaries agreed as to what happened but they did not agree on why or what it meant. Much depended on whether the observer was tory or whig, imperial official or local citizen. Stories about what occurred did not conflict, but emphasis did and contrary interpretations were sent to Great Britain explaining why certain actions had been pursued and others avoided. John Temple, surveyor general of the customs, wrote his superiors that "had the Civil Authority proceeded with that Firmness that (I think) their Duty requires, there is no reason to doubt that a Seizure would have been made of whatever was clandestinely lodged there." The inhabitants of Boston, writing to their agent in London, emphasized quite different facts. Daniel Malcom, they said, had locked himself in his house that afternoon because he believed Hallowell and Sheaffe would return. If they did and attempted to gain entry, he was determined that "it sh[ould] be forceably." His justification was that he had been "assur[e]d from the Declaration of the Person who hired the aforesaid Cellar & his own knowle[d]ge of the other Apartments that no Contraband Goods were there."[2]

We will never know if dutiable items had been hidden in that cellar room, although if we rely on Malcom's reputation as a smuggler, attributed to him largely by officials of the revenue service, the best guess is that there were. But whether there were or not, the questions that deserve to be answered are why (in the words of the surveyor general) the sheriff of Suffolk County did not act with "Firmness," and why (in the words of the inhabitants of Boston) Captain Malcom created a situation in which the customs men could enter his house only if they did so "forceably."

Malcom is the one to consider first, and there are three aspects of his conduct that deserve to be underscored. First, he may have wanted Hallowell and Sheaffe to resort to violence, but he did not initiate any nor did he seek an excuse to start it. Second, as soon as he had the opportunity, he sent for witnesses whom he kept with him until the officers departed. And third, he did not fear prosecution. The collector and comptroller needed evidence before they could proceed by criminal information against him in the admiralty, and unable to get into the cellar room they had no evidence. There was even less concern about the common law. It probably never occurred to Sheriff Greenleaf that Malcom might be charged with an offense. He had long since ceased thinking of such possibilities during controversies involving the customs service. The whigs controlled the Suffolk County juries; the grand jury would not have indicted Malcom and the traverse jury would not have convicted him. When considering the veracity of Malcom's statements, it can be said that whatever other reasons he may have had for coloring the truth, he was not shielding himself from prosecution.

Malcom had waved a pair of pistols but, he insisted, they had neither powder, ball, nor flint. He did not tell that to Hallowell—he had reason not to—and we may suspect that to his dying day Hallowell believed he would have been shot had he tried to force his way into the house. It would be interesting to know what the sheriff thought. There were whigs who warned Greenleaf not to go too far, as Malcom was a resolute man, capable of shooting him. But those who admitted making such statements insisted that they had qualified them by saying Malcom would fire only at a person who broke "open his Doors without first showing him legal Authority."[3] Those who were in the house with Malcom said he had no intention of resorting to violence. "It is my Opinion," one wrote, "that had the Officers shewn Captain Malcom proper Authority he would have opened his Doors, or had they broke his house open there would not have been a hair of their heads hurted by him or anybody in the House."[4] If the officers broke in, Malcom was quoted by another man, "he did not intend to kill or even abuse them but if they proceeded wrong he would trounce them at Law."[5] Or, as Malcom himself said, he intended "to pursue them in Law as far as Justice would go"; that is, he added, if they acted legally "I never would say no more, but was fully determined if they broke open my House to pursue them according to Law, as Long as I had a penny left."[6]

There is a second aspect of Daniel Malcom's conduct that day which must be given a paragraph of attention: his preparations. After Hallowell and Sheaffe left to see the governor and before they returned with the sheriff, Malcom consulted some friends and it was agreed that two of them—John Pigeon and Captain Enoch Rust—would join him and Mackay inside the house. He wanted "Witnesses," Malcom told Pigeon, in the event the customs men "took any measures the laws would not bear them out in he was determined to prosecute them to the utmost Severity of the Law." No firearms were prepared, nor was there to be "any Sign of any Opposition in said House." They would shut themselves in "as fast as possible" and let Hallowell make the first move.[7]

There seems no avoiding the conclusion that Malcom was preparing to fight with law, not with weapons. He said as much to Hallowell and Sheaffe when they asked him to compromise, or so he later claimed. According to him, they not only offered to give up their shares but promised that if any dutiable goods were found in the cellar room "they would not do me any harm." He replied that "if they had a Right to break open my House they might, but if they persisted in breaking open my House I would take all Legal Methods to have myself righted." Every one of the witnesses who said that they had spoken to Malcom agreed that he told them much the same, all of them, that is, except Hallowell, who did not believe Malcom planned a legal case but instead intended to kill whoever battered down his door. Everyone else, including the two tidewaiters, reported that Malcom challenged Hallowell's authority and most knew why he did so.[8]

Reading the depositions almost a century afterward, Horace Gray, a distinguished lawyer who later became a justice on the United States Supreme Court, marveled at the understanding of legal issues displayed by laymen. "The testimony taken on this occasion," he remarked, "shows how well instructed the people were in the principles of law applicable to the case." There was no doubt in Gray's mind that James Otis had been giving lessons.[9]

Bernard said that Malcom sent for Otis, but no witness mentioned seeing him at the house. There had been no need for him to come as he had briefed his client very well. Had Malcom a lawyer whispering advice into each ear he would not have acted differently than he did. His words might have been less passionate, but his deeds would have been the same. The emphatic denial of the customs men's authority backed by gestures that left no room for misinterpretation, the gathering of witnesses, the locking of the house, and the refusal to acknowledge the sheriff out by the gate, all bear indications of acting on legal advice. He had a right to resist illegal entry even under color of authority. His actions, however, had to be reasonable under the circumstances. Thus we may believe Malcom's assertion that his pistols were not loaded. To threaten the officers by blocking their way was one thing, to have used deadly force when his own life was not in danger was another.

Under the circumstances, loaded pistols would have been unreasonable, constituting an offense answerable to an in personam action in the court of admiralty. Had one discharged accidentally, wounding an officer or even a bystander, the bearer could have been indicted at common law and a whig jury would have had to extend the doctrine of self-defense to "unconstitutional" seizures in order to acquit. The wisest course was to stay indoors, not appear at any window, and ignore the shouts from outside. Such conduct not only avoided accusations of refusing to deal with crown officers, it meant that Malcom could not be drawn into an argument that might end in blows.

Perhaps the most telling point is that Malcom provided himself with a factual defense. Moreover, he may have gone to lengths to make certain the customs officers heard and understood that defense because we know all four were impressed by it. The two tidewaiters as well as the collector and comptroller mentioned it in their summaries of the evidence. "Malcom said," they asserted, "that he supposed we Came for his Money and if he had not been at home he imagined we should have taken it out of his Chest."[10]

Could Malcom have meant that he believed these customs men, whose movements were watched by the entire town, had come to his house in broad daylight to rob him of his cash and coins? They would have been arraigned before Justice Ruddock within half an hour. The charge was ridiculous as an explanation of Malcom's reasons for resistance, but not altogether senseless and we may suspect the fine hand of James Otis or some other whig attorney behind it. A lawyer could well have told Malcom to say what he did or something similar. While unlikely, it was not impossible that Malcom might be charged with a crime. At the least, someone could have been accidentally hurt and if Malcom was not acting lawfully he would have been responsible. As a defendant he could not testify in his own behalf, others would have to put his defenses into evidence and there was no better way than by the prosecution's own witnesses during cross-examination. Malcom's lawyer in his summation would have elaborated on the theme that the customs service was a den of thieves from whose grasp no money was safe. It would not have mattered to the Suffolk County jury that the whole idea was absurd. They would have had an excuse to acquit Malcom on the ground he had believed he was defending his property.[11]

We are not yet finished with the Malcom affair. The most important question of all remains to be considered. What has not yet been answered is why Malcom and perhaps Otis planned and executed the particular legal strategy that was followed.

One explanation, of course, is that Malcom had uncustomed goods in his cellar and did not want Sheaffé to seize them. It is surely the most obvious possibility. The fact that a crowd had gathered in front of the house may be evidence that the people of Boston thought Malcom had something to hide and were prepared to defend him against the enforcement of imperial law. But if Malcom had time to consult with a lawyer he probably had time to remove the goods, especially with so many friends on hand. Moreover, why bother with witnesses or go to such lengths to arrange affairs so that the customs officials would have to commit an overt act of force before they could get into the cellar?

It could be argued that by making them break down the door Malcom hoped to guarantee that the crowd would come to his aid. But had he needed to arouse the mob, a passionate, open confrontation on the top step, accompanied by a rousing speech, would have better served his purposes. He had other reasons for the trap he laid.

Considering the evidence as a whole, the question whether there were uncustomed goods in the house becomes immaterial. Whether there were or not, there is no escaping the fact that Malcom was setting the stage for a lawsuit. That is why he had witnesses on hand and wanted Hallowell and Sheaffe to use force. He might have lost any goods seized but would have been able to bring an action for damages had they proceeded without legal authority and, perhaps, he also planned to sue even if they had been acting lawfully under an imperial statute which the whigs of Boston thought unconstitutional.

When the evidence is examined in all its aspects, it is difficult to escape the conclusion that a constitutional principle was being asserted. Hallowell and Sheaffe claimed authority to see what was behind the cellar door, as they themselves put it, "by Virtue of a Writt of Assistance." The writ of assistance was a general writ—that is, a writ issued once and good for innumerable executions—the issuance of which Boston merchants had retained James Otis to oppose earlier in the decade. Charles Paxton had petitioned for its issuance and Otis, in the first significant whig argument before a Massachusetts court, contended that general writs of this type could not legally be granted by colonial judges. Thomas Hutchinson had ruled that they could and issued writs, first to Charles Paxton and later to Benjamin Hallowell.

THE USES OF LAW

There is good reason for thinking that Malcom intended to challenge the validity of writs of assistance. After all, Malcom's lawyer was James Otis, a man who had serious doubts about the legality of general warrants. The writ of assistance was general, not special—granted to a specific customs officer to be used whenever he wished to conduct a search of private property without applying to a court in each instance or even stating his grounds for suspicion. It was, moreover, secret and not subject to delays.[12] The name "assistance," as explained by an English attorney general, came from the fact that the writ was directed to officials and citizens alike, "commanding them to be aiding, assisting and helping the Commissioners of the Customs and their Deputies, Ministers, Servants and other Officers in the Execution of their Duty"; "to see," said Hutchinson, "that the Officers of the Customs are protected & aided & assisted whenever they shall be obstructed in the discharge of their duty." It was, in summary, a search warrant, authorizing customs men during daylight hours to enter and, if necessary, break into warehouses, stores, and homes to search for smuggled goods.[13]

Issued in Massachusetts since 1755, there had been little opposition to the writs until about 1760, probably because they had previously been used to suppress treasonous commerce with France during the Seven Years' War. The sugar act changed the emphasis. Customs officers now demanded that certificates of importation accompany all dutiable goods. Even storekeepers had to have them, especially for such common items as tea, wine, molasses, sugar, and rum—items that changed hands frequently as they were used in money-short America to settle accounts. What the writ of assistance now meant was that officials could enter any store and, on finding customable goods, demand a certificate. Without the document a shopkeeper faced the presumption of illegal importation. As a result there was even greater opposition to the writs of assistance in 1766 than there had been at the time when Chief Justice Hutchinson rejected Otis's argument and issued one to Charles Paxton.[14]

There had been much controversy surrounding Hutchinson's decision. His colleagues had expressed doubts whether general writs were constitutional and the chief justice, suspending judgment, had written London seeking a ruling that might clarify the question. He did not, however, write to the attorney general, to a judge on the competent court, or even to a lawyer active in revenue practice. Instead, Hutchinson relied on William Bollan, the colonial agent, who once had been advocate general of the Massachusetts admiralty court and was an active proponent of raising an American revenue by reforming and extending the customs service. The chief justice wanted to issue the writs and knew the right man to ask for the "opinion" needed to persuade his fellow judges. It was less a judicial action than political and when it became known had serious consequences for the prestige of the superior court. Bollan provided the information expected of him and the writs were issued.[15]

Much had happened since Hutchinson's opinion. Not only had the sugar act been passed, making writs of assistance even more obnoxious to Americans, but courts in other colonies had refused to issue them. Only in Massachusetts and New Hampshire had petitions for the writs been granted; to the south tory judges were as determined in their opposition to general warrants as were their whig associates. It was a development that may have given Boston merchants hope that Hutchinson's colleagues could be persuaded to change their minds. About four months prior to the Malcom affair, it had been learned that the highest court in neighboring Connecticut not only refused to issue a writ of assistance but also that the judges expressed doubt of its legality in America: "As the Act of Parliament had made Express provision that it shall issue under the Seal of the Court of Exchequer: And we have no Statute here relative to it."[16]

The Connecticut court had based its ruling on a jurisdictional consideration far narrower than Otis's sweeping argument that general writs were not legal under English constitutional law. Indeed, the grounds for the decision may be thought rather technical. The statute of parliament authorizing issuance of search warrants to revenue officers in England had specified they be granted by "the lord treasurer, or any of the barons of the exchequer." In other words, they were to originate in the court of exchequer, one of the three central courts of common law sitting at Westminster Hall and whose judges were called barons. A later statute had been understood to extend writs of assistance to the colonies, and still another specifically gave to customs officials in America the "like assistance" in making searches that the earlier act had provided to their counterparts in England. But parliament did not indicate which courts were authorized to issue the writs and Connecticut's judges held that, as they were not an exchequer court, they were not empowered by law to grant general writs.[17]

A similar argument had been made in the Massachusetts case. Jeremiah Gridley, representing the customs service petitioning for the writ, had agreed that exchequer's process did not run in the province, but asked what parliament could have meant by authorizing to revenue officials a "like assistance" if it did not also intend to empower a local court to issue like writs. In Massachusetts that court had to be the superior court of judicature over which Hutchinson presided as chief justice. Moreover, there was a provincial statute specifically vesting in that court "cognizance of all pleas . . . whatsoever as the courts of king's bench, common pleas and exchequer within his majesty's kingdom of England have or ought to have." Thus by local, not imperial, legislation the superior court of judicature was an exchequer court and had authority to issue writs of assistance.[18]

Agreeing with Gridley, Thomas Hutchinson relied specifically on the provincial statute. He did not write an opinion, but in the first writ of assistance issued, the chief justice quoted from the act conferring exchequer powers on the superior court, apparently accepting the premise that such a grant of jurisdiction carried with it all extraordinary and statutory powers, not merely those traditionally vested in exchequer by common law.[19]

The whigs did not allow Hutchinson's ruling to settle the matter. Both arguments continued to be heard, the broad one on constitutional principles and the narrow one about exchequer jurisdiction. When Connecticut's decision was learned, James Otis may have been emboldened to try having the writs already granted quashed. Daniel Malcom, one of the merchants who retained him to argue the earlier case, would have been a willing client. We may be certain, too, that Otis would not have limited himself to the technical argument. Recently the whigs had been raising objections to Hutchinson's assumption of exchequer jurisdiction that had constitutional overtones. The superior court of Massachusetts, they were saying, did not and could not function in the same manner as the exchequer in England. There, writs of assistance were not granted to all officers but issued at the discretion of the barons. Moreover, the designated officer remained under the control of the court as did the disposal of any seizures, which was not the case in the colonies. And finally, in London it was exchequer that issued the writ of delivery, the "sister" writ of the writ of assistance, restoring goods illegally seized. Due to the interposition of the admiralty jurisdiction in Boston, the superior court of judicature did not and could not enforce similar constitutional safeguards.[20]

Had Otis and Malcom intended to test the legality of Hutchinson's writs of assistance, there is no doubt they would have won. The superior court might not have reversed its earlier ruling, but an appeal to London would have prevailed. A month after Hallowell decided not to break into Malcom's house, the Connecticut decision had been referred to William de Grey, England's attorney general, by the commissioners of the customs. He was the proper law officer, for the United Kingdom of Great Britain had no attorney general, and it was English not Scottish or British legal principles that prevailed in the colonies. Writs of assistance could not be issued in America, de Grey ruled, because they were statutory writs which only exchequer was empowered by parliament to grant, "and the Court of Exchequer in England do not send their Process into the Plantations, nor is there any Process in the Plantations that corresponds, with the description in the act." Asked to reconsider his opinion at least in regard to Massachusetts, he refused. The provincial statute vesting the superior court with exchequer jurisdiction was not relevant. Only exchequer had been given authority to grant writs of assistance.[21]

William de Grey, who had been sworn in as attorney general the month before the Malcom affair, was a conservative politician and a lawyer who tended to dwell on narrow technicalities. Soon he would find himself baffled by the ability of American whigs to defy British authority while relying on legal and constitutional arguments as justification. "Let gentlemen look into the papers on the table," de Grey told the House of Commons two years later, pointing to documents provided by Bernard and Hutchinson, "and they will see how well these Americans are versed in the Crown law. I doubt whether they have been guilty of an overt act of treason; but I am sure they have come within an hair's breadth of it."[22]

De Grey's ruling on the Connecticut decision may be typical of his legal reasoning, but it cannot be faulted as technical legalism. He was, it should be noted, interpreting revenue statutes imposing serious penalties on violators. They were, therefore, criminal in nature and by the canons of construction it was his duty to construe them strictly. Parliament may have intended to extend the writs of assistance to the North American colonies, but it had been careless, neglecting to vest the power of issuance in any existing tribunal. The Massachusetts statute granting exchequer jurisdiction to the superior court was too narrow to rectify the oversight. The writs that Hutchinson had signed were illegal.

What was law for the state during the eighteenth century was law for the individual. When news of the Malcom affair reached the ears of revenue officials in London, there was general wonder that Daniel Malcom was not in jail. Even the lords of the treasury expressed interest by asking England's attorney and solicitor generals "whether the resistance made by Mr. Malcom to Mr. Hallowell the Officer of the Customs armed w'th such a Writt, does not subject him to the punishment directed by the 13th and 14th of Ch[arles] 2nd to be inflicted on persons forcibly hindering the Off'rs of the Customs in the execution of their Office." The law officers replied that there was no possibility of bringing criminal charges against Daniel Malcom or anyone else concerned in the affair. The customs officers may have been obstructed "in the execution of their office," but they could not even file a "Civil Action," let alone prosecute, "inasmuch as the Writ of Assistance by Virtue of Which they entered the House and Cellar, was not in this case a legal Authority."[23]

The attorney and solicitor generals had been given all the information: they knew of Malcom's threats, the fact he had been armed, and the raising of the mob. But Hallowell and Sheaffe presented no evidence that unreasonable force had been used or even that they had suffered the slightest injury. It was they who had acted illegally, not Malcom or the Boston crowd.

New law was being made although the British failed to notice what was happening. At its next session, parliament corrected the mistake uncovered by de Grey and provided that "writs of assistance . . . shall and may be granted by the said superior or supreme court of justice having jurisdiction" within each colony. Thomas Hutchinson and the chief justice of New Hampshire responded by signing new writs, but in the colonies south of Massachusetts all courts rejected the petitions of the customs officials. The reason, Attorney General de Grey was told, was "that no informations had been made to them of any special Occasion for such Writ, and that it will be unconstitutional to lodge such Writ in the Hands of the Officer, as it will give him a discretionary Power to act under it in such Manner as he shall think necessary." De Grey wrote another opinion, affirming that the writs were constitutional. It was to no avail. Colonial judges outside of Massachusetts and New Hampshire still refused to sanction writs of assistance. It hardly mattered for even in Massachusetts they were soon dead letters. The Malcom case seems to be the last time a writ was employed in Boston.[24] As customs officers could not "enter into any House, Shop, Cellar, or Warehouse" without having a writ of assistance, it became the rule that houses, shops, cellars, and warehouses were no longer broken into.[25] The explanation, Thomas Hutchinson thought, was that whig law had nullified imperial law. "Writs of Assistance are issued whenever they are applied for, but the Civil Officers are not regarded," he wrote. "The laws have lost their force, & upon the rising of a mob I should have no dependance upon any civil or military officer to suppress it; the only chance would be from private persons of spirit, who being alarmed with the fear of having their property destroyed might perhaps combine together & make resistance; but this is very uncertain at any time, and when a mob is raised meerly to rescue seized goods, such a combination is not to be expected."[26]

It does not seem to have occurred to Hutchinson that the "persons of spirit" upon whom he counted did not fear for property when an anticustoms mob was on the streets. From their legal and political perspective, the whig crowd that opposed customs officials was out to preserve private property, not destroy it.[27]

If Malcom wanted to test the legality of Hallowell's writ, he would not have been thinking of being arrested, prosecuted, and then appealing to London. He would have been planning to sue for damages Hallowell, or Sheaffe, or possibly Greenleaf—most likely the first two. In fact his main objective may have been a civil suit, not the constitutional issue of general warrants. Moreover, fear of a civil suit, not doubts about the legality of writs of assistance or apprehension of the mob, was unquestionably the main reason why the customs men did not dare even open Malcom's gate that afternoon. He would have brought an action of *trespass*, and they would have had to pay a generous judgment.

Massachusetts law gave Malcom several grounds for suing the officials, although under the rules of pleading he would have been permitted to select only one. To make a search or seizure without a lawful warrant was an actionable wrong. "Probable Cause" was "no Excuse"; the writ had to be valid and if the plaintiff's attorney manipulated the pleadings the issue of legality could be made one of fact to be determined by the whig jury rather than of law for the tory judges—one reason why even after the English attorney general had ruled the new writs valid customs men were reluctant to employ them in Massachusetts Bay.[28]

It is more likely, however, that the lawyer advising Malcom was thinking of an action of *trespass*. Officials could be sued in Massachusetts for damages whenever in the exercise of their duties they committed a wrong that resulted in an injury. It they omitted to perform some task required of them by law (a nonfeasance), the action of *case* lay. If they acted in a manner that caused injury to the plaintiff (a misfeasance), and what they did was not privileged, they were answerable to a writ of *trespass*. By shutting himself in the house and ignoring pleas that he come outside, Malcom invited the customs men to commit an overt act upon which he might start a lawsuit. We may be certain the officials were aware of the legal trap. We need only note that Greenleaf did not even open the gate. He persuaded two neighbors to call out to Malcom over the fence, but neither he nor anyone else took the logical step of knocking on the door.

Surely there is an explanation why the customs men did not do what others wishing to speak to Malcom would have done. It can be no accident that during the entire afternoon Hallowell, Sheaffe, and Greenleaf did not go beyond the fence or put a foot on Malcom's property. To have opened the gate would have been "trepass"; a mere step onto his land would have provided Malcom grounds for commencing a suit. With the whigs in control of Suffolk County juries, there would be no need to prove a material injury. When customs officials were defendants and seizures or attempted seizures were in the background of the litigation, jurors employed the civil law to impose criminal-law type sanctions, in effect using damage judgments to punish revenue men for enforcing "unconstitutional" imperial statutes.

It may be thought that Greenleaf, in his capacity as sheriff, would have been privileged to have opened the gate. That is, had he been sued, he could have defended himself by pleading that he had been performing an official duty. In legal theory he was privileged, although in this case the privilege depended on the legality of the writs of assistance which, as we have seen, were invalid. But assuming for the sake of argument that there was no doubt about the legality of the writ, and it does seem that Hallowell and Sheaffe believed they were acting under lawful authority, we may be certain that none of them—the sheriff, the comptroller, or the collector—would have opened the gate. They knew the plea of official privilege might not prevail in a Suffolk County court.[29]

Had Malcom sued Hallowell for breaking into his house or even for opening his gate, Hallowell would have answered that his action had been privileged by virtue of his writ of assistance and he would have cited the appropriate statutes authorizing him to enter private buildings to search for contraband goods. The answer, if denied by Malcom, would have created a question of law and Chief Justice Hutchinson, ruling that the writ was valid, would have dismissed Malcom's action. But as Hallowell and Greenleaf knew, Malcom's lawyer would not have traversed the answer, he would not have denied that the defendant's alleged offense was privileged. Instead, he would have avoided the question of law by traversing the answer with an issue of fact. There were several possibilities: to deny that the defendant was an officer; to deny that the attempted entry of the house occurred during daylight hours as required by law; to deny that the defendant had a writ of assistance; or to deny that the defendant produced the writ, also a requirement for valid service.

We may assume Malcom would have asserted the last defense as he had carefully prepared the groundwork for it, making the claim in terms as strong as could be asserted. "I never saw any Writ of Assistance nor any other Power or Authority whatsoever to break open my House, and if I had I am sure I would be the last Man in the World that would stand against it." The defendant would then have to reply, either by admitting that he had not produced his writ or by traversing the allegation. If he made the admission he would have provided the court with a question of law—did an official acting by authority of a writ of assistance have to produce that writ on request? Even tory judges would have ruled his defense insufficient; writs had to be produced, and the defendant would have lost the action. Thus he would surely have adopted the second alternative, and denied the plaintiff's allegation. But again that would have been a question of fact for the jury—was the writ produced and shown to the plaintiff?[30]

In truth, all the options were in the hands of the plaintiff's attorney. If he wished a jury trial he could always obtain one by raising a factual issue. Both Hallowell and Sheaffe were well aware of their dilemma; they had learned by experience the year before during the stamp-act crisis. They also knew the consequences of a jury trial, that in whig Boston whig juries made whig law.[31]

It is remarkable how well the participants in the prerevolutionary struggle understood private law—Boston merchant as well as imperial official. The Malcom drama was repeated too often for the legal maneuverings to be regarded as mere coincidences.[32] Historians who have assumed that fear of mob violence kept Greenleaf, Hallowell, and Sheaffe from breaking down Malcom's door have been wrong. Fear there may have been, but fear of whig law was a strong enough deterrent. It would be farfetched to suggest that every member of the crowd gathered about the house was there to see if the officers would dare risk an action of *trespass*. Yet it seems that many were, and those who were not had been carefully briefed by the time they gave their evidence. Every deposition placed Malcom's actions within the margin of legally permissible conduct. Thus it seems safe to conclude that had the customs officials and the sheriff physically forced their way through the front door, the crowd would not have intervened to keep them out of the cellar. Perhaps it would have, but the event is doubtful and there was no chance the sheriff would have tested the people's reaction. He knew, as did Hallowell and Sheaffe, that even if they entered the house and found that Malcom was hiding uncustomed goods, they would not have made a seizure. Had they, Malcom would have forfeited what they confiscated, true enough, but the judgment of a valid seizure obtained by the officials from the admiralty court would not have barred suit at common law. Malcom still could allege *trespass* and expect that a whig jury would award damages sufficient in amount to cover his losses and to "penalize" the defendants. There was no appeal from a Massachusetts jury verdict except to the Privy Council in London, an expensive procedure that lay only if the judgment had been for £300 sterling or more.[33]

Had Hallowell and Sheaffe been bold and willing to risk their own fortunes, they might have tested the strength of the Suffolk County jury. In the sugar act, parliament had recently attempted to protect customs officials from harassment by local law. Should an action be brought against a revenue man for seizing goods in the line of duty, the statute provided that the presiding judge could certify "probable cause" and even though the plaintiff won his case, he "shall not be intitled to above two pence damages, nor to any costs of suit; nor shall the defendant in such prosecution be fined above one shilling."[34] The language was as unambiguous as any drafted by the eighteenth-century parliament. There was no mistaking either the intent or spirit, yet it must be asked if it gave comfort to Hallowell and Sheaffe. No lawyers of reputation would have ventured to advise them that they were now judgment proof.

Had Malcom sued Hallowell and Sheaffe by a writ of *trespass,* the action would have been filed in the inferior court of common pleas for Suffolk County. While by collusion the two parties could bypass that tribunal and go directly to the superior court, ordinarily the matter would have gone to trial, the whig jury would have returned a verdict for Malcom, and the whig judges would have refused to certify "probable cause." Hallowell and Sheaffe then would have appealed to the superior court where the original judgment would not have been reviewed for errors of law as today, but the matter would have been retried before a different jury. Again Malcom could have anticipated victory, but now Hallowell and Sheaffe would have moved that the tory judges grant a certificate of "probable cause." While Chief Justice Hutchinson surely would have been willing to do so, it was by no means certain he had the power. The defendants in their answer could have placed on the record the defense that the alleged trespass arose from a legal seizure and that defense should have brought them within the provisions of the sugar act limiting damages to "two pence." But the plaintiff, it will be recalled, would have denied the probative fact and the jury's verdict for the plaintiff would have been tantamount to a finding that the defendants had not been customs officers or had not been acting in their official capacity. On the record it would have been an ordinary case of trespass, not, as the statute required, an "action, or other suit or prosecution . . . commenced and brought to trial against any person or persons whatsoever, on account of the seizing [of] any . . . ship or goods."[35]

Whether Hutchinson could or would have gone outside the record to certify probable cause was the question no attorney could yet answer. We might assume that he would, but contemporary lawyers would have been less certain. Hutchinson was a law-minded man, troubled by close distinctions and immobilized by mere technicality. We may think he would have found an excuse because we expect a tory judge to serve imperial interests. That was not Thomas Hutchinson's way. The law in its narrowest points was his constant guide, as any Massachusetts lawyer advising Hallowell and Sheaffe would have known.[36]

In other colonies where the sugar act was tested, customs men discovered that it did not always protect them. They and naval officers were not only sued, they left court owing large judgments to merchants whose property they had seized. And there is more. Even if the sugar act provided the protection intended by parliament, it would not have done the full job. There were other grounds for suing revenue officials than those covered in the statute. Agents inspecting goods legally imported kept in mind the possibility they might be sued if any item was broken, a strong likelihood after 1767 when a duty had to be paid on every piece of glass entering the colonies and each piece had to be individually unpacked and examined as there were several grades of glass with a different tax on each grade. Even if the official made a seizure and the court certified probable cause, the statute did not offer full immunity. Had Hallowell and Sheaffe forced their way into Malcom's house, seized illicit goods, had them condemned in admiralty, and obtained a certificate of probable cause, they still could have been sued at common law by anyone who suffered an injury or even by a person who had been merely brushed aside. Again the action was *trespass*. Nothing had to be proved except physical contact, and the issue went to the whig jury. Should we wonder that customs men were reluctant to make seizures even after passage of the sugar act? And if the possibility of being sued was not bad enough, consider the reverse situation. What if the person injured during a seizure was an agent? "The officers," Commissioner Henry Hulton complained, "had no probability of obtaining redress for any injuries they received, by a process at Law, before a Jury of the People who held the very Laws under which the officers acted, to be Unconstitutional."[37]

We should not be surprised that the "two pence" proviso of the sugar act failed to embolden customs officials. History was in fact repeating itself. For over a century a parliamentary statute had been on the books permitting defendants who faced either a civil or criminal charge stemming from enforcement of the imperial revenue laws to cite the appropriate law as a defense and plea the general issue. The presiding judge was then enjoined "to acquit and indemnify them and every [one] of them and from all such suits, indictments, informations or prosecutions, for or concerning any matter or thing acted or done in the due and necessary performance and execution of their respective trusts and imployments therein."[38]

Again the spirit and intent had been unambiguous and again the statute failed in its purpose. Within ten years Massachusetts courts had returned large verdicts against customs officials, even threatening to sell into bondage an agent unable to satisfy a judgment. It was a judicial pattern repeated throughout the North American colonies during the early decades of the eighteenth century. More recently Thomas Hutchinson had been unable to invoke the statute to dismiss an action against the collector of Boston for a seizure that had been adjudicated as legal and proper in admiralty—a decree that was in imperial legal theory an absolute bar to suit at common law. And just after the siege at Malcom's house, a naval officer who had been arrested in New York on a civil warrant following a seizure and spent about four months in jail awaiting trial, had judgment returned against him for £4046 damages and costs of suit.[39]

There is another possibility to be considered, small but interesting as a further illustration of how imperial statutes could handicap customs officials. The fact has been mentioned that the people in the street and Malcom in his house said the informer had to be identified publicly, and the point was made that they surely knew the law did not support them. But that was customary law, for the practice was that informers' names were kept secret and they did not accompany revenue men on raids. Statutory law was not so clear. The act of parliament authorizing writs of assistance provided that if the information upon which a search was conducted "prove to be false" then "the party injured shall recover his full damages and costs against the informer, by action of trespass to be therefore brought against such informer."[40] The right was a nullity if the identity of the potential defendant remained unknown. Had Malcom sued Hallowell and Sheaffe and won, establishing on the record that the information had been "false," he would have had grounds for suing the two officials again, this time for depriving him of a statutory right to bring a writ of *trespass* by refusing to disclose the name of the potential defendant. For Hallowell or Sheaffe to have done so would have damaged the service, but if they did not they faced an expensive lawsuit no matter the outcome. It was a dilemma that may furnish another explanation why officials were reluctant to make seizures and why they thought they needed either new imperial statutes or the direct intervention of British law enforcement.[41]

Over the years imperial law had never proved strong enough to protect customs officials from local American law. The threat that they would be taken to court or even the mere implication, as the Malcom affair demonstrates, was often enough to dissuade revenue agents from doing their duty. Parliament had given Hallowell and Sheaffe the authority to enter Malcom's house, but they could not execute that authority in Boston. It may be, as they said, that they were fearful of mob violence. More likely they were afraid of the uses that Daniel Malcom and James Otis would have made of local law.

5

An Implacable Enmity

THE DEVELOPMENT OF FACTS

Events must not be seen in isolation. Just as the affair at Daniel Malcom's house was related to the rescues of seized goods at Newburyport and Falmouth, and to colonial constitutional theory about the illegality of parliamentary taxation, so the town meeting held in Boston shortly after the commissioners landed owed its call to issues more complex than mere rumor that the mob might soon be on the streets. We have seen the result of that meeting—a resolution urging the inhabitants "to preserve Peace and good Order"—but what occurred tells only a third of the story. There are also the questions *why* and *what* it meant.

James Otis spoke that day and what he said was ambiguous and somewhat controversial. He would later deny printed reports, but there is reason to believe that if he was misquoted he was not misquoted by much. "[L]et our burthens be ever so heavy, or our grievances ever so great," he is supposed to have said, "no possible circumstances, tho' ever so oppressive, could be supposed sufficient to justify private tumults and disorders, either to our consciences before God, or legally before men."[1]

We must not dwell on side issues: the words "private tumults," if used, could make all the difference. People would have understood that Otis was condemning riots not sanctioned by public opinion, that he was urging the mob to restrain itself until there were politically useful reasons for it to go on the streets. But we cannot be certain Otis used those specific words. All we know is that he was moving away from the more militant of his whig colleagues, for he was slowly succumbing to the occupational disease of his profession by being too law minded. The concept of sovereignty and the British constitutional doctrine of parliamentary supremacy would soon entrap him in a net of legalism. He told the people that the crown had authority to appoint the commissioners, and we must assume that he meant what he said. Current legal theory demanded that sovereignty be vested in some person or institution. It must not be divided, for it had to be whole or it could not exist. Parliament was the sovereign lawmaker for the empire and once you stumbled on that concept it was difficult to escape from the conclusion that even bad or "unconstitutional" statutes had to be obeyed.[2]

It is well to be realistic; most whigs were not lawyers. Violence could trouble them, not sovereignty. The legal dilemma lay beyond their recognition. English legal history did not teach them that parliament was supreme; it taught them that arbitrary government was unconstitutional. Resistance to arbitrariness had been an established right since the time of Magna Carta, long ago made constitutionally respectable by Lord Coke, the Puritan rebellion, and the Glorious Revolution. The American whigs' own opposition to the stamp act, employing violence to persuade the stamp distributors to resign, was but the latest event in a long, honorable tradition. Jared Ingersoll had told a mob demanding his resignation as the designated stamp agent for Connecticut that it should "think more how to get rid of the *stamp act,* than of the officers who are to supply you." Otis echoed Ingersoll when he warned Boston's town meeting that to "get rid" of the commissioners of the customs would not repeal the Townshend duties. Even so, it would not do to conclude that because the people adopted Otis's resolution and "unanimously agreed to exert themselves on all Occasions, to support good Order," they repudiated tactics used successfully during the stamp-act crisis. Institutional realities may have changed; principles remained the same.[3]

The dynamics of the stamp controversy made mob action necessary. The stamp excise was a new tax with special officers appointed to collect it and depriving London of those officers through forced resignations meant no tax could be collected and no precedent established for internal taxation. Under the premises of the new crisis, "*violent* Efforts must be unnecessary."[4] The reason was not that the Townshend duties were part of a familiar line of statutes—they were in the whig view of the constitution as much an innovation as the stamp act—but that the long-established revenue apparatus was to be utilized to collect them. Removing the commissioners would not have the same result as removing the stamp agents. Every subordinate customs official had to be driven out as well, and that fact alone made "*violent* Efforts" unnecessary. There were too many men to be intimidated. Rioting would have been so widespread, their enemies could easily persuade London they were in rebellion.

By our definition, the word "inexpedient" would have been more accurate than "unnecessary," although an eighteenth-century whig knew what it meant. The people of Boston urged one another to be calm not because they were less opposed to the Townshend duties than they had been to the stamp act, but because political realities had changed during the two years since they last saw a mob. A new wave of rioting might one day be necessary, but for the moment it could produce more harm than benefit, a risk that in whig parlance made it "unnecessary."

Boston's whig leadership was thinking in terms of nonimportation, economic pressure for repeal of the Townshend duties by boycotting merchandise of British manufacture. "No Mobs and Tumults, let the Person and Properties of our *most* inveterate Enemies be safe," was the whigs' new slogan, "*Save Your Money and you save the Country*." Five days after the town meeting, the selectmen issued a statement urging the citizens to sign a subscription pledging the use of "our own Manufactures, and the disuse of foreign Superfluities."[5]

Nonimportation lay in the future, and though important as a promised alternative to crowd action, it was not the chief consideration explaining the town's resolution for calm and order. More compelling in the minds of those who voted was the realization that, for the moment at least, riots would be more likely to serve tory than whig ends. Indeed, there was a strong suspicion that Governor Francis Bernard and the commissioners were attempting to provoke trouble. The night before the meeting some unknown person has posted on the liberty tree a call to direct action, apparently urging that the commissioners be driven from town. We need not stretch our imaginations to guess it was the work of an overzealous whig; the town condemned it as a tory scheme but made no attempt to implicate a specific tory. The notice, the inhabitants voted, was "a *dirty Trick*," calculated "to irritate the Passions, at a Time when ALL depends upon our being *cool, deliberate* and *firm*."[6]

The action by the town was more revealing than may be thought. Resolutions were not passed on whim or fancy. They were drafted by leaders who knew what arguments were tolerable with the people and adopted by a majority that thought those arguments sound. The suggestion that someone had posted a notice hoping "to irritate the Passions" and incite a riot may strike us as absurd, but we did not vote at that town meeting. Those who were there did not find the idea ridiculous, by voting for the resolution they were saying it made sense.

The selectmen, after several days of reflection, provided a stronger indication of whig thinking when they warned the people there were enemies in town seeking to incite them to riot. Someone unknown who had written "a Piece" in the *Evening-Post* discussing the town meeting seemed to have had "such an Aim." Every individual who had been "at the two last Meetings of the Town, must know that he has misrepresented Facts, and that in so irritating a Manner, as every Reader must observe the Tendency thereof is to raise the Passions." Therefore, the selectmen pleaded, "keep your Tempers, and study Moderation, when you meet with incitements artfully thrown out to beguile you into illegal Measures. Believe us—they are intended so highly to excite your Resentment that you may thereby, before you can take a second thought, be thrown into such Expressions of it as may be improved by designing Persons to Ends that will tend to the Gratification of their own Avarice and your Ruin."[7]

The selectmen may have been relying on rather tenuous evidence to prove there was a tory plot to incite Boston to riot, but they were not the only ones. Each side, in fact, seized on rumors and mere suspicion to prove the other was plotting its ruin. That same month Governor Bernard wrote London that the whigs had planned a demonstration against the customs commissioners, similar to the stamp-act riots, aimed at forcing them to resign, which for some unexplained reason had been abandoned. Later he informed the secretary of state, Lord Shelburne, that there was "such an opposition to the Commissioners and their Officers, and such a defyance to the Authority by which they are appointed, continually growing" that "the most dangerous consequences are to be expected."[8]

The commissioners were reporting much the same, though they made a greater effort to establish a conspiracy than did Bernard. Charles Paxton lost no time informing the lord lieutenant of Ireland, a member of the British cabinet, that on the very day he and his colleagues landed in Boston he had been burnt in effigy. While his facts were correct, they were also shaded. Bostonians had been celebrating Guy Fawkes Day, an annual occasion, during which the crowd paraded effigies of the pope and the devil through the streets before throwing them into a great bonfire. When the commissioners landed, the name "Charles" was fixed on the breast of the devil and that was the effigy burnt. By not mentioning these particulars, Paxton implied that a mob had been raised to threaten him and left the impression that he was in danger. He also repeated the governor's charge that "great pains was taken before our arrival to raise a Disturbance but the better sort of people interposed and prevented it."[9] Paxton provided no facts supporting this assertion. If he had we may be certain that his evidence would not have been sufficient proof to establish the allegation in a court of law, a consideration that, under the circumstances, did not matter for there was no need to overcome a reasonable doubt. What Paxton said was self-evident to a tory or imperial official and soon would be to the British ministry as well.

Given the political predilections of the jury that they were seeking to convince, anyone could have sustained the onus of proof and among imperial officials almost everybody tried. Mobs had been forming in Boston ever since the first stamp-riot, Paxton's colleague Henry Hulton asserted, and Samuel Adams "was their Political Dictator." The conclusion was logical to a tory: "our lives and property depend on the caprice of our Sovereign Lords the people."[10]

Had we been able to ask Paxton and Hulton for evidence, they probably would have referred us to the memorials, letters, and dispatches that they and other officials had sent to London. They certainly thought them persuasive for they were puzzled by the ministry's failure to respond. We may gauge the probativeness of the facts upon which the commissioners relied by considering their first report to the imperial treasury. In it, they attempted to convince their superiors that under the present circumstances they faced danger in Boston.

> The minds of the people scarcely composed after the late [stamp-act] tumults, were susceptible of every impression, and these doctrines agreeing with their democratic principles, were received with applause, and in a little time the frenzy of the people of this town was raised to such a height, that a forcible opposition to the execution of the new [Townshend] Laws was threatened; but . . . no act of violence was then committed, tho' every inflammatory act had been practiced, to stimulate the people thereto, and we have ever since remained in safety, tho' not without some apprehentions, Mr. Paxton having undergone the indignity of suffering in Effigy.[11]

Why "no act of violence was committed" even though "every inflammatory act had been practiced, to stimulate the people," is a question that did not trouble the commissioners. Instead of probing issues that would interest us, they avoided confusing analysis and made the most of the one concrete piece of evidence they had to support their case, the effigy of Charles Paxton. With such questionable direct proof, they had to rely on circumstantial evidence to sustain the assertion of danger and counted on London's prejudices against the town of Boston to make it convincing.

There were two other ministerial prenotions not overlooked—"exploited" would be too strong a term as the commissioners held these views as sincerely as did the ministers. One concerned the seditious recklessness of the colonial press, the other the partisan irresponsibility of the political opposition at home. "The people," Paxton wrote, "are continually taught in the publick papers that they are not Oblig'd to Obey the laws of Great Brittan [sic] because they are not represented in parliament, and since the opposition to the Stamp Act there has been a general relaxation of the laws of trade." Local leaders and Boston newspapers were not alone to blame although they "retail the most licentious publications, denying the right of Parliament to lay any taxes whatsoever on the Colonies: and some went so far as to assert the most unlimited independence." Also culpable were members of parliament such as William Pitt and Lord Chancellor Camden who opposed taxing Americans on constitutional grounds. "Everything that is said, or published in England, in favour of the Colonies, is peculiarly prejudicial, as the people in this Country are led to believe, that their cause is powerfully espoused at home."[12]

Due to America's reputation for excessive democracy, circumstantial evidence of this sort was more probative coming from the colonies than it would have been from Great Britain or Ireland. "Every man," Paxton asserted, "seems to think he ought to be at liberty to do what he pleases without any restraint from Law, especially from Acts of parliament."[13] It was a wild, sweeping indictment that we have every reason to think Paxton believed was true, but few whigs would have understood what he meant and those who did would have said he was inaccurate. They did not seek freedom from legal restraints, nor did they quarrel with legitimate acts of parliament. It is necessary to reemphasize a point that has been made before: only if one defines "law" from the imperial perspective does Paxton's statement have validity. As seen by the whigs that was too narrow a perspective.

A few months after Paxton wrote that Americans wanted to be free of law, the people of Abington, Massachusetts, held their annual town meeting. We need not catalogue them to be certain they considered themselves law-abiding citizens, opposed to illegal activities and respectful of legitimate authority. Yet they passed a series of resolutions that Paxton and his fellow commissioners would have characterized as lawless. The seventh is the most germane as it concerned the controversial new taxes—the Townshend duties—which, the inhabitants of Abington resolved, were "*a mere nullity*." It was a bold, defiant assertion that might well have been enough for a town so small, but there was even more. "Voted, as the opinion of this Town," the resolution continued, "that he who, *vi & armis,* seizes the property of an American subject, for not paying the duties imposed on him by said acts, ought to be deemed no better than a highwayman, and should be proceeded against in due course of law."[14]

We may mark the resolution's call that customs men be "proceeded against in due course of law" and conclude that the town was commending the example set by Daniel Malcom. In fact the resolution goes much further. The analogy to "a highwayman" leaves no room for ambiguity. Malcom had intended to use the civil law to apply a criminal-type of punishment against Hallowell and Sheaffe. The people of Abington had moved beyond that stage and were saying that enforcement of unconstitutional revenue laws was a criminal act and should be prosecuted like any other robbery. They were not seeking freedom from the restraints of what Charles Paxton called "law." Rather they wanted to apply what they called "law" to restrain Charles Paxton. Little wonder the commissioners of the customs would conclude that "While it is the general received opinion that the Acts imposing the late duties are unconstitutional, the People will be easily persuaded not to pay any."[15]

The point too often overlooked is that the commissioners were building a factual case that depended largely on proving the whigs defined law differently than did London. The Abington resolution was a perfect example of what Paxton meant by lawlessness, while many (though yet not all) whigs would have said it was a statement of legal principles. The commissioners' definition, however, was London's definition and that fact alone made their case persuasive. Moreover, because they were speaking of law in the imperial or parliamentary sense they were able to charge that all of the colonies, not just Massachusetts Bay, were guilty, for everywhere "the people seem to be as ripe for riot, and mischief, as they are here." Evidence to sustain such an important and damaging allegation was similar to that offered with regard to Boston; proof was not direct, it was circumstantial.

"At New York," for example, "sundry seditious papers have been dispersed, stirring up the people to a resistance." In Philadelphia the culprit was John Dickinson, whose *Letters from a Pennsylvania Farmer* began appearing in the public press just after the board arrived in Boston, "denying the right of Parliament to lay any tax whatsoever on the Colonies, and as the Author affects moderation, and a parade of learning, we consider them of the most mischievous tendency." And "At Rhode Island," the commissioners reported, indicting an entire colony for an incident occurring in just one community, "it was proposed in an advertizement posted upon the town-house, to stop the revenue money, which the officers there were about shipping home."[16]

The last charge deserves attention. When we consider its background we learn something of the quality of evidence furnished London by imperial officials to support allegations of American lawlessness. The Newport advertisement had not said precisely what the commissioners implied. The lords of the treasury recently had refused to remit funds that Rhode Island claimed it was owed. The notice called on the people to seize the money in the customshouse as reprisal, a balancing of accounts so to speak. A town meeting was immediately convened and the "Advertisement" condemned as an attempt "to interrupt the Peace and good

Order of the Town, by promoting Tumults and Riots." Furthermore, it was voted, the author had intended "to bring the good people of this Town and Colony under the Imputation of contriving to rob his Majesty's Revenue, and of throwing off all the Restraints of Law and Government." A reward was offered "out of the Town-Treasury" for information "against the Author or Authors of the said infamous Advertisement, upon his or their Conviction." The commissioners, in their report to London, did not mention the meeting or that the whigs took steps to prevent robbery of the customshouse. Instead, they implied that the advertisement was symbolic of the times. It alone was the probative fact.[17]

We would do well not to forget the Newport affair. It demonstrates more than that the commissioners were capable of mentioning only evidence supporting their case, much as a lawyer cites favorable precedents while ignoring precedents favorable to the other side. Also important is the fact that other towns besides Boston had reason to think imperial officials hoped to incite riots. Indeed, there were some that made the charge. Boston became the focus of attention because that was where the commissioners were located. They had, a committee of the town asserted in a report adopted by the inhabitants, "from their first arrival discovered Such an arrogance and insolence of Office as let many Persons to apprehend that they aimed at nothing less than provoking the People to such a degree of intemperance as to make an appearance of it." The word "appearance" conveys the whigs' greatest fear. If the commissioners were unable to raise the mob, they would continue to press their case. Where direct evidence was lacking, "appearances" would do as well.[18]

The controversy had not been initiated by the commissioners. Before the American board was even created, the whigs of Boston had been complaining that their views and activities were misrepresented in reports sent to London by Governor Bernard.[19] They proved the charge by replies Bernard had received from the secretaries of state. The king, Lord Shelburne wrote a year after the stamp act's repeal, "is extremely sorry to observe any degree of ill-temper remaining in his colony of Massachusetts-Bay, or, that points should be so improperly agitated as to tend to the revival of disputes, which every friend to America must wish to be forgotten." What representations of "ill-temper" had he made, the house asked the governor, and demanded to see his original reports. When they were not delivered the whigs assumed the worst. "The People of this Town and Province, are under this great Disadvantage," a Boston clergyman complained, "that living so distant from the great Fountain of Government, they Know not what has been alledg'd against them, nor in what Light their Conduct has been plac'd, and consequently it is out of their Pow'r to vindicate themselves till the Misrepresentation has had its

Effect." It was not just, he concluded, that London "act upon Accounts stated ex parte" and "industriously conceal'd from the People who are essentially interested in them."[20]

As time went on, enough of Bernard's dispatches reporting alleged colonial conspiracies were published for the whigs to build a counter case of conspiracy. Their enemies had been unable to provoke the mob, they contended, and so "more shifts & pretensions are to be sought after" by Bernard, who surely would continue to send London "frequent reports of insurrections intended."[21] And that is just what Bernard did. Unable to report riots he reported rumors, unable to report a rebellion he reported that rebellion was in the air.

The quality of proof the governor furnished to support his apprehensions may be gathered by considering a paragraph from one of his reports to the ministry and then part of an answer voted by the town of Boston. They are long quotations and deal with an event to which we must return. Even if placed out of chronological context, they belong here for they are not only the best example of how the two sides argued facts but also of what the whigs thought of the facts upon which London was formulating the colonial policy. Bernard wrote:

> It is some time since there have been frequent reports of insurrections intended, in which it has been said the houses of one or more of the commissioners and their officers would be pulled down; two were more particularly fixed upon. Upon one of these nights a number of lads, about 100, paraded the town with a drum and horns, passed by the council chamber whilst I was sitting there in Council, assembled before Mr. Paxton's (a commissioner's) house, and huzzaed; and to the number of at least 60 lusty fellows (as I am assured) invested Mr. Burch's (another commissioner's) house for some time, so that his lady and children were obliged to go out of the back door to avoid the danger which threatened. This kind of disturbance was kept up all the evening and after all, was treated [by local whigs] as the diversion of a few boys, a matter of no consequence.[22]

To these facts, typical of the type of evidence Bernard compiled to prove that Massachusetts was teetering on insurrection, the town of Boston answered:

> But to give a colouring of these Ideas of an Insurrection, there must be something more alledged than barely that there had been frequent Reports of its being intended; and therefore his Lordship is told of an event which in part took place as some few remember,

but the story is wrought up by the Governor with all the strokes of masterly invention to serve the purpose "A number of Lads says he peraded the Town with a Drum and Horn" And what possible harm could there be in that? Why among other Houses, "they passed by the Council Chamber when he was Sitting in Council" And did they stop to insult the Governor and Council? Such a circumstance would doubtless have embellished his Excellencies Narrative. There [sic] passing by however carried the air of an insult, tho' in all likelihood the unlucky Boys might not know that his Excellency was there—But they had "assembled before Mr. Paxtons House" and least it should be forgot his Lordship is reminded that Mr. Paxton is a "Commissioner"—And did they do Mr. Paxton the *Commissioner* any injury, yess truly "they huzzard" & went off then they "invested Mr. Burchs House" And his Lordship is also told that Mr. Burch is "another Commissioner"—and "his Lady & Children were obliged to go out of the back door to avoid the danger that was threatened" . . . Whether this Lady whom Governor Bernard has *politely* ushered into the view of the public, *really* thought herself in danger or not, it is incumbent on him to show that there were Just grounds for her apprehensions, that Mr. Burch's House was in fact "invested" and that "the most dangerous consequences were to be expected" The World may be assured there was not the least appearance of this kind; and yet, these are Mr. Bernards own declarations to his Majestys Ministers, grounded upon vague and idle Reports, beneath one of his rank and station to take any notice of, and especially with a design to misrepresent.[23]

The tone may seem frivolous, but the parties were serious. The questions at issue were whether the province had a right to see the evidence so it might defend itself and whether the evidence was entitled to weight.[24] Especially annoying was Governor Bernard's habit of indicting the entire colony by the actions of one town or counting everyone present at an event to give weight to a statement made by a single person. Thus he incriminated the town of Boston by saying that at one of its meetings "many wild and violent proposals were made." A careful reading of his facts, the inhabitants of Boston contended, showed that "Governor Bernard constantly represents bodys of Men, even the most respectable, by proposals made by Individuals." The technique was similar to judging the conduct of both houses of parliament "by every motion that has been made, or every expression that has dropped from Individuals in the warmth of debates."[25] In sum, Bernard's facts were not evidence at all but prejudice, "meanly *felching* from Individuals belonging to those Bodies, what had been drop'd in the course of Business or Debate: Journalizing every idle Report brought to him, and in short acting the part of a Pimp rather than a Governor."[26]

The suspicion of collective paranoia may lead us to question causes but not sincerity. If it was a factor it was due not to whig propaganda so much as to the study of constitutional history. The past was a beacon that guided eighteenth-century Americans as they responded to political predicaments. "No one that has read our *English History*," Boston's *Evening-Post* reminded its readers, "can be ignorant, that most of the *grand Mischiefs*, which our nation has suffered in *former reigns*, have been brought on by means of *wicked ministers*, and *evil counsellors about the King*." We may find these suspicions overblown, but by the standards of the times they were less eccentric than normal. The anxiety dominating the votes of Boston's town meetings was also voiced in contemporary Britain. In a petition, the freeholders of Middlesex warned George III about "the endeavours of certain evil-minded persons, who attempt to infuse into your royal mind, notions and opinions of the most dangerous and pernicious tendency, and who promote and counsell such measures as cannot fail to destroy that harmony & confidence, which should ever subsist between a just and virtuous Prince, and a free and loyal people." If in Massachusetts, whigs such as John Adams suffered from a touch of political paranoia, they did not suffer alone. When the king in a speech from the throne condemned rioting in the colonies, John Wilkes's *North Briton* echoed thoughts earlier expressed by Boston. "These disturbances," it told his majesty, "owe their rise to the Ministry, not to the Americans."[27]

The ministry was to blame as it was responsible for sending to America officials who misrepresented colonial conditions, misinformed the British public, and misled the very men who had appointed them. Benjamin Franklin knew the breed well. From his vantage point in London, where he served as agent for Massachusetts Bay as well as Pennsylvania and several other colonies, he saw them leave for their posts and read the reports they sent back. Many Americans wrote of their faults, their prejudices, and their vices, but none described them better from the whig perspective than did Franklin. They were, he said, "needy men" whose "necessities make them rapacious, their office makes them proud and insolent, the insolence and rapacity make them odious, and being conscious that they are hated, they become malicious; their malice urges them to a continual abuse of the inhabitants in their letters to administration, representing them as disaffected and rebellious." Then the ministry usually made a second mistake, compounding the error of having appointed such men: it "believes all; thinks it necessary to support and countenance its officers; their quarrelling with the people is deemed a mark and consequence of their fidelity; they are therefore more highly rewarded, and this makes their conduct still more insolent and provoking." Eventually the inevitable happens. "The resentment of the people will, at times and on particular incidents," Franklin concluded, "burst into outrages and violence upon such officers, and this naturally draws down severity and acts of further oppression from hence." Provocation was the greatest danger.[28] Sufficiently provoked Americans would forget their resolutions "to exert themselves on all Occasions, to support good Order."[29] They would act, the ministry would react, and prerogativism would replace liberty as the foundation of colonial law.

6

A Counter Work

THE ARGUMENT OF FACTS

We may make too much of law. There is a danger that politics and political propaganda may be distorted by casting them in a legal mold. If too much emphasis is placed on the analogy to law, it may be argued that we run the risk of obscuring not only the true context of the debate but also what the participants thought about the issues. Undoubtedly, it is well to be cautious, but there is also danger on the other side. Those who would ignore the legal implications have missed a vital dimension. Law was on the minds of both colonial whigs and imperial officials to a greater extent than has been thought. They saw their opponents not merely manipulating law but violating it as well. "There is a set of men in America," the people of Boston voted as early as 1766, "who are continually transmitting to the mother country odious and false accounts of the collonys; which is a crime of the most dangerous tendency."[1]

We might easily dismiss the word "crime" as mere rhetoric, a descriptive expression thrown out in the heat of political discussion without intending to convey its legal meaning, but we would be wrong. Three years later the Suffolk County grand jury indicted General Thomas Gage, Governor Francis Bernard, the commissioners of the customs, the collector, and the comptroller of the port of Boston, "for writing certain letters to the secretary of state and other [of] the King's ministers, and therein slandering the inhabitants of the town of Boston, and of the province of Massachusetts Bay." Nor should it be supposed that the jurors were not serious. Chief Justice Thomas Hutchinson believed that they were. "The attorney-general," he wrote, "had refused to draw the bills, when requested by the grand jury, and they either drew them themselves, or employed some other lawyer, unknown, and presented them to the court."[2]

48

THE ARGUMENT OF FACTS

Nothing, of course, came of the indictments. Hutchinson wrote for and received from the king orders that the attorney general enter a nolle prosequi upon each bill.[3] That fact is irrelevant. The important point is the indictments themselves and what they reveal about contemporary attitudes. American whigs may not have used terms such as "criminal," "legal," or "slanderous" in a manner acceptable to an English lawyer, but they had meaning for a growing number of colonists. The concept of illegality committed by government officials was still imprecise, for during the years between 1766 and 1770 it was only emerging; but soon it would have a precision in what can be termed "whig law": any threat to colonial privileges and immunities was "criminal."

Should we wonder why the vocabulary employed by American whigs was often the vocabulary of law in a situation that seems more political than legal, two answers are readily apparent. First, the realization they were arguing a case much as they would a lawsuit which depended primarily on the presentation of facts countering or mitigating those argued by their "enemies"—and on legal principles. And second, they usually channeled their defenses through legal institutions. In many colonies, where the governor or the crown appointed the council, the only voice whigs had was the lower houses of the provincial assemblies which could draft petitions and vote protests, but could take little positive action. In Rhode Island, where the governor was elected by the legislature and was a whig, it was possible to enact statutes nullifying acts of parliament and provide a color of legality to people resisting or disobeying imperial law.[4] Governor Bernard would have vetoed similar enactments in Massachusetts. There, legislation could not be so effective as in Rhode Island though the institutions able to formulate factual arguments, send them to Great Britain, and publicize them at home were greater than in most other colonies. In addition to the house, the executive council, and the selectmen of Boston who often issued statements or defenses, there were the people themselves who assembled in town meetings. In strict constitutional theory, a town meeting in Springfield or Salem had no more standing to make pronouncements on imperial laws than did mass meetings in New York or New Castle upon Delaware. But they were legal gatherings and when they issued arguments of fact, denying allegations made by imperial officials or making counter accusations of their own, they spoke through a legal institution that in southern colonies could be imitated only by grand-jury pronouncements.

The chief and most obvious factual defense was the assertion that Americans were law abiding, always "well dispos'd to assist the Civil Magistrate in the lawful Exercise of Authority, without the Aid of Military Troops, as any of his Majesty's Subjects in England." If disturbances had occurred it was not their fault but parliament's. "[J]ustice impels us to declare," the Massachusetts council stated, "that the people of this town and province, though they have a high sense of liberty, derived from the manners, the example, and constitution of the mother country, have, till the late Parliamentary taxations of the colonies, been as free from disturbances as any people whatever."[5]

The whig defense depended upon your point of view. It was valid from the whig perspective. Before the constitutional controversy began, Boston had been the best-regulated community in the colonies, perhaps in the entire empire, due in large part to the active participation of an unusually high percentage of the population in the processes of government, especially by attendance at town meetings. It was that very fact, however, that made the place suspect in tory eyes. "[T]he principal cause of the Mobbish turn in this Town," William Shirley had contended following the only serious riot that occurred during his governorship, "is its Constitution, by which the Management of it is devolv'd upon the populace assembled in their Town Meetings; one of which may be called together at any time upon the Petition of ten of the meanest Inhabitants, who by their Constant attendance there generally are the majority and outvote the Gentlemen, Merchants, Substantial Traders and all the better part of the Inhabitants; . . . and by this means it happens . . . that a factious and Mobbish Spirit is Cherish'd." Statements such as this, drawn from tory definitions of good government, enraged whigs. Bostonians were "universally uneasy," they might admit, but to call them "mobbish" was "a vile abuse of them."[6]

Governor Bernard was one official who publicly made the accusation. After the second stamp-act riot—the one occurring on 26 August 1765, during which the homes of Benjamin Hallowell and Thomas Hutchinson were looted by an uncontrollable mob—he charged that "the disordered State of the Province had affected its very Councils." The accusation was false, the house of representatives replied, and moreover Bernard was relying on the fact of a single, isolated incident to impute guilt to the entire province by telling the world "that the whole Body of the People had justified the Violence committed by a few Persons in the Town of Boston, tho' publicly detested by its Inhabitants—that they were upon the very Borders of Rebellion." The next day the inhabitants assembled in a town meeting—"the largest ever known on any Occasion"—where they voted unanimously "that the Selectmen and the Majestrates of the Town be desired to use their utmost endeavors agre[e]able to Law to suppress the like disorders for the future, and that the Freeholders and other Inhabitants will do everything in their power to assist them." Thus, the house was able to claim, the riot of 26 August, while the result of "a general popular discontent upon good grounds," had been the work of only "a few villains" and "the virtue of the people themselves finally supressed the mob."[7]

Whigs knew one version of what had occurred, tories another. It was the tory account that gained currency at home, for reasons that will later be considered. When the inhabitants of Boston learned what was being said in Great Britain about the riot of 26 August, they called yet another town meeting, this time to tell their side of the story. A committee was appointed to write a letter to their agent in London recounting the details. When the first draft was read it was voted to recommit because some people thought significant facts had not been emphasized. The committee was instructed "to represent the suddenness of the Mob rising in the Night of the 26th of August 1765, and the exertions immediately made by some of the Inhabitants to suppress or quiet those People." That point was stressed in the final version of the letter. "A number [of concerned citizens]," the letter said, "went to the governors house to take his excellencys orders but he Was not in town—from whence one would conclude that he was no more apprehensive of such a tumult from any appearances than others were." The people of Boston summed up their defense by not only denying responsibility for the second stamp-act riot but by claiming that the events of that week showed them worthy of praise not blame. They had, the inhabitants voted, "ever held the violent Outrages of Persons unknown in the late Times of Distress in the Utmost Detestation and Abhorrence, and from a Sense of Duty, as well as just Indignation at the Ravages committed on the Properties of divers of their Fellow-Subjects and Citizens on the 26th of August 1765, took the earliest Opportunity to exert their strenuous Endeavors, in aid of the Civil Authority, to restore Peace, Order and Tranquility; which were accordingly in one Day restored, and have been ever since preserved."[8]

Whig statements were no less self-serving than reports to London from imperial officials. Facts were shaded by the people of Boston just as they were by the commissioners of the American customs. Some of the rioters who did the damage on 26 August were known to the authorities. Public opinion might detest their actions but not to the extent that they could be prosecuted. The whigs had reasons to call them "Persons unknown" just as Charles Paxton would have reasons not to mention the Newport town meeting that condemned the "Advertisement" urging an attack on the customshouse. Other facts too were glossed over or ignored, but the main argument was not only valid, it would remain true for the future. The destruction of Thomas Hutchinson's house was a whig aberration never to be repeated. It had been too vicious, too disorderly, and even militant whigs called it "lawless." The event would not be repeated in prerevolutinary Boston. Crowd actions were henceforth more limited, more directed at specific political targets, and more orderly in their execution.

The shock experienced on the night of 26 August gave rise to the second of two criteria by which whigs legitimized and justified employment of the mob to prevent the execution of whig law. The first was that the crowd served a public, not private function, taking to the streets to oppose unconstitutional statutes of parliament such as the stamp act. Now the second test was that the mob confine its actions to harassment of imperial officials, commit no unnecessary destruction of property, and act with what the whigs described as "decency" and "decorum."[9]

Order, decency, and decorum became standard terms of description for whig mobs in every part of the continent. On the day that the stamp act was to take effect, the inhabitants of Kittery, Maine, joined the people of Portsmouth, Greenland, and Newcastle, New Hampshire, in a long funeral procession after which they buried the "stamp act." "The whole," it was reported, "was conducted with the utmost Decency." Earlier, "effigies of a Distributor of Stamps" had been carried through the streets of New London, Connecticut, "by the principal part of the inhabitants," cannons were fired from the fort, and ten or eleven effigies were burned. " 'Tis said the most perfect decorum was observed in all their behaviour, and no person received the least injury." A few weeks later men in Newburyport, Massachusetts, learned of a ship in the harbor that had been cleared at Halifax by stamped paper. Forced to surrender the clearance, the captain of the vessel was escorted to a justice of the peace "where he was sworn before some Hundreds, that he had no other stamp Papers, nor knew of any other in Town, nor would make use of any again untill allow'd by the Province." He was then released but not forgotten. The next morning the captain's effigy hung on the liberty tree and during the afternoon was carried about town "with Drum beating and Flag flying." The "whole," we are told, "was conducted with the utmost Decency and Order."[10]

The resignations of the stamp distributors were reported in much the same fashion. The New Jersey mob appointed a committee of two to obtain the resignation of that province's agent. Whether he agreed or not, their written orders specified, the two committeemen were to "treat him with that complaisance and decorum, becoming a gentleman of honour." George Meserve, New Hampshire's stamp distributor who already had publicly promised not to serve, received a notice from Portsmouth's sons of liberty that they wanted his written resignation signed "on the Drum Head." Before a large number of witnesses, "several of whom were men of property" (a fact often mentioned to impress the British that a whig crowd was not a "mob"),* Meserve swore he would never sell stamps. Then, according to the *New Hampshire Gazette*, "these *Sons of Freedom*, satisfied with their conduct, retired to their respective places of abode, without the least disturbances or injury offered to any person in town." Andrew Oliver, Massachusetts's stamp agent, experienced similar humiliation at Boston's liberty tree. About 2000 gathered, including "the Gentlemen Selectmen of the Town, with the Merchants and principal Inhabitants," to hear a justice of the peace administer the oath of resignation. "After which three Cheers were given and Hanover-Square was clear in 10 minutes."[11]

Events unconnected with the whig political movement or the controversy with the mother country were even reported in these terms. During 1766 a New York mob, "without the least tumult, noise or previous notice," arrived at a jail to set free the leader of a recent uprising by tenant farmers. Expecting a pardon the man told his rescuers that he did not wish to leave and "the company withdrew as suddenly and quietly as they met, without doing the least mischief of any kind."[12]

The emphasis upon order within disorder became so pervasive that even Boston's traditional day of violence, Guy Fawkes or Pope's Day, was reported in these terms. The celebration of 1765 occurred just nine days after the Hutchinson riot and fears "were great least it should prove another 26 of August." Instead, "the Town remained the whole Night in better Order than it had ever been on this Occasion," a period of "Peace and Quietness," for although the popes and devils were paraded and burned "every Thing was conducted in a most regular Manner, and such Order observed as could hardly be expected among a Concourse of several Thousand People," proof that the second stamp-act riot "was not agreeable to the Sentiments of the Town, but was only the lawless Ravages of some foreign Villains, who took Advantage of the overheated Temper, of a very few People of this Place, and drew them in to commit, such Violences and Disorders as they shuddered at with Horror in their cooler Hours."[13]

Bostonians knew they had a reputation for violence to live down. The riot of 26 August 1765—destroying Thomas Hutchinson's house, damaging the home of Benjamin Hallowell, and threatening the property of Charles Paxton—may have been an isolated event but it had made a

---

*When a crowd forced Virginia's stamp distributor to resign, the governor did not know how to describe the event. "This concourse of people," he wrote the board of trade, "I should call a mob, did I not know that it was chiefly if not altogether composed of gentlemen of property in the Colony, some of them at the head of their respective Counties, and the merchants of the country . . . for few absented themselves."

deep impression in the mother country. When the stamp act was repealed, friends in Great Britain warned them to celebrate with decency and decorum. "See that your rejoicings be within bounds, and that no person be burnt in effigy," one man wrote from Bristol. Assembling in town meeting, the inhabitants voted that bonfires and fireworks would be under public supervision. While private houses were to be illuminated by candles, exceptions were made for the poor, sick, and those with "Religious Scruples." It was, moreover, resolved "that all Abuses and Disorders on the Evening for Rejoycings by breaking Windows, or otherwise, if any should happen, be prosecuted by the Town." When the celebration occurred Bostonians were on their best behavior. "To the Honor of the Sons of Liberty we can with Pleasure inform the World," the *Boston Gazette* boasted, "that every Thing was conducted with the utmost Decency and good Order, not a Reflection cast on any Character, nor the least Disorder during the whole Scene."[14]

Eighteenth-century Boston deserves admiration. It had to marshal facts and argue them, and showed it was capable of doing both. To undo the damage of the stamp-act riots, the town set about proving that it was law abiding. Propaganda to historians, it was a plea in abatement to the people of the town, begun as a serious program after the repeal of the stamp act when tensions were relaxed and further controversy not expected. Had they known that the Townshend duties would soon be passed, they might have been less optimistic. But as events would soon prove, new imperial legislation was not needed to raise apprehensions and feed antagonisms. Before the Townshend duties were enacted and the commissioners of the American customs were even a rumor in Boston, the town found itself challenged again to argue facts in its own defense. Benjamin Hallowell and William Sheaffe, the comptroller and deputy collector of the port, charged the inhabitants with riot and the rescue of dutiable goods.

The Daniel Malcom affair may have been, as the whigs claimed, "an *Occurrance,* which in the City of *London* would scarce perhaps be thought worth the notice of a common Constable,"[15] but in Boston it commanded the attention of a royal governor. Francis Bernard, when the sheriff, comptroller, and deputy collector reported to him that they had been unable to get into Malcom's house that afternoon, ordered that depositions be taken of the officers, their subordinates, and certain selected witnesses.

The town was immediately alarmed. The depositions, people feared, would be "a partial Account" tending "to corroborate the Designs of our Enemy, & might be made the Ground of further misrepresentations." Besides, they claimed, it was "unreasonable & a Grievance that Evidences should be taken ex parte touching the Conduct of any of their Inhabitants," especially when the deposing officer was Governor Bernard, a writer of "defamatory Letters." Whigs may really have believed the Malcom affair a minor incident, but there was apprehension—fears summed up by James Bowdoin when he wrote that Bernard had made it his task to put the "Ministry up on revenue projects and other disgustful measures, and [was] eternally agitating them by his representations, in which he has a peculiar knack at making mountains of mole hills, & idle chitchat, treason."[16]

As soon as Bernard's plan became known, a "legally qualified and warned in Public Town-Meeting" was called. Two committees were created, and James Otis, the moderator, was appointed to both. The first was instructed to wait on Bernard and request copies of his depositions "that so the Town having Knowledge of their Accusers, and of the Nature and Design of the Testimonies taken, may have it in their Power to rectify Mistakes, and counter work the Designs of any who would represent them in a disadvantageous Light to his Majesty's Ministers." The second was to study the depositions and, if necessay, produce evidence for the town. That James Otis was the only practicing lawyer appointed indicates that he was expected to guide the "counter work."[17]

Bernard had little choice except to make the depositions public, and they did not prove as damaging as whigs had feared. Only crown officers had seen a "mob" on the street in front of Malcom's house; every other witness said the crowd had been orderly and respectful, merely curious spectators whiling away the time. Reading the testimony as a whole, what is said seems rather harmless, but our impressions are immaterial. The inhabitants of eighteenth-century Boston found more to alarm them than we do today. The depositions, they charged, "tended to corroborate the designs of our enemies and might be made the grounds of further misrepresentations," for "they contained a partial account of the behavior of the people who from mere curiosity had got together," and were an "endeavour to magnify a bagatelle opposition to a custom-house officer, to the enormous size of a general contempt of all King's officers."[18]

Small details that escape our eyes caught the attention of James Otis and his committee. It was a grievance, Bostonians asserted, that in his deposition the informer, Ebenezer Richardson, had been "dignified" by Governor Bernard "with the title of Esquire" so "that the evidence of this detestible person might have its weight." More important it was found "that a number of Persons of Credit, who were able to set the whole matter in a clear Light, had by *some means or other,* escaped his Excellency's Notice." And so the committee obeying the mandate of the town meeting, "of their own Accord took the Depositions of those Persons" to be sent, "together with those taken by the Governor, to their friend at Home, to be produc'd as *Occasion* shall require."[19]

The committee did not interview any of the officers who had deposed before Bernard. Perhaps they would not cooperate, but just as likely they were not asked. Otis's task was not to refute their testimony by direct examination. It was to modify or clarify the statements made by average citizens in response to what he was sure had been the governor's leading questions. William Nickells is a good example. In his deposition before the council he admitted advising Sheriff Greenleaf not to enter Malcom's house. Now he swore he had only been expressing the opinion "that said Sheriff had no lawful authority so to do." He had also cautioned Greenleaf that Malcom was resolute and posed a danger. Too much should not be made of such a warning, Nickells now explained to Otis. "[H]e only meant that Capt. Malcom would resist to Violence, an unlawful Entry into his House; but that he believes he Capt. Malcom would not have made the least Opposition to Lawful Authority."[20]

Otis, in his questions, did not depart from the previous legal strategy. The defense Malcom had devised to give his actions a coloring of legality was again asserted. He had not been challenging lawful authority but unlawful authority. Now that defense took on the added dimension of having been understood by members of the crowd gathered outside his house. They had not been a mob ready to defy the sheriff and customs officers, but people who knew the law and had reason to believe that despite their numbers there would be no violence committed that afternoon.

The most damaging evidence gathered by Bernard from witnesses other than customs officials had been furnished by William Wimble. In his first deposition he corroborated testimony given by Sheriff Stephen Greenleaf. Wimble told him, Greenleaf had said, that if the officers made an overt move against Malcom a bell would be rung and the streets filled with people. The statement was serious as it amounted to, or seemed to be, a threat that the mob would rise and resist the enforcement of imperial law. Although he had not said so to Greenleaf, Wimble told the governor and council that he had not meant that the bell would be rung to summon the inhabitants, but that if it were rung the result would be to bring people out into the streets. They could, for example, think they were responding to a fire. He even had an explanation why he thought the bell might be rung. Ebenezer Richardson, not the whigs, would have rung it.[21]

Wimble related most of these facts to the governor and council. Otis must have felt that the damage done by the statement to Greenleaf was not overcome by Wimble's qualifying explanation. He had the witness sworn by the committee and received for the record a rather splendid specimen of how whigs argued facts in answer to tory facts. What the sheriff said was true, Wimble admitted. He had told him the bell might be rung and the streets filled. But "he meant and now explains it that it was the Opinion of the People that the Informer had hid himself in the old north meeting House and that he would ring the Bell in order to make his Escape in the Crowd which would be collected thereby, that he had no apprehension that any other Person would Ring the Bell or take any other Method to raise a Collection of People to oppose the Custom House Officers, every body appearing to him to be very quiet and peaceably disposed."[22]

It is important to understand precisely what Otis was doing. As already noted, the Malcom affair was referred to the attorney and solicitor generals of England and would even be brought up in parliament. Bernard had collected his depositions in the hope London would be persuaded to take action. If that occurred Otis knew, the determining question would not be whether Malcom had acted lawfully but whether the crowd in front of his house had been an unlawful mob engaged in a riot with which local officials had been powerless to deal. To counter the evidence that Bernard had gathered, and to prevent an adverse ruling by the attorney general, it was necessary to "counter work" at least enough facts creating a reasonable doubt whether there had been a mob, or, if there had been a mob, that it had threatened the officers with either an actual or potential riot.

That specific facts were disputed should not surprise us. The size of the crowd depended on who saw it. Hallowell and Sheaffe claimed that when Greenleaf returned from his abortive attempt to persuade Justice Ruddock to come to Malcom's house it numbered "between 3 or 400 people." Their two tidewaiters said the same. More damaging was the estimate of John Tudor, the one justice of the peace present and who was questioned only by Bernard. He put the figure at "near 300." Daniel Malcom, on the other hand, made a much lower count. "I only peeped out of my Window," he swore, "but believed there was not more that fifty if quite so many, and all appeared in good order." Enoch Rust, who was one of Malcom's "witnesses" stationed inside the house, also "looked out of the Windows once or twice." He thought there were no more "than fifty Persons" on the street, "but mostly Boys as far as I could Judge." One of those who made up the crowd said it "did not exceed one hundred," while another did not "suppose there was above twenty or twenty-five Men there besides the Officers and about as many School Boys."[23]

The size of the crowd was a fact bearing on Boston's reputation for rioting at a moment's notice, but proved little concerning the issue at hand. There were only two peace officers, four customs men, and a single justice present, and by everyone's estimate the crowd was large enough to intimidate so small a force. The probative fact in London would be its nature, its mood, or what one tory called its "moberenes."[24]

Hallowell and Sheaffe testified directly to that point. They had, they claimed, received "repeated Intimations from several persons of Credit . . . that if there should be any force offered to be used by us in breaking into said Malcoms house the Officers would be insulted and ill used, and it would be attended with fatal Consequences to them . . . by means of which we should certainly run the hazard of our lives." Sworn separately, Sheaffe was asked "whether if you had proceeded in opening the house, you think that your lives would have been in danger."

"Ans: Yes Certainly."

"Q. Whether you think the Danger woul'd have come from within the House or without?"

"Answer: From Both."

"Q. How come you to be of this Opinion?"

"Answer: From the information of diverse credible people who came to us for that purpose."[25]

The subordinate customs men, the two tidewaiters, also said they had been threatened with serious bodily harm had they attempted to force their way into Malcom's house.[26] No one else supported Hallowell and Sheaffe. Surely Governor Bernard was disappointed. Their charges would have been more damaging had they been corroborated by Sheriff Greenleaf or Justice Tudor, two native-born officials unconnected with the revenue service.

While somewhat helpful, Greenleaf did not furnish Bernard the quality of factual data expected of one in his position. He said there had been a mob and that it would have reacted violently had he tried to enforce the law, but he was annoyingly indefinite, accusing more by inference than by positive evidence, never, for example, identifying any of the individuals whom he quoted. Typical of his testimony was an answer to the question whether any person in the crowd had threatened him or the other officials with violence should they attempt to enter Malcom's house. He thought so, he replied, at least when he asked if any men would give him assistance should he call on the *posse comitatus*. Greenleaf remembered "one Voice from behind him say Aye we'll assist you, but by the manner of the pronunciation and tone of voice he took it to be Ironical and either by way of Ridicule or threatening."[27]

Justice of the Peace John Tudor was even less cooperative. Acquaintances had told him there might be trouble if the officers broke into the house and he had gone with Greenleaf to mingle with the people hoping to prevent trouble. He had, he swore, not been needed. "I Went in Amongst them and Asked some Questions they Answered me in a Very Pleasant Manner and All of them whilst I staid with them behaved very Quietly and some of them said very Pleasantly they Came to see how Affairs was Like to go, etc., etc. I left them in all Appearance in Good Humour and Quiet."[28]

Tudor's statement set the tone that Otis needed,[29] corroborated by all the other witnesses questioned by his committee. "I am certain," Paul Revere deposed, "the people that were gathered had not any intent to hinder the officers in the discharge of their duty but would have protected them all that lay in their power." Caleb Hopkins said much the same. Far from having any thought of opposing Greenleaf, he had joined the crowd only "to see such a thing as the breaking open of a mans house which thing was not common in this Country." According to Nathaniel Barber, Hallowell's "mob" had not been a mob at all, but "worthy Gentlemen and good sort of People, there was not the least appearance of disorder, much less Opposition to any legal Authority." There had occurred, two other witnesses agreed, "nothing riotous or tumultuous among them."[30]

The theme of all the depositions was the same. If the officers faced any danger it was from within the house (where, it will be recalled, Malcom had a right to resist unlawful entry), not from the crowd which was "as Quiet as tho they were at Church" or "going to a Funeral." The testimony was uniform and so was the language. Certain set phrases appear in most depositions indicating that James Otis thought the matter serious enough to brief every witness whom he questioned. "[T]he people assembled behaved with decency and good Order and had not the least appearance of a Riot," was a recurring description, although it would be wrong to think words were put into the deponent's mouth by Otis for they also are found in depositions taken by Bernard. We can only guess, but it seems safe to assert that with or without prompting from Otis, eighteenth-century Bostonians were familiar with the criminal law. They knew what constituted an illegal mob and the crowd scene they described was anything but a mob. "The People in the Street appeared to be in good order and sober," was one way they put it, although the words "decency and good order" were more popular, repeated in almost every deposition.[31]

If Otis, seeking to establish a legal defense, made any contribution to the evidence it most likely was the testimony given by all those questioned that Malcom had not gathered the crowd, did not request its aid, and wanted no one to help him. "Capt. Malcom never asked me to assist him in anything at all in regard to making any resistence against the

Officers breaking open his house," a neighbor asserted, "nor did I ever hear he ask'd any person as I live next door to him the said Malcom." Other witnesses were as emphatic: Malcom neither asked for nor wanted help. Hallowell had made the charge, saying Malcom had told him he would have "assistance enough" and that "the said Hallowell would be served as he was before by the Mob." It was an important allegation, bearing not only on the question why the crowd had gathered but also on whether it was reasonable for the customs men to fear violence. Malcom, of course, denied he ever uttered such a statement.[32]

There were, to be sure, claims made that defy credibility. Enoch Rust, for example, was in the house that afternoon but had no knowledge that Malcom was defying imperial authority. "I never heard anybody call to Captain Malcom to open his Gate or Door that afternoon." And Malcom himself testified "that I never saw any Writ of Assistance nor any other Power or Authority whatsoever to break open my House, and if I had I am sure I would be the last Man in the World that would stand against it." Such assertions were a bit farfetched but nevertheless useful. They had no bearing on the question of Boston's collective responsibility for preventing the customs men from making a seizure, but did raise factual doubts whether a genuine, lawful attempt had been made to obtain entry to the house.[33]

We must not permit ourselves to be led astray. The issue was not the conduct of the officials but the conduct of the crowd. Hallowell, Sheaffe, the two tidewaiters, and to a lesser extent Sheriff Greenleaf, all said the mob, to prevent law enforcement, threatened violence. That was the case they sought to prove and they had facts to prove it: that imperial customs statutes could not be enforced in Massachusetts. Otis's "counter work" was not to establish conclusively that this contention was wrong. He did not have to demonstrate that imperial writs ran freely in the colony. All he had to do was cast doubt on the evidence; to show that the Malcom affair was immaterial to the question, that it neither proved nor disproved that parliament's statutes were unenforceable in Boston.

The probative fact for the whig side was not the lack of violence for none had been charged. Spoken threats and implied intimidation were the grounds of the tory case, and an important fact contributing to the "counter work" was that no one reported seeing weapons. Even that was not a determinative consideration if the crowd consisted "of fifty or upwards." Then "whether armed or not" it could have been proclaimed a riot if, and only if, it was "unlawfully, riotously or tumultuously assembled." Justice Ruddock, by refusing to accompany Greenleaf to the house, and Justice Tudor, by saying he would go only to mingle with the people and report their attitudes, nothing more, had seen to it that no magistrate was in a position to proclaim a riot. Greenleaf, by provincial law, was empowered to do so, though it was not customary for a sheriff to proclaim riots in Massachusetts.[34] He did not, and the inference Hallowell and Sheaffe attempted to draw from that fact was that he had been intimidated by the mob, that he knew a proclamation would be ignored, was afraid it would precipitate violence, and expected that the *posse comitatus* would turn upon him rather than the rioters.[35] To overcome that inference, Paul Revere and other witnesses testified that the people "had not any intent to hinder the officers in the discharge of their duty but would have protected them all that lay in their power." By saying everyone had been as quiet as if at church or going to a funeral, a counter inference was established: that a riot had not been proclaimed because there was no mob "unlawfully, riotously or tumultuously assembled." The crowd had not even been sullen.[36] It had been peaceful, outwardly friendly, and in no way threatening.

There is a temptation to draw definitive conclusions that must be resisted. We can never be certain which version came closest to the truth or even if either side knew that it was exaggerating or fabricating facts. It is possible both whigs and imperial officials thought their accounts accurate. It would not even be wise to draw suppositions from the testimony of Sheriff Greenleaf, who apparently sought to please his superior, Governor Bernard, by saying he thought he had been threatened with violence, yet failed to furnish any damaging evidence substantiating the charge. If he was cautious in his deposition, he had reason to be. It might be thought he did not want to antagonize local whigs, for no matter the outcome he had to continue to live in Boston. If so, that was only one consideration. Greenleaf had a sound legal reason to play down the fact that he had been stopped by the crowd from entering Malcom's house, if indeed he had. It did him no good to prove that there had been a riot. English law did not permit a sheriff to plea as an excuse for failure to serve a legal process that he had been prevented by a mob. It was "a libel on the Government" to say that its civil officers were "not strong enough" to do their duty, and had Greenleaf given direct evidence that he had been afraid to act he would have been admitting a breach of office.[37]

The importance of the Malcom affair and its aftermath for the history of the American Revolution is not whether the crowd was a mob on the verge of a riot but how and why specific facts were argued by the parties concerned. One side sought to prove that imperial law could not be enforced in whig Boston. The other side did not have to prove the contrary, but rather that there was no evidence that the complaining officials had been kept out of Malcom's house by the mob or even by the threat of a mob. Considering how well law was understood by whigs, and that many probably surmised that Malcom had set a legal trap in order to sue Hallowell and Sheaffe, it is quite likely that the crowd was as quiet as whig witnesses testified. The fact that Greenleaf never went near the front door and did not even open the gate makes it reasonable to suppose, as he said, that threats spoken were in an "ironical" or sarcastic manner, not direct boasts of violence or assertions that he would be attacked. The customs officers could easily have concluded that there was more menace than actually existed. The people were hostile to the revenue service. Threats did not have to be spoken to be felt.

Both sides thought its case had been established, but each was reading only selected evidence. The commissioners of the customs, after they arrived in Boston, assumed everything Hallowell and Sheaffe told them had been proven, and more than once reminded London that the Malcom affair was evidence that they were "unsupported" by existing law-enforcement agencies.[38] Although the whigs would learn that many people in London believed the tory version of what happened—that a mob had opposed the customs officers while performing a lawful duty[39]—they continued to insist nothing damaging had been proven against their reputation by the "mighty pains . . . taken to work up this trifling matter, into an important *Narrative,* for a confirmation of what had before been slanderously reported of the Americans." The depositions gathered by Otis and his committee not only exposed the falsehoods of their "enemies," whigs asserted, they "afforded an instance of the authority with which the *people* speak, when their voice is united and they speak with decency."[40]

7

A Time of Mobs

THE USES OF FACTS

It does not do to leave a tale half told. We have seen that Americans were afraid they were being misrepresented, but we do not know what they feared. Suspicion alone would not be enough to explain why rational merchants in Philadelphia declared "that every sly art has been used to incense the ministry against the colonies; every argument that malice could invent has been urged to induce them to overturn the ancient foundations of liberty." There had to be some purpose, some reason motivating those unnamed "men" whom the Massachusetts house believed "will not cease to sow the seeds of jealousy and discord, till they shall have done irreparable mischief."[1]

It was not necessary to believe that governors and customs men wanted to suppress American liberty for them to be suspected of misrepresenting colonial legal behavior and social order. The desire for personal gain and official favor were incentives enough. "Governors and other officers of the crown, even the little officers of the revenue sent from hence" were said to color accounts of "their own loyal and faithful conduct" with exaggerated tales of American opposition in order to place their own activities in a better light. A governor would claim credit for every pro-imperial vote in a colonial legislature, but when things went wrong "he is never in fault; the assembly and the people are to bear all the blame;—they are factious ... turbulent, disloyal, impatient of government, [and] disrespectful to his *Majesty's Representative*." The average customs official was much the same, representing "the people as all inclined to *smuggling*," which was prevented by his "*extream vigilance*," for which he deserved "a *larger salary*." The British ministry listened to such men, its own puppets, and the troubles of America could be attributed to the fact that the ministers gave "full credit to what is reported to them concerning the dispositions and conduct of the people respecting the new [customs] regulations, by those who first projected them, and whose salaries, pensions, and expectations, are wholly founded upon the establishment of an American revenue." In fact, James Bowdoin blamed the imperial government's decision to tax the colonies, the policy precipitating the current constitutional controversy, upon false notions of colonial wealth "encouraged by persons here who expected to share in the revenue by an increase of salary or appointment to office."[2]

It is not necessary to ask if these charges were true. We may suspect they were for some individuals; human nature being what it is, officials surely curried favor with distant superiors by exaggerating difficulties and attributing failures to local conditions beyond their control. Truth does not matter and proof does not have to be detailed. What counts is that many colonists believed the charges and understood the consequences. They were not only certain that London was flooded by official misrepresentations of their conduct and attitude, they knew the dangers misrepresentations entailed.

Constitutional reform was one hazard, as for example Governor Bernard's urgent pleas that membership on the Massachusetts council be made appointive by the crown rather than elective by the house of representatives, a small step toward Bernard's goal of remodeling all governments in America on the Irish pattern.[3] More immediate was the evident fact that the reports sent home about American conduct by imperial officials caused the ministry and parliament to adopt unsympathetic attitudes toward colonial assertions of privilege or colonial petitions for constitutional redress. And third, they threatened that sooner or later London would respond by demanding that the whigs conform to imperial law or they would be compelled to do so by force.

Two ideas were gaining prevalence in Great Britain. First, that Americans believed opposition to an act of parliament justified violence and, second, that law and order had broken down in the colonies. People in Boston received letters from London warning them that though many in the mother country approved resistance to internal taxation they were shocked and dismayed by "the destruction and plunder of private property." The town was guilty of "flagrant Breaches of public Order," John Hancock was told by British merchants doing business with Americans who had petitioned parliament to repeal the stamp act. "You must know better," they warned, "than to imagine that any well regulated Government will suffer Laws, enacted with a View to public Good, to be disputed by lawless Rioters, with Impunity." Bostonians protested that they were misrepresented, that when riots broke out in Suffolk County it was they, the people, who acted immediately and decisively to restore order. "[O]ur most inveterate Enemy," they replied, "dare not openly assert that the civil Authority in this County & even thro the Province has not as good reason to be assured of the Assistance of the People in the legal Exercise of Power as in any County in England." That, of course, was precisely what their enemies were asserting.[4]

Words were carefully measured. The whigs of Boston said the people would support the government "in the *legal* Exercise of Power" and they meant exactly that. Illegal usurpations such as the stamp act were a different matter, a distinction tories could not sanction. "The Mob was so general & so supported," Governor Bernard had complained at the time of the riots, "that all civil power ceased in an instant & I had not the least authority to oppose or quiet the Mob." The "multitude," a tory Bostonian wrote home, "among which are many men of figure and fortune, imagine that such proceedings will surely procure a Repeal of the [stamp] Act." Thomas Gage, the army's commander in chief in America, reported a "general Scheme, concerted throughout" all the colonies by the use of "Menace or Force to oblige the Stamp Officers to resign."[5]

Boston would later list Gage among its "enemies," accusing him of eagerness "to receive unfavorable Impressions" of the town, and charging that "the publick Testimony he was prevail'd upon to bear against it, before he could have Time to make an impartial Enquiry, betray'd a want of *Candor* unbecoming his Station and Character." Whether whigs had good reasons to doubt Gage's veracity, they at least had grounds for questioning his sources of information, and recent debates in parliament had taught them that his comments on conditions in America had great influence at home. That had especially been true in the house of lords where some members opposing repeal of the stamp act had quoted reports received from Gage and other imperial officials. Their dispatches described conditions close to insurrection. Colonial resistance was not directed against one statute only, they asserted, nor was it limited to the issue of internal taxation, but questioned the authority of parliament itself. Repeal, they warned, far from making Americans grateful, would foster more daring opposition in the future and encourage what some implied was the beginning of a movement toward independence.[6]

American newspapers published two formal protests issued by thirty-three members of the house of lords opposing the repeal of the stamp act. In one, Gage was quoted as having written that the people in the colonies "are averse to Taxes of any Kind; and that the Merchants of that Place think they have a Right to every Freedom of Trade which the Subjects of *Great Britain* now enjoy."[7] It was such evidence, furnished by imperial officials like Gage, that persuaded these dissenting lords to vote against repeal. It was, of course, a matter of respect for the sovereignty of parliament, but not to be overlooked was the problem of law enforcement. Reports from America indicated that colonial opposition to the stamp act amounted to "Tumults and Insurrections" and that "the total repealing of that Law, especially while such Resistance continues, would (as Governor *Barnarde* [*sic*] says is their Intention) 'make the Authority of *Great Britain* contemptible hereafter.' " From this evidence—evidence based on impressions and surmises—it followed that "the Appearance of Weakness and Timidity in the Government and Parliament of this Kingdom" would have "a manifest Tendency to draw on further Insults." To repeal the stamp act without first suppressing lawlessness, "may greatly promote the Contagion of a most dangerous Doctrine, destructive to all Government, which has spread itself over all our *North American* Colonies, that the Obedience of the Subject is not due to the Laws and Legislature of the Realm, farther than he, in his private Judgment, shall think it comformable to the Ideas he has formed of a free Constitution."[8]

American whigs did not have to read between the lines. They understood what was meant. The dissenting lords might argue that repeal of the stamp act was a demonstration of weakness, a relinquishment of parliament's supremacy, but the thrust of their discontent was directed at law enforcement. Parliament was sovereign in theory, but no one would know it by looking at the conditions of law in British North America. "Repeal of the Stamp Act, without any previous Submission on the Part of the Colonies," would "in Effect, annul and abrogate all other Laws and Statutes relating to our Colonies," while, conversely, failure to enforce the stamp act would not only promote disrespect for law in general but resistance to future efforts at enforcement.[9]

The dissenting lords made no effort to placate whig anger or protect imperial officials in the colonies by relying on general arguments rather than specific information. They cited and quoted reports and documents furnished the ministry by its agents in America. They were, the lords said, "convinced from the unanimous Testimony of the Governors, and other Officers of the Crown in *America*," that the riots of 1765 "might easily have been quieted before they attained any dangerous Height," had the government there been armed "with proper Orders and Powers, repeatedly called for in vain." Numerous letters expressing "the Opinion" not only of British agents but of "many of the most intelligent and respectable Persons in those Provinces" became evidence proving that the stamp act would not have failed had it been properly "tried."[10]

The dissenting lords dismissed fears expressed by some members of parliament that enforcement of the stamp act would have led to bloodshed. On the contrary, they asserted, enforcement would have resulted in compliance, not defiance. Someone in America had written the secretary of state that there was no danger and the lords quoted what was said as proof that their colleagues were being intimidated by empty threats. The American people, the writer had contended, "dare not oppose a vigorous Resolution of the Parliament of *Great-Britain*." Had the imperial legislators "thought prudent to enforce their Authority" the colonists would have obeyed. The name of the correspondent was not revealed. There was no need—the evidence was in his words, not in his identity. The fact he wrote from America was proof that what he reported was based on firsthand knowledge and, as it was what the dissenting lords wanted to believe, was accepted as true. Indeed, what was said was familiar, following a pattern American whigs would soon recognize as part of the conspiracy of misrepresentation. Imperial officials described them not only "as disaffected and rebellious," but also "(to encourage the use of severity) as weak, divided, timid, and cowardly."[11]

Americans had been warned by friends in Britain that many promoters of the stamp act "were for enforcing it by a Military Power," information confirming their suspicions. The protest of the dissenting lords told them nothing new. Tories in Boston were already saying that the town was ruled by the mob, and it was common knowledge that Governor Bernard felt—or pretended to feel—unsafe in what he called "my difficult and perilous situation . . . without a force to protect my person."[12]

Whigs thought the governor wanted troops so he could rule by prerogative, but in truth the stamp-act riots were the cause of his anxiety. They had been an unnerving experience. Reflecting on his situation the day after the second of Boston's two riots, Bernard realized "how extreamly weak an American Governor is in regard to popular tumults, without a file of Men at his Command & having no regular troops, at present, within call." The provincial militia was no alternative for it was one with the mob. He had not even been able to use it to reinforce Castle William where he planned to store the stamps. It was the only fortress in the colony, the one public building in which they might be kept safe from destruction. The militia, Bernard feared, could "be the Means of betraying the place." His best hope was "to hold out, untill Orders come from England, which probably will be accompanied with forces." His majesty's royal governor could not believe "that so Violent an Opposition to an act of parliament can fail of meeting with general resentment there."[13]

As soon as London learned of the stamp-act riots, Bostonians began to receive rumors that the ministry would dispatch soldiers to enforce the law. Nothing came of such stories. While there is no way of being certain, it is possible that the first time any high-ranking official threatened or even suggested to a Bostonian that troops were needed to coerce obedience to imperial law was during the Daniel Malcom affair—that is, if we believe Malcom's partner, Captain William Mackay. "Mr. Hallowell told me," Mackay reported, "that this Affair would be of bad Consequence to the Town and Province, that they must have a Regiment of Soldiers to assist them in doing their Duty." If so, Mackay replied, "it would be his Fault and not ours as we wanted none." All Boston agreed but whigs feared that their wishes would not weigh heavily in the decision and as time went on rumor that the military was on its way continued to be heard.[14]

American whigs did not have to guess. They knew that a minor incident in a colonial town could be swelled into a major event by the time it was reported in London. Even the paltry Malcom affair was used as a fact to argue that something had to be done to strengthen law enforcement in the colonies. The English commissioners of the customs thought that the incident was evidence proving that their American officers were "not vested with sufficient legal Authority for carrying into execution the Acts of Navigation, Trade, and Revenue." They wanted new laws, but parliament dismissed the matter, saying it did not have time for every violation brought to its attention. After the American commissioners took up residence, the emphasis shifted from the need for stronger laws to the need for an armed force. While in London lobbying for the creation of the board, Charles Paxton had insisted that regular troops were necessary to maintain the authority of imperial government in Boston, and claimed, probably with justification, that Thomas Hutchinson agreed. Within a few months Paxton had Robinson, Hulton, and Burch convinced that he was right. Troops were needed not only to end mob rule, they wrote, but to give heart to the tory party as "there are many people of property in this town, who might be induced to shew their countenance in support of Government, if the executive power had strength to protect them." It was, of course, their opinion; they had not consulted the potential tories for whom they spoke. "We have not made any one privy to the contents of this memorial, as a Subject of this delicate nature, requires the utmost secrecy, in the present feeble, and unhinged state of Government."[15]

Privy or not, the whigs had an idea what was occurring and were worried. A visitor to Boston during 1768 wrote a London newspaper that they "were much more concerned at any mobs that happened than the Government people. These last seemed pleased with them, as countenancing their representations—the necessity of sending soldiers to keep them in order."[16]

Today, looking back at the evidence, we may wonder why American whigs were so concerned. They may have been certain that the commissioners had "calumniated them to Government," but why should they have thought the ministry would believe what was written? They may have claimed that the British public "[h]aving by a series of iniquitous and irritating Measures provok'd a loyal People almost to Desperation . . . magnify every act of an American Mob into REBELLION," but why should they have expected to be harmed by such impressions? The evidence sent to London was not strong, the facts were largely circumstantial—hints, suggestions, rumors of mobs—in only a few cases accounts of actual rescues of property seized by customs men, unlawful perhaps but, like the Malcom affair, largely minor occurrences that could be called "rebellion" only by stretching definitions and only by inference made part of a concerted conspiracy.[17]

One answer, of course, was the prestige office gave those making the "misrepresentations." Even if the evidence lacked probative weight, the reporters did not. Their dispatches were studied by the ministry and shown to members of parliament and to the king. Petitions, answers, or defenses from the colonies, by way of contrast, were not always given countenance and when read were often ignored. "Moreover, it is worth particular notice, that in all disputes between power and liberty in America, there is danger that the greatest credit will always be given to the officers of the Crown, who are the men in power," the Massachusetts house charged. "This we have sometimes found by experience; and it is much to be feared, that the [British] nation will fall into some dangerous mistake, if she has not already, by too great attention to the representations of particular persons, and a disregard to others."[18]

The danger was compounded by conditions in the British Isles. It was not to be wondered, whigs were warned, that the ministry could be persuaded that Boston was in the hands of the mob, for that was precisely the case of London and Westminster. At the time the commissioners were urging that troops be sent to America to suppress riots, the government at home was using soldiers for just that purpose. The worst riots in Irish history took place during the very month the ministry decided that the situation was in fact dangerous at Boston and responded to the pleas of the customs men by ordering the army to occupy the town. There were also crowds roaming in every area in Scotland and England. Two thousand hungry poor people arose in Bristol alone, and elsewhere noblemen and magistrates were mobbed. Most menacing of all, the supporters of John Wilkes, a political crowd, had taken over the streets of London. It is not difficult to imagine the exaggerated visions that raced through the minds of British ministers reading reports of the Malcom affair, when we realize they only had to look out of their windows at Whitehall to see riots far more extensive than anything experienced in America. The same month London learned of Malcom's defiance, the government was faced with "the greatest & most dangerous mobs and insurrections all over England, that ever was known, great numbers of mills and houses were destroyed, and many lives lost—in some places the civil magistrates, with the county militia, in others, parties of soldiers had for the present suppressed several parties of rioters but had by no means allayed that spirit of tumult and discontent, that had generally spread thro' the land, occasioned by the long continued hardships and oppressions, with which the poor have been burderened [*sic*]."[19]

There had been two stamp-act riots in Boston, one on the evening of 14 August 1765, the other twelve days later during the night of the twenty-sixth. Between those two dates there had been general calm, yet the usually well-informed board of trade told the king that the crowd had been on the streets from 15 to 26 August, implying that for eleven days Boston had been subjected to mob rule. We would be wrong to think this assertion a deliberate misrepresentation of the facts. It was a natural mistake to assume that what was happening at home also occurred in the colonies.[20]

More serious than misconceptions of the dimension of riots were misconceptions about their suppression. In Great Britain troops had to be used or the crowd might stay on the streets for days on end. Surely it was difficult for a British minister to contemplate a society in which civilians undertook the task of terminating a mob. Thus when Bostonians reported that they had done so, the claim passed unnoticed and the king was told that there had been one, long, continuous riot in Massachusetts. A fact that whigs tried to establish and that never was taken seriously in London was that Americans would not have tolerated the conditions that existed in British cities.

Perhaps British social realities made it impossible for the imperial government to understand American legal conditions. But even had that problem not existed, the principles guiding the people of Boston would have been too outlandish for an official with tory predilections to have taken seriously. Bostonians differentiated between the two stamp-act riots in their town and did so on grounds that led to the conclusion that only the second had been illegal. They, and many other American whigs as well, approved of the first riot for, though some property had been destroyed, "no violence had been offered to any one" and the stamp distributor for Massachusetts Bay had been intimidated into resigning, making it both "justify[e]d" and a date to be celebrated by all Americans. The twenty-sixth, by way of contrast, had been destructive—"villainous Proceedings" and "shocking Transactions"—clearly distinguishable in the minds of Bostonians from the previous riot: a mob which they not only condemned but by authorizing citizen assistance "in the Suppression of all Disorder," made certain did not reoccur.[21]

There may yet have been another fact on the minds of British ministers making it difficult for them to see American crowds as they were seen by whigs: the thought of bloodshed. Historians generally agree that eighteenth-century British mobs were more threatening than those in contemporary Massachusetts, though some believe that they were better controlled as they "were dealt with forcibly and speedily." It was that very fact, the use of troops resulting in counter violence, that made British crowds more dangerous than those in America. Because they were not opposed by armed police power, whig colonial mobs were less likely to be distracted from the political purpose that had brought them onto the streets and once it was accomplished they invariably dispersed on their own accord.[22]

The sister of Commissioner Henry Hulton saw another distinction between the mobs she had witnessed at home and those she encountered in Boston. In England, she explained, "a few lights put into the Windows will pacify, or the interposition of a Magistrate restrain them, but here they act from principle & under Countenance, no person daring or willing to suppress their Outrages, or to punish the most notorious Offenders." Miss Hulton did not realize it, but she had mentioned a fundamental difference between crowds in the home islands and the colonies. In Great Britain and Ireland the magistrates spoke with authority because the mob knew they would order the troops to fire. In America few magistrates would think of suppressing a political riot because they were whigs and agreed with the crowd's objectives. In a sense that was what she meant by "lights." Homeowners who did not want their glass panes smashed by men rushing through London streets shouting "Wilkes and Liberty" put candles in their windows to signal support for John Wilkes even if they detested him. Benjamin Franklin, who kept his house illuminated for several nights in succession, would have been amused at her statement as he reckoned the cost of candles an expensive consequence of British riots.[23]

It is unnecessary to describe the destruction, terror, or scope of eighteenth-century British rioting for the story has been masterfully told elsewhere.[24] The views of Franklin should be considered, however, as he was an American whig living in London and appreciated how easy it was for officials there to equate reports received from the colonies with conditions personally experienced at home. "In America," he complained, "if one mob rises, and breaks a few windows, or tars and feathers a single rascally informer, it is called REBELLION; troops and fleets must be sent, and military execution talked of as the decentest thing in the world."[25] In Great Britain crowds were far more destructive, assaulting people who would "not roar for Wilkes and liberty," tearing down houses, wrecking boats, threatening bridges, "soldiers firing among the mobs and killing men, women, and children," and yet "we hear no talk of England's being in *rebellion;* no Threats of taking away its Magna Charta, or repealing its Bill of Rights," as when reports of more minor affairs were received from the colonies.[26] "I have seen, within a year, riots in the country about corn; riots about elections; riots about work-houses; riots of colliers; riots of weavers; riots of coal-heavers; riots of sawyers; riots of sailors; riots of Wilkesites; riots of government chairmen; riots of smugglers, in which custom-house officers and excisemen have been murdered, the King's armed vessels and troops fired at, &c."[27]

There had been mobs in Franklin's hometown of Philadelphia, but nothing in America prepared him for what he encountered in the mother country. Ironically some of the accounts he sent to colonial friends read much like the reports Henry Hulton and Francis Bernard were sending in the reverse direction. "All respect to law and government," Franklin wrote Joseph Galloway, "seems to be lost among the common people, who are moreover continually inflamed by seditious scribblers, to trample on authority and every thing that used to keep them in order." Can it be a coincidence that on the very day Franklin wrote this gloomy appraisal of conditions in London, Lord Hillsborough, the colonial secretary, was so concerned about conditions in Boston that he ordered Bernard to protect customs officers from lawlessness?[28]

Just as it was easy for British officials to magnify the extent of rioting in the colonies, so it was easy for them to imagine that the American customs service was in greater danger than it actually was. In the colonies revenue men could be roughly handled, but they were not killed. It was a point whigs appreciated but could the ministers in London? When they heard of mob resistance they surely associated it with violent deaths. Customs officers in England and Scotland risked their lives when inspecting ships for dutiable goods. Smugglers fought "regularly the King's cruizing Vessels," drove them ashore, and burned them, even killing revenue men. Much is revealed about legal conditions in both countries when we learn that the only proclamations issued by Governor Bernard offering rewards for the capture of fugitives "charged with the Murder of . . . one of the Officers of his Majesty's Customs" concerned incidents that occurred in England, not in the colonies. Even more is told about attitudes when we note that the edition of the *Boston Gazette* containing one of these proclamations carried the story of a customs official in America being visited by a mob—a mob that boasted it had not abused its victim and had destroyed no property.[29]

It would not do to think the boast a bit of whig political propaganda. They were arguing a fact, true enough, but they were also asserting a point of law. Violence was sometimes justified and therefore not unlawful, they were saying, when used for certain purposes and under certain circumstances. The distinction drawn between the two stamp-act riots in Boston was not a convenient aberration. It was basic to an emerging whig theory of law, a legal theory that tories could not accept and perhaps did not understand. We would do well to think of a gulf separating the legal mind of the American whig from the legal mind of the imperial official, a gulf that is widening as time goes on. They are arguing facts true enough, but they are also arguing law, and when the legal theory justifying and explaining whig facts is unacceptable, indeed incomprehensible to the men who govern the empire, those whig facts are falling on deaf imperial ears.

8

A Fearful Quiet

THE CONSTITUTIONAL DILEMMA

Expectations often seem unbelievable in retrospect. When the commissioners of the American customs first took office, an Englishman expressed optimism. If "they escape hanging," he wrote, their appointment "will be found . . . a very wise and beneficial measure."[1] Hanging, one danger they did not face, was just about the only inconvenience they escaped. The creation of the board did not prove as "wise and beneficial" as the ministry had hoped. It tightened procedures and raised more money, true enough, but by adding to American grievances it may have cost more than it was worth.

To seek the origins of causes would be a useless quest. The commissioners may have commenced their tenure as prejudiced against Americans, as colonial whigs believed. It is just as possible they reacted only after sensing the hostility surrounding them. Henry Hulton was not long in office before realizing that with the exception of Scots merchants there was virtually unanimous opposition to the revenue statutes of parliament. Symbols of the new imperialism on arrival, their activities and public attitudes soon transformed the commissioners into personal enemies in the eyes of most Massachusetts whigs. After the Boston massacre of 1770, the social ostracism was just about complete. "[T]here is no safety in conversing with them, or showing them the least respect," the pastor of the new north meetinghouse told a friend. The plain fact is that the board simply did not belong in Boston. Even Joseph Harrison, the collector of the port and the board's chief local subordinate, wished they were somewhere else. "My present situation is indeed very distressing and truly pitiable," he told the Marquis of Rockingham. "The Commissioners [are] not very friendly (on account of my being an Advocate for temperate Measures till such Time as the Hands of Government shall be strengthened.)"[2]

Harrison's words interest us, not because of his unhappiness, but because they illustrate the ease with which revenue officers stationed in Boston threw out hints for troops and stronger laws when writing to men of influence at home. Commissioner Charles Paxton was a master at the technique. While in London he had lobbied for soldiers, and once setting foot back in Boston he apparently thought them more urgent than ever. The revenue statutes, Paxton warned a member of the British cabinet, would never be obeyed by American merchants for one reason: American merchants could not be made to obey. "The Officers [are] no way to blame for they have no power to Enforce them," he explained. "The Authority of this Government has been found to be quite ineffectual and impotent. . . . Unless the hands of Govert. are Strength[e]ned I fear that the people wont easily be persuaded that Great Brittan [*sic*] is in earnest to Support her own laws." He was only repeating what Bernard had been saying, and what the board was collectively telling London. The commissioners had been in America just three months when they reported that the situation was virtually hopeless. We may think they knew they were exaggerating but we will never be sure. That very same day they asked Commodore Samuel Hood at Halifax for his aid. "We are of Opinion," they wrote, "that it is essentially necessary to the Service that a Frigate should be stationed in this Port."[3]

Daniel Malcom may have been responsible for the request to Hood. A few days earlier, according to the commissioners, several local merchants applied to John Williams, inspector general of the revenue service, for what the commissioners called "the usual Indulgences, and among the Rest the famous Mr. Malcom, and being answered that the full Duties would be required, he went away, and said he should take his own Measures."[4]

We must marvel at the scene. Daniel Malcom of all people requesting favors from customs men! Could he have thought they would consider it? Could he have been serious? There is even a question whether they were able to grant what Malcom asked. The commissioners had authority to "compound," that is, after a seizure had been made, to return the goods to the owner and settle for a fine lower than their value.[5] It is not, however, clear they could agree to a prior "indulgence." The idea has the scent of bribery to twentieth-century noses, but it had been the practice of colonial collectors and comptrollers before the creation of the board and, if not strictly legal, had been sanctioned by custom. Not any longer, the board was saying.

Whatever Malcom had in mind is a mystery. A conservative guess is that he was testing the waters, seeing how strict the new enforcement was to be before resorting to smuggling. He is believed to have had Madeira wine aboard a ship and had no intention of paying the exorbitant duty. "On the next day," the commissioners reported to London, "his Vessel arrived near the Harbour, where she was unloaded of about Sixty pipes of Wine into Lighters, which were conducted into Town at Night by a great Number of people—the Master nevertheless, the next day, reported his Vessel in Ballast, and though the Affair is notoriously known and our Officers have endeavoured to procure an Informer, yet no one dares to appear." It was, Bernard observed, "a strong-handed landing . . . which still remains unpunished for want of Power rather than Discovery."[6]

The feeling of helplessness, absolute, frustrated helplessness was a prime reason the commissioners believed they needed military support. What could be more demeaning to their pride than the boldness of Daniel Malcom? They knew his reputation, yet he walked in and asked an indulgence. When they refused, he replied that he did not need it. Then Malcom proceeded to prove the fact by running a valuable cargo ashore and bringing it into town. Indeed, he flaunted the insult. The very next day, while his captain was filing a patently false entry, Malcom called a merchants' meeting to propose that Bostonians cease importing products of British manufacture until the Townshend duties were repealed. The deliberations, Bernard reported, "were sanguine, and full of high Pretensions," and though little was decided, the meeting "may be said to be the first Movement of the Merchants against the Acts of Trade."[7]

The commissioners had expected stronger measures; they may have even hoped that their refusal to grant "indulgences" would lead the whigs to raise a mob. We will never be certain, but what they wrote to London gives the impression of being disappointed at Malcom's mild reaction. "Instead of opposing the execution of the new Laws by violence, as had been threat[e]ned," the board explained, "a Plan of *economy and industry,* was set on foot, at one of these town meetings, the apparent design of which, is to allarm the trading and manufacturing people of Great Britain, and to engage them in their interest, so as to obtain a repeal of the [Townshend] Laws."[8]

A nonimportation agreement, publicly promulgated and generally subscribed to, may have been a combination for the purpose of opposing a statute of the realm and not a "legal measure" as whigs would insist, but it was nonviolent and did not bode ill for the commissioners' physical safety. The fact that Boston merchants could enter into a nonimportation movement, announce its details in the press, use the post office to urge other seaports to adopt similar agreements, print those agreements, and publish the names of "importers" as "Enemies to the Constitution of their Country" was more evidence of the weakness of imperial law and the need for stronger legislation. It did little, however, to strengthen the commissioners' case for having troops sent to Boston. Even Daniel Malcom was furthering the whig policy of restraint. If imperial officials believed violence necessary to prove their case for military support, the whigs would not accommodate them.

It is well for the historian to remain neutral. The story should not be intruded upon by the reporter. Yet the more one looks at the evidence the more one is drawn to the conclusion that Governor Francis Bernard and a majority of the commissioners were so fearful of the whig crowd and so convinced they needed military protection that they actually desired the very event they dreaded, a riot in Boston. What the whig mob would not provide, imperial officials would have to invent.

The task of convincing London, never difficult considering Boston's reputation in government circles, was made easier by two events destined to alter Massachusetts history. The new office of American secretary was created and the Earl of Hillsborough named to that position. On the very day Boston newspapers announced the appointment, Governor Bernard wrote a letter to Hillsborough's undersecretary warning that while Boston was quiet it was a most fearful quiet. "The officers of the Customs are still threatened with Violence and Vengeance; nor are the Commissioners spared." There had, in fact, been one case of "violence," the running ashore of Daniel Malcom's sixty pipes of Madeira wine. Five days later, writing directly to Hillsborough, the governor recalled that there had been another serious riot. It was the event we have already seen when examining Bernard's standards of proof—the "boys" who surrounded the homes of commissioners Burch and Paxton, making noise and frightening the ladies, evidence that the Boston town meeting would ridicule.[9]

Rumors were flying among imperial officials in Boston and all were reported to London. The resignation of Andrew Oliver as stamp agent was to be reenacted with the commissioners playing the principle role. They "had certain Information," they wrote the lords of the treasury, "that, on the next day, being the Anniversary of the Repeal of the stamp Act, which has been observed as a Day of Triumph over Great Britain, certain Images would be affixed to a Tree called the Tree of Liberty, that the Mob would assemble and bring the Commissioners and the Officers of the Board to the Tree, to oblige them to renounce their Commissioners [*sic*]."[10]

They were correct about the planned celebration. Boston had commemorated the repeal of the stamp act the year before, and would do so again in 1768. The original festivities had brought the largest crowds the town could remember onto its streets. They were expected to be even more numerous for the second anniversary as the date, the eighteenth of

March, fell immediately after Saint Patrick's Day. During the second half of the eighteenth century, Saint Patrick's Day in Boston was an occasion for "elegant Entertainments." In 1767 the Irish and their friends had celebrated on the evening of the seventeenth, but now—and Bernard thought this an ominous fact with which to enlighten Hillsborough—the whigs arranged to postpone Saint Patrick's Day for twenty-four hours insuring a larger and, for tories, a more threatening mob.[11]

The eighteenth of March 1768 began much as the crown officers expected. The first sight that greeted them at the break of dawn were effigies of Commissioner Charles Paxton and Inspector General John Williams hanging from the liberty tree. The figures were soon removed, apparently by whigs, but that fact did not calm the nervous commissioners. "[T]he Morning," they wrote, "was ushered in with Guns firing Drums beating, and a Display of Colours in several parts of the Town." The board immediately sent a note to Bernard praying his protection. The governor summoned the council and received the answer he expected. "At Council I set forth in strong terms the atrociousness of this insult [the effigies], the danger of its being followed by actual violence, and the necessity there was of providing for the preservation of the peace of the town. But all I could say made no impression upon the Council; they persevered in treating the affair as of no consequence, and assuring me that there was no danger of any commotion."[12]

There is no need to examine the council's arguments. They said there was no danger because there was no riot, a day of rejoicing should not be confused with insurrection.[13] What interests us is not the defense but the imperial complaint, and it was Bernard even more than the commissioners who argued facts to build a legal case. It would be well, therefore, to consider the quality of his evidence and the probativeness of his presumptions. The quotation is long, yet should be considered with care, keeping in mind that this was the presentation that won the tory case, this was the letter that persuaded Lord Hillsborough that Massachusetts was in rebellion and that troops would have to be sent to Boston. Bernard begins with one of his favorite inferences: if the event had not proved as dangerous as expected it was because some unnamed whig leaders were able to keep the situation under control—at least on this occasion.

[G]reat pains were taken by the selectmen of the town and some other gentlemen, that the festivity should not produce a riot in the evening, and so far it succeeded that it produced terror only and not actual mischief. . . . These prevented the lighting a bonfire in the street, which was several times attempted, and would probably have been a prelude to action. But the assembling a great number of people of all kinds, sex, and ages, many of which showed a great disposition to the utmost disorder, could not be prevented. There were many hundreds of them paraded the streets with yells and outcries which were quite terrible. I had in my house Mr. Burch, one of the commissioners, and his lady and children, who had the day before moved to our house for safety. I had also with me [Hutchinson and Sheriff Greenleaf]. But I had taken no steps to fortify my house, not being willing to show an apprehension of danger to myself; but at one time there was so terrible a yell from the mob going by that it was apprehended that they were breaking in, but it was not so. However it caused the same terror as if it had been so, and the lady, a stranger to this country who chose our house for an asylum, has not recovered it as yet. They went on and invested Mr. Williams' house, but he showed himself at a window and told them that he was ready for their reception, and they went off, and either did not intend or dared not to attack his house. They also at two different times about midnight made outcries about Mr. Paxton's house out of mere wantonness to terrify his family. The whole made it a very terrible night to those who thought themselves objects of the popular fury; and yet if I should complain of it, I should be told that it was nothing but the common effects of festivity and rejoicing and there was no harm intended.[14]

Bernard's last sentence would prove correct. The whigs did make the argument he predicted. The crowd of 18 March had not been a mob, just "a few disorderly persons mostly boys." In his diary Selectman John Rowe estimated that 800 people had gone to the house of Inspector General Williams, "but did him no damage, which the greatest part of the gentlemen in town were very glad off [sic]." "Whether their design was to do him an injury or not," a gathering of elected whig leaders argued, "by his address and soft treatment of them, together with the interposition of some of the neighbouring householders, they soon retir'd & dispers'd, without doing any mischief at all."[15]

General Thomas Gage later reported to Hillsborough that it had been a "trifling" affair. With that judgment the council agreed. The activities of the eighteenth were "too inconsiderable" to deserve attention except for those "persons disposed to bring misery & distress upon the town & Province." Even after troops arrived in Boston and the commissioners had won their case, the whigs continued the argument. The fact that soldiers had been sent "in consequence of some Children hallooing on the 18th of March last, must be owing to the most unkind and injurious Representations."[16]

Once again the imperial evidence does not seem to sustain the imperial case. If the mob was dangerous why had no injuries occurred? If the plan was to force customs officers to resign why had they not been summoned to the liberty tree? The commissioners had an answer. The insurrection planned for the eighteenth of March had been postponed. The general court had sent London a petition praying repeal of the Townshend duties, and it was judged politically wise to await a reply before resorting to more violent protests, or so the commissioners claimed. "It does not appear that it is their plan to molest us immediately, as the last Mob was prevailed upon to disist from proceeding to Outrage until the Answer of Government to the remonstrance of their Assembly could be received," all five members of the board explained ten days after the riot of the eighteenth of March.[17]

We might expect that having survived the night the commissioners felt somewhat secure, but of course they did not. The restraint of the crowd was evidence of the precarious situation in which the king's officers and all other loyal subjects found themselves. In a marvelous, paragraph-long sentence, the commissioners summed up the case for troops based entirely on inference, conjecture, and rumors, the sources of which were not revealed.

> Though no immediate Outrage should be committed on ourselves or Officers, yet if the answer from Government to the Remonstrances of the lower House of Assembly should not be agre[e]able to the people, We are fully persuaded that they will proceed to violent Measures; In the mean Time we must depend on the favour of the Leaders of the Mob for our protection and in such Circumstances we cannot answer for our Security for a day, much less will it be in our power to carry the Revenue Laws into Effect.

Governor Bernard told the same tale to Lord Hillsborough: the whigs had postponed physical violence until parliament had time to answer the colony's petition. "But it is inferred, and sometimes expressly declared, that when they have advice that the redress which they expect is denied, they will immediately proceed to do themselves justice."[18]

When it is realized that facts of this probative quality constitute the evidence, the argument, the case that will bring the regular army to Boston, one may well draw back in puzzlement, if not astonishment. Yet there was as much wonderment on the other side. The commissioners' facts seem weak, yet they thought them convincing for they went to great lengths to argue them. It must be asked why they had to take the trouble. There can be little doubt that they and their colleagues in the imperial service did not face a difficult task persuading official London that Americans were ripe for revolution and that troops were needed to maintain the king's laws. The ministry did not read between the lines. It did not note that little violence was reported or that evidence was mostly circumstantial. Even more telling, the government was conditioned by riots and smuggling at home to believe the worst about riots and smuggling in the colonies. The commissioners, if they wanted troops sent to Boston, did not have a heavy factual burden to carry, the onus of proof was light. What they offered seemed immaterial and unconvincing to American whigs and their British supporters, but it would win the case with the ministers at home.

Yet the evidence that they offered had, until now, not been enough. To prove the factual case gave but half a victory. We might think it sufficient to persuade the British ministry that troops were necessary in Boston: once that was done, soldiers would be dispatched to protect the commissioners and maintain order. Ironically it was not. Sustaining the factual burden was one thing, the legal burden was a different matter. Massachusetts constitutional law stood in their way, and the whigs knew how to manipulate that law to protect themselves from military intrusion.

There were two constitutional facts of life that placed on those imperial officials seeking troops for Massachusetts Bay a heavy factual burden if they wished to establish a legal justification. The first was that for purposes of maintaining order and policing the inhabitants, soldiers would not be sent into the old English colonies lying south of the former French possessions in Canada and north of the former Spanish settlements in the Floridas unless requested by the local government. The second was that in Massachusetts the request could not come from the governor alone. It had to be made by the governor with the advice and consent of the council.

Francis Bernard knew the law and appreciated the predicament in which it placed him. It was, in fact, his greatest grievance, expressed in letter after letter to London: the power of the local institutions of government, especially the veto of the council. The imperial constitution itself bound his hands. Lord Barrington, who was Great Britain's secretary at war and also Bernard's wife's cousin and political patron, had told him emphatically that he could expect military support in peacetime only if he made a formal, legal application stating that soldiers were needed to prevent rioting or to enforce the law. Current imperial policy, Barrington explained, was that troops "should not be quarter'd in the old Colonies which have been long settled and inhabited, unless call'd for by the Civil Magistrate or Government of the Province, as necessary to preserve the publick peace."[19]

Barrington had said "unless call'd for by the Civil Magistrate or Government" by which he meant the governor or the governor and council, depending on the provisions of the charter of the colony making the request. Massachusetts's charter said nothing directly on point, but long-established practice had created a constitutional rule that the governor could not act in any important matter without the advice and consent of the council. Calling for troops to maintain law and order during peacetime clearly fell within that category. It was a convention of the local constitution that Francis Bernard did not question. "All the king's governors," he explained to the colonial secretary, "are directed to take the advice of the Council in military movements, and in this government where the governor is in a more peculiar manner obliged to have the advice of the Council for almost everything he does, it would be dangerous to act in such an important business without such advice."[20]

Bernard accepted the validity of the colonial constitutional convention, even though it meant that his hands were legally tied, he could not send for soldiers to suppress whig dissent no matter how desperate he thought the situation. The fact bears repeating that members of the council, subject to veto by the governor, were elected by the house of representatives. The house, in turn, was elected at town meetings. As a majority of the town meetings were dominated by voters of the whig persuasion, so was the house of representatives which was not about to fill the council with tories. As a result of the constitutional apparatus of power and the political realities of the 1760s, the council gave the whigs a veto over the governor. One situation in which the veto would certainly be exercised was a gubernatorial request for advice and consent that troops be brought into the colony to coerce the inhabitants into obeying imperial customs statutes or other laws imposing parliamentary taxation.

Governor Bernard had learned from experience that he could not initiate a call for military assistance, or, as he expressed the situation, "it is in vain to put such a question to the Council; for, considering the influence they are under from their being creatures of the people, and the personal danger they would be subject to in assisting in the restraining them, it is not probable that the utmost extremity of mischief and danger would induce them to advise such a measure." The whigs would have said the governor was once more misrepresenting facts. The council would refuse consent not because of fear but because of conviction that troops were not needed. That issue is, for the moment, beside the point. During the stamp-act crisis, the governor had believed military aid necessary and wanted to ask for it. He had, in fact, been told by London to apply to General Gage for whatever forces were needed to restore order should persuasion fail and the situation get out of hand. These instructions arrived after the disturbances had abated, but even had Bernard received them in time they were constitutionally worthless. Following the second riot, that of 26 August when the houses of Hallowell and

Hutchinson were attacked, he asked the council that it consent to a request for troops. The councillors refused, and there was nothing the governor could do.[21]

The constitutional predicament was an imperial grievance summed up by Bernard in a letter to Lord Barrington. "The Commissioners have asked me what Support I can give them, if there should be an Insurrection," he wrote. "I answer none at all. They then desire me to apply to the general [Gage] for Troops; I tell them I cannot do it; for I am directed to Consult the Council about requiring Troops; & they will never advise it let the Case be ever so desperate."[22]

There was only one constitutionally viable way by which the military could be ordered to Massachusetts Bay as a police force preserving law and order. That was for the ministry in London to rescind the rule that a request had to come from the governor and council, and give the command itself for the military to march. That was another constitutional fact of life, known to Francis Bernard, to the commissioners of the customs, and to the local whigs. It was also why the whigs believed their enemies wished to incite them to riot and one of the reasons Boston's town meeting urged everyone to remain calm. For the commissioners to sustain the legal burden of proof necessary to overcome London's constitutional reluctance to interfere with colonial government, they needed more than rumors of "insurrections intended" and threats implied. An actual riot was necessary or, if they failed to obtain that, a disturbance that could be reported to the ministry as a mob rising would have to do. Should there be no violence during the disturbance then noise could be emphasized and the potential of what might have been and surely will eventually occur would be the dominant theme.

We need not wonder why the affair of 18 March was the incident upon which the agents of British imperialism sought to rest their case. One might say it was because Bernard and the commissioners had nothing else to report, which is true. But there is also the fact that they were writing to the Earl of Hillsborough who had just taken office. Hillsborough's predecessor as the secretary of state responsible for colonial affairs had been Lord Shelburne and his departure meant more than a changing of the guard. Shelburne was a constitutional traditionalist and would have settled the American controversy through established institutions. He was opposed to using armed forces to support either royal or parliamentary prerogativism in the older English colonies, and (or so contemporaries believed) he was not a man to be taken in by Bernard's representations.[23]

The Earl of Hillsborough was made of different stuff. Long familiar with American affairs, he was an official less encumbered by constitutional restraints. George III would one day declare that he did "not know a man of less judgement than Lord Hillsborough," and at least one historian has suggested he "was quite unqualified for the post."[24] His abilities need not detain us. What is important is that time would prove, as one biographer put it, that Hillsborough "took his opinions of American affairs very much from Francis Bernard."[25]

It has been mentioned that on the day the new appointment was announced in local newspapers, Bernard wrote to Hillsborough's undersecretary telling of Boston's restless quiet. It is not a coincidence that just a few days earlier he had also written to Lord Barrington reiterating his grievance of constitutional restraints. The war secretary was reminded by the Massachusetts governor that he did not dare initiate a request for soldiers. "Ever since I have perceived that the Wickedness of some and the folly of others will in the End bring Troops here," Bernard asserted, "I have conducted myself so as to be able to say, and swear to, if the Sons of Liberty shall require it, that I have never applied for Troops." The implication was clear enough, he did not have to spell it out. He might be mobbed if he again approached the council. The fact he had never been personally threatened was not mentioned, and we may doubt if he felt such fear. In less than five months he would ask the council to consent to an application for armed assistance. The council would once more refuse, everyone in Boston would know what had occurred, but no mob would appear to make him swear.[26]

A few days after writing Barrington, Bernard sent a long letter to the new colonial secretary, making certain that he, too, understood the situation. "His Majesty's ministers have within these three years been fully acquainted with the defenceless state of this government," Lord Hillsborough was told, "and therefore I trust that I shall be excused leaving it entirely to the administration to determine upon a measure which they are much more able to judge of and be answerable for than I can be. I shall have trouble and danger enough when such orders arrive, though I keep ever so clear of advising or promoting them." "I have," Bernard would later reiterate, "constantly sent home accounts of all occurrences which could influence this question, I have concluded, that a change of measures must originate at Westminster, and that the first orders for quartering troops at Boston, would come from thence."[27]

One cannot help but marvel at Bernard's presentation of the case. Troops were inevitable to solve the legal dilemma of rebellious Boston. The risk of requesting them was too much to ask of him; Hillsborough could be "answerable," he could not. The decision was up to London, the king's servants in America must await the event.

We may indeed admire the astuteness of the beleaguered governor, but not at the expense of ignoring what is being argued. British officials serving in Massachusetts Bay have attempted to marshal facts to prove they need the support of the army to maintain both imperial law and the revenue service. So far they have failed, partly because the conditions of local constitutional law prohibit that they make the decision alone. As a result they must sustain an even heavier burden of proof as London has to be persuaded not only that soldiers are necessary but that necessity justifies modifying or even abandoning a long-established constitutional arrangement that left internal police matters to individual colonies. The ministry is being asked to usurp powers it had never before exercised and which American whigs will contend it does not possess.[28] Finally, in an ironic twist to the argument, Governor Bernard relies on the constitutional predicament itself, as the most probative fact for sustaining the legal burden and overcoming the constitutional dilemma.

If we are puzzled it is because we forget that the British constitution spun a different course than postrevolutionary American constitutions: it was unwritten, based on existing institutional realities and established conventions defining the proper exercise of governmental power. Whatever could be plausibly argued and forcibly maintained, the eighteenth-century imperial constitution was legitimately altered, expanded, or reformed by a broader spectrum of officialdom than merely the judicial. Francis Bernard was a lawyer and knew what was plausible. He argued a constitutional convention as a legal fact to change the constitution.

9

In a Distressed State

THE DOCKING OF LIBERTY

Francis Bernard had a unique perspective of the American world. For him the situation was always desperate. One reason was surely a sense of helplessness, not from facing the Boston crowd but from trying to convince London that the constitution had to be changed. All his letters repeated the theme and no one at home seemed to listen.

When the situation called for decisive action Bernard remained immobilized and critics said he lacked courage or vigor. The fact that he could not act, that he possessed little power was universally ignored, misunderstood, or thought somehow irrelevant. Every commentator seemed to assume that he, not the law, was at fault. The commissioners had asked him "what support to their office, or protection for themselves, I can afford," Bernard told his superiors. We have seen the reply that he reported to Lord Hillsborough. In a similar letter to the Earl of Shelburne he furnished a more elaborate explanation. "I answer, None in the world," the governor wrote. "For tho' I am allowed to proceed in the ordinary business of the Government without interruption; in the business of a popular opposition to the Laws of Great Britain founded upon the pretensions of Rights and Privileges, I have not the shadow of authority or power." A month later Bernard acknowledged that his colleagues in the imperial service had given up hope he could seize the initiative. "The Officers of the Crown & Friends of the British Government are now in a distressed State hoping that, but not knowing how or when, they shall be relieved."[1]

Ever since the stamp-act crisis Francis Bernard had been sending one message to London: the constitution had to be reformed. His argument was clear. Without substantial additions to gubernatorial authority he should not be blamed for failing to suppress whig outbursts, the ministry must not assume that a colonial governor could show the decisiveness long expected of a lord lieutenant of Ireland. The customs commissioners understood the grievance. "[O]f this we are well convinced," they wrote the lords of the treasury, "that the Governor and Magistracy have not the least Authority or power in this place, that the Mob are ready to be assembled on any Occasion, and that every Officer who exerts himself in the Execution of his Duty will be exposed to the Resentment of the Populace, without the least probability of receiving and [sic] Protection."[2]

There were no ambiguities. The message should have been understood had only London been listening. An American colonial governor was dependent on local institutions to enforce the law and those institutions were under the constitutional control of men who would not enforce imperial law.

The constitutional dilemma should have been understood by the ministry, but it was not, at least not fully. Imperial government officials occasionally noted the governor's predicament, yet ignored the problem whenever action was thought necessary, even issuing orders with which Bernard could not possibly comply.[3] We may be surprised but we should not be. The problem was not even understood by some officials much closer at hand.

Up in Halifax, Commodore Samuel Hood thought the commissioners ill-served by Bernard, that he was indifferent to the abuse they received from the mob. "They were, as I am told," Hood wrote George Grenville, "never properly supported by the Governor, and in no one instance did he ever have recourse to the civil magistrates for putting a stop to any riot or unlawful meeting." The truth is that Bernard often had "recourse to the civil magistrates," repeatedly asking them to suppress riots. They did not have to obey and he had no way of making them comply. But even had they a constitutional duty to suppress every riot called to their attention, the political situation would have remained the same. They defined gatherings differently than did Bernard and would not have cooperated on those occasions he wanted to suppress the crowd. Where he saw a riot, they saw a few "hollooing" boys, noisy perhaps but harmless.[4]

Commodore Hood's misunderstanding of Massachusetts Bay's legal realities has been cited for more than merely a sampling of official attitudes. His belief that Bernard suffered an advanced case of constitutional abulia endangering the commissioners would play a role in prerevolutionary events. Hood responded to the customs board's call for naval assistance and did so with more in mind than collecting the king's revenue. He received their request late in March and promptly sent the frigate *Hope* to Massachusetts Bay. Her commander carried the message that as soon as possible H.M.S. *Romney* would be permanently stationed in Boston Harbor.

Romney was a man of war which had been resheathed early in 1767 for service at Halifax. It had carried Hood's broad pendant across the Atlantic when he first assumed the North American naval command, arriving in Nova Scotia about two months before the commissioners got to Boston. Now, under the command of Captain John Corner, she was placed in their service. "You are hereby required and directed," Hood instructed Corner, "to be aiding and Assisting unto the Commissioners of the Customs, to the utmost of your Power upon the water, in the Due and legal execution of the Laws of Trade and Navigation according to the true Intent and meaning of the said Laws, and the several Acts of Parliament made in that behalf."[5]

Enforcement of the revenue acts was the excuse for *Romney*'s being sent, but customs duty was only part of her mission. Keep the political situation of Boston constantly in mind, Corner was told. "[Y]ou should be always upon your Guard," Hood reminded him, "against the Mischievous humour of the populace." Shore leaves, for example, were to be supervised closely. "You are never to suffer a Boat to go from the Ship without two Petty Officers in her, that one may have nothing to do, but to attend to the keeping her safe."[6] The British navy apparently did not trust Boston's crowd even with the king's property.

Romney arrived at Boston on 17 May 1768. The commissioners were disappointed at such an inadequate display of force, but they had little time to brood. Eight days earlier John Hancock's sloop *Liberty* had also come into port, carrying wine ordered from Madeira the previous November. The following morning, the tenth of May, Nathaniel Barnard, master of *Liberty,* went to the customshouse and made entry of 25 pipes of wine. Soon the commissioners would believe that when she docked, there had been 127 pipes aboard the sloop, and would be happy to have *Romney* at their service.[7]

The legal and political situation that greeted these two ships was summed up by Charles Paxton, who already had begun a campaign to convince the cabinet that the presence of *Romney* in Boston Harbor was but a token gesture, not the answer to the imperial dilemma. The people of the colony, he warned Viscount Townshend, were saying that if the Townshend duties were not repealed, "they will put the Governor and the Commissioners of the Customs on board a Ship and send them to England." It was "the Opinion of wisest Men here that unless we have immediately three or four men of war and at least one Regiment every thing will be in the greatest confusion and disorder."[8]

Thus matters stood when *Liberty* docked at Hancock's wharf. On one hand the imperial side was convinced, as Bernard said, "that it is the intention of the Faction here to cause an Insurrection against the Crown officers, at least of the Custom house, as soon as any kind of Refusal of their extravagant Demands against Great Britain shall furnish a Pretext." On the other side, as Mercy Otis Warren later wrote, there was some thought that the revenue officials were capable of concocting "a design to raise a sudden ferment, that might be improved to corroborate the arguments for the necessity of standing troops to be stationed within the town."[9] It was in the midst of this charged political atmosphere of mutual suspicion that the commissioners of the customs, after delaying a month, decided to seize John Hancock's sloop *Liberty*.

10

A Dangerous Hour

THE LIBERTY RIOTS

The question why *Liberty* was seized need not detain us. It seems that by using the sloop as a temporary warehouse to store goods for which he did not have a loading permit, John Hancock was in technical violation of imperial customs statutes. What concerns us is that *Liberty* was ordered seized by the commissioners of the customs. It is the manner of the taking and the time of day that interest us, not the reasons why.

It has been conjectured that Collector Joseph Harrison objected to the time *Liberty* was to be seized. It did not seem wise to make a stir between six and seven in the evening for that was an hour "when the lower class of people were returning from their day labour." The objection was over-ruled by Commissioner Henry Hulton, who told the collector and comp-troller to call for aid from H.M.S. *Romney,* perhaps even have *Liberty* towed away from Hancock's wharf and moored near the man of war. It is not clear what the original plan had been. Some contemporary accounts say that when the two customs officials boarded the vessel and an-nounced seizure by blazing the king's board arrow on her main mast, Harrison wanted to leave the sloop where it was, while Hallowell in-sisted that it be moored under *Romney*'s guns. Harrison had asked the navy to stand by "in case a Rescue should be attempted," and may not have intended any action more drastic than putting one or two minor customs men on board *Liberty*. In any event, whatever was planned, both could contend that the seizure had to be made at that unfavorable hour—unfavorable due to the likelihood of attracting a crowd—because the tide was then near full. Should naval aid be needed, or should it only be necessary to have royal marines stand by to discourage interference with the seizure, high tide was the time when *Romney*'s barges could most easily be maneuvered about the wharf.[1]

Romney, according to Commissioner Hulton, had been sent to Massachusetts because "frequent disturbances" put him and his colleagues "under continual apprehension for their safety, as the Governor had often told them he could give them no protection."[2] A question remaining to be answered was just what difference *Romney* would make. The attempt by Harrison to seize *Liberty* was to be the first test of imperial "protection." As soon as they stepped upon Hancock's wharf, the collector and comptroller probably realized that the question might soon be answered. There waiting was Hallowell's adversary of 1766, Captain Daniel Malcom.

Most likely coincidence placed Malcom on Hancock's wharf at that hour. There is no evidence that Bostonians were aware *Liberty* was about to be seized. Also present was Captain Caleb Hopkins, who had been a witness for Malcom in his house the day Hallowell tried to get into his cellar with a writ of assistance, and Captain John Matchet, a man who had joined Malcom in removing a customs official from another of John Hancock's vessels just a month or so earlier. These three men were known to Hallowell and he identified them. Others who were there and who, he said, tried to obstruct the seizure of *Liberty,* were "unknown" to him.[3]

Identification of individuals was not to be a major factor in the coming dispute. Their actions, not who they were, created controversy. Bostonians claimed that no one on the wharf attempted to interfere with the revenue officials. It is remarkable how reasonable Malcom and his supporters were, but before doubting his account it would be wise to recall how well informed he had been on other occasions about the fine points of imperial revenue statutes. They protested the method of seizure, argued issues of law, but did not seek to obstruct the planting of the king's arrow. The customs men were told that employment of naval personnel as a police force within the harbor was unprecedented and therefore of dubious validity. Moreover, there was no need to have *Liberty* towed away from the wharf, even if such a step was legal, which was also doubtful. The *Boston Evening-Post* summed the discussion up in one sentence: "Several Gentlemen present advised the Officers not to move her, as there would be no Attempt allowed by the Owner to rescue her out of their Hands."[4]

"I'll be damned but she shall go," Harrison told Malcom—or so Malcom later claimed. The collector was giving a rather curt answer to the suggestion that the seizure was illegal, unnecessary, and likely to cause a disturbance.

Malcom, as usual, described himself as the soul of discretion, arguing legal points in hopes of avoiding violence. "I am afraid," he told Harrison, "it will make a great disturbance in town, as I think your proceednigs [*sic*] are contrary to custom, and I believe contrary to law."[5]

We should not be surprised that Benjamin Hallowell recalled a different conversation.

Malcom, Matchet, and Hopkins said, that the before-mentioned sloop should not be taken into custody; and declared they would go on board, and throw the people belonging to the Romney overboard; and made use of every means in their power to interrupt the Officers in the execution of their duty; saying, if this work was going forward, it was high time to begin; and these people, with many others, swore revenge upon the King's Officers, holding the vessel by the ropes and sides until she was forced from them.[6]

Romney lay a cable's length from the shore. As soon as Hallowell appeared on the wharf, according to Malcom, he gave a signal to the man of war and pointed to *Liberty*. Marines immediately boarded Hancock's vessel, "having their guns and other arms." If we can believe Malcom, they were spoiling for a fight. "I was then along side the said sloop," he asserted under oath, "and heard said master of the man of war give orders to fix their bayonets, and take their places, and that the first damned rascal that said a word to blow his brains out, or run him through with the bayonet." These threats were spoken at a time no whigs were opposing the seizure. Malcom did not admit he took overt action against the sailors. It was Hallowell who made that accusation, on the strength of which a biographer has asserted that then and there, on Hancock's wharf, Malcom "led the patriots in the first clash with the armed forces of England." If the claim is true, it cannot be proven by the words of Daniel Malcom. He denied it under oath.[7]

Perhaps Joseph Harrison, as well as Hallowell, inadvertently contributed to Malcom's fame. Several men, among whom he must have included Malcom, "got on board [*Liberty*] in order to regain Possession," Harrison asserted, "just as the Man of Warrs Boat well Man'd and Armed had got along side: They soon drove the Intruders out and I delivered the Vessel into custody of the commanding Officer."[8] The implication is that there had been a struggle. If so, it was a remarkably tame one, for not even Benjamin Hallowell claimed that any person had been hurt.

With Harrison's order that Captain Corner take custody of *Liberty,* the matter might have ended, but for the crowd assembled on the waterfront, growing every minute. We must not think that only militant whigs or friends of John Hancock had gathered to watch *Liberty* rowed away. Those there, the *Boston Evening-Post* reported, "were joined by a number of Sailors, and vagrant Persons who were suspicious of an Intention to put them on board the Ship." What apparently happened was that the sight of armed marines and sailors rowing toward land from *Romney* had raised an alarm along the waterfront that a press gang was coming ashore. Mere rumors of impressment were sufficient to raise mobs in eighteenth-century New England and fears that men were about to be seized for service in the British navy surely contributed to the swelling of the *Liberty* crowd.[9]

No matter why the crowd had gathered, two facts are certain: it was sizable and it was "combustible." It also, Thomas Hutchinson charged, "insulted the Custom H[ouse] Offic[ers] and carried them in triumph as trespassers up the Wharffe." That statement was not quite true according to Joseph Harrison. He and Hallowell "walked off the Wharf without any Insult or Molestation from the People, who were eagerly engaged in a Scuffle with the Man of Warrs Men and endeavoring to detain the Sloop at the Wharf." It was after *Liberty* left her berth that the assembled people turned on the customs men, apparently to their surprise even though Harrison had boasted that any attempt to seize Hancock's vessel "must necessarily be attended with the utmost Risque and Danger." They had "scarce got into the Street before we were pursued by the Mob which by this time was increased to a great Multitude. The onset was begun by throwing Dirt at me, which was presently succeeded by Volleys of Stones, Brickbatts, Sticks or anything that came to hand."[10]

Harrison's eighteen-year-old son attempted to protect his father but the two were separated after running about 200 yards, "pelted with stones" most of the way. The older man was soon hurt, struck by a rock or a club. The facts are not clear even from his own account. He was too intent on describing the extreme danger he had faced to bother about small details. And it was extreme danger too, Harrison believed, for had the mob caught him, the prerevolutionary Boston crowd for the first and only time would surely have killed a man.

> I received a violent Blow on the Breast which had like to have brought me to the Ground, and I verily believe if I had fallen, I should never have got up again, the People to all appearance being determined on Blood and Murder. But luckily just at that critical moment a friendly Man came up and supported me; and observed that now was the time for my Escape as the whole Attention of the Mob was engaged in the Scuffle about my Son who he assured me would be taken out of their Hands by some Persons of his Acquaintance.[11]

The attack took place at about seven o'clock and, Harrison added, "it was hoped that the People would have dispersed without doing any further mischief." Instead, by nine o'clock "the Mob had increased to such a prodigious Number that the whole Town was in the utmost Consternation and Confusion." A whig newspaper reported that the crowd consisted of merchant seamen, an exaggeration to some extent but an assertion reflecting the belief that impressment was the root cause of the *Liberty* riot.[12] Governor Bernard in a report to the Earl of Hillsborough told what happened after this second crowd was formed.[13]

The first victim was a man named Irvine, inspector of imports and exports for the board of customs commissioners. He was, Bernard wrote, "attacked" by that second mob, "very much beat and abused, and would probably have been killed if he had not been rescued by two of the mob, and enabled to escape through an house." Next, the crowd

> went to Mr. Hallowell's house, and began to break the windows and force an entry, but were diverted therefrom by assurances that Mr. Hallowell was almost killed, and was not at home. They then went to Mr. Harrison's and broke his windows, but he not being at home, and the owner of the house entreating them to depart, they left it. Then they went to Mr. William's house, one of the Inspectors general [of the customs], who was then at a distance from Boston, and broke near an hundred panes, and did other damage to the house; but upon Mrs. Williams appearing and assuring them, that he was absent, and only she was at home, they departed.[14]

Thus, while Bernard had the satisfaction of reporting that the crowd attacked only customs officials, the most visible symbol of imperial taxation, and that some windows had been smashed, he had less to tell than earlier when writing about the riots of March. Then, at least, the wife of one of the customs officials had been badly frightened. On this occasion, at each of the houses it visited, the mob pursued a limited purpose— harassing its victims, destroying some property, and letting its opponents know who ruled the streets. The governor could not even report any frightened English ladies. Mrs. Williams came out and addressed the mob, showing that she at least had not been sent into hysterics. Bernard, however, did not miss the opportunity to end with one of his familiar conjectures, proving that even if serious violence had been avoided it was due not to whig restraint but to luck and remarkably good fortune. "Happily," he wrote of the crowd, "they did not break into any house, for if they had got at a cellar, the mischiefs would have been greater and more extensive."[15]

One more event took place that evening. A sailing boat belonging to Harrison, one in which he took great pride, was dragged out of Boston Harbor and burned on the town common. "By this time," Bernard wrote, "there were about 500, some say 1,000 men gathered together whilst the boat was burning." Despite the large numbers—one out of every three or four men in town was present—nothing else occurred. "They consult[e]d what was to be done next," a tory wrote home to England, "& it was agreed to retire for the night. All was ended w[ith] a Speech from one of the Leaders, conclud[in]g thus, 'We will defend our Liberties & property, by the Strength of our Arm & the help of our God, to your Tents o Israel.' "¹⁶

The *Liberty* riots occurred on Friday, the tenth of June. For the next two days the town was quiet, probably out of respect for the Sabbath. Sometime during this period the commissioners of the customs took shelter on H.M.S. *Romney,* bringing with them as many imperial officials as they could persuade to flee. Boston, they argued, was no longer a safe place for servants of the crown.

On Monday, Bernard reported to Hillsborough, "a paper was found stuck upon the Liberty-tree, inviting all the sons of liberty to meet at six o'clock, to clear the land of the vermin which are come to devour them, &c. &c." The governor thought the notice an ominous sign. The whig editors of the *Boston Gazette* thought it evidence that an aggrieved people would still harken to moderate measures and petition for redress. "[T]he Expectation of this Meeting," they wrote, "kept the Town in Peace."¹⁷

Perhaps it was just as well that matters remained quiet for a few days. When people gathered at the liberty tree on Tuesday, there were 4000 men on hand according to Bernard, nearly 2000 according to a report received by the departed customs commissioners. The whig *Evening-Post* gave no figures, merely asserting that the assembled crowd consisted "of a larger Number than was ever known on any Occasion," while Thomas Hutchinson wrote of "Vast numbers of the populace, and others," particularly stressing the troublesome fact that many of those present were from out of town.¹⁸

It would seem that even whigs were surprised by the turnout. Many more men gathered at "liberty hall" than could be handled in an orderly fashion. It was soon found impossible to do business out-of-doors and the meeting was adjourned to Faneuil Hall.¹⁹

Once in Faneuil Hall the whig penchant for legality and legitimacy surfaced. Someone objected that the meeting had not been called according to law. Almost immediately it was voted to adjourn so that, as Bernard correctly stated, "the Select-men might call a town-meeting to legalise the Assembly." Whigs were insistent on the forms of law. The tory *Boston Chronicle,* for example, reported that James Otis had been elected moderator before adjournment. The next week it had to retract the story, conceding that no irregularity had occurred. Otis had not been elected until after warrants had been issued and the meeting legally called. Interestingly, before the original story and retraction were printed, Bernard had also written Hillsborough that a moderator had been chosen during the morning session at Faneuil Hall. He did not, however, think the fact important enough to emphasize. Not sharing the whigs' penchant for legality, Bernard did not appreciate how he might have scored a point against them.[20]

The selectmen issued warrants to the constables, the town was duly warned to meet, and at three o'clock in the afternoon everyone was again in Faneuil Hall. It was soon discovered that the multitude was too large for that building, and a second adjournment was voted so that they could move to the Old South. That fact provides our most reliable estimate of the size of the crowd. Faneuil Hall, Samuel Adams believed, was "capable of holding 1200 or 1300 men," while Old South could hold between 5000 and 6000.[21]

As usual the revenue officers were certain Boston was plotting against them. The inhabitants, Harrison wrote the Marquis of Rockingham, had assembled "to concert measures for totally expelling the Commissioners of the Customs and several wild and strange Propositions for that Purpose were then made; but nothing more was done than appointing a Committee of 21 Persons to wait on the Governor with a Demand for the Redress of what they call Grievances." While Bernard agreed that "[m]any wild and violent proposals were made, but warded off," and, like Harrison, emphasized the radicalism of an unnamed few rather than the moderation of the majority, he did admit that the meeting had not been concerned with the commissioners or the customs services. Explaining to Hillsborough what transpired, he outlined two of the many "wild and violent proposals." One was "that every captain of a man of war that came into this harbour, should be under the command of the General Court." The second was "that if any person should promote or assist the bringing [of] troops here, he should be deemed a disturber of the peace, and a traitor to his country."[22]

It would be well to consider those two proposals for they provide an indication of what Governor Bernard was reporting to London as the ultimate in whig political radicalism. The first had to do with impressment and its purpose is obvious. If naval captains were under the authority of the whig legislature, they would soon stop sending out press gangs. The second, of course, expressed the persistent whig fear, now magnified by what had occurred on Friday. Bostonians knew that those wanting troops sent to the Bay colony would use the *Liberty* riot to advance their argument.

Instead of adopting a call to arms, the town meeting drafted a petition to the governor, praying for redress of current grievances. In keeping with the whigs' own self-image, it was a legal document raising issues of law. A "humble petition" was the description of merchant John Rowe, "and I think a very smart petition." In truth, it was more than merely "smart." As were so many other statements voted by Boston whigs during the prerevolutionary era, the petition was a very lawyerlike production. The voters of the town meeting sought only the possible, they did not demand the unobtainable. Radicals might have asked Bernard to keep the departed commissioners on *Romney* and ship them back to London. The petition adopted by the town meeting pretended that issue was moot. The commissioners had fled town and as whigs could think of no other reason for them to do so, it followed that they left because they had resigned their posts.

> As the Board of Customs, have tho't fit, of their own motion, to relinquish the exercise of their commission here, and as we cannot but hope, that, being convinced of the impropriety and injustice, of the appointment of a Board, with such enormous powers, and the inevitable destruction which would ensue from the exercise of their office, will never re-assume it.[23]

Instead of hounding the commissioners or complaining about the seizure of *Liberty,* Boston's whigs went directly to the main issues: the rumor that troops had been requested by Bernard's government and impressment. They combined the two under one grievance: the presence of *Romney* in Boston Harbor. After all, *Romney* not only was pressing men, it might be the precursor of a regular military establishment. They had, the people complained, petitioned George III many times against unconstitutional laws to no avail. They had waited patiently "to receive a gracious answer to, with the greatest attention to the public peace, untill we find ourselves invaded with an armed force, seizing, impressing and imprisoning the persons of our fellow-subjects, contrary to express acts of parliament." They would, the petition concluded, assume that the commissioners of the customs had left Boston forever. They had, therefore, but one prayer.

> We flatter ourselves, your Excellency will in tenderness to this people use the best means in your power, to remove the other grievance, we so justly complain of, and issue your immediate order, to the commander of his Majesty's ship Romney, to remove from this harbour.[24]

To be sure, the request was directed more to the governor's political capacity than his legal authority. Whigs knew what the answer would be. No one desired a military presence in the colony more than Francis Bernard. Besides, a governor did not possess the constitutional power to order a naval vessel to leave Boston or Massachusetts Bay, and that is precisely what Bernard told the committee sent by the town meeting to visit him at his country estate. Impressment, however, was another matter. Again unable to issue direct orders, on this question the governor could promise to employ his good offices and persuade the navy to consider Boston's petition. Impressment, Bernard argued, "is practised in Great-Britain, and all other [of] his Majesty's dominions, and therefore I cannot dispute it in this part of them. But I shall use my utmost endeavours to get it regulated so as to avoid all the inconveniences to this town, which you are apprehensive of."[25]

Bernard's political persuasion was stronger than his legal authority. Captain Corner agreed that *Romney* would impress no men "belonging to or married in the Province, nor any employed in the Trade along Shore, or the neighboring Colonies." A little later he announced that the Bostonian recently pressed "is dismissed, and will be ashore this day."[26]

Whig law, backed by the threat of a mob assembled in an undeniably legal town meeting, had won an important victory. Perhaps even more significant than the apparent curbing of impressment, was the fact that Bernard had been forced to deal directly with the people by receiving a committee from the most democratic and legally uncontrollable body in local government. It was a step he had long dreaded. To make matters worse, while the people were awaiting his answer, they appointed a second committee to draft instructions to their representatives in the lower house of assembly. John Adams wrote them, and they not only raised the issue of the legality of the seizure of *Liberty,* they made clear that more basic issues were to be pressed in the future.

> We have the mortification to observe one act of parliament after another passed for the express purpose of raising a revenue from us; to see our money continually collecting from us, without our consent, by an authority in the constitution of which we have no share, and over which we have no kind of influence or control; to see the little circulating cash that remained among us ... appropriated to the maintenance of swarms of officers and pensioners in idleness and luxury, whose example has a tendency to corrupt our morals, and whose arbitrary dispositions will trample on our rights.[27]

Notice was served that Bernard and the commissioners were not forgotten. Nor was parliament. They continued to maintain, Adams wrote and people voted, "a reverence and due subordination to the British parliament, as the supreme legislative in all cases of necessity, for the preservation of the whole empire."[28]

Adams's words shocked Thomas Hutchinson. "This is," he mused, "a singular manner of expressing the authority of parliament." If anything, such thoughts, publicly, indeed boldly expressed, proved that troops had to be sent to Boston. The whigs were convicted by their own words. Mobs were not the only cause of alarm. "It must be supposed," Hutchinson concluded,

> that the town intended the world should know that they acknowledged no greater degree of subordination. The governor, nevertheless, for representing the men who led the people to the declaration contained both in their address to him and in their instructions to the representatives, as aiming at independency, has been charged with misrepresentation, in order to bring a military force into the province.[29]

Indeed, Francis Bernard had now more reason than ever to wish the military close at hand. He had not only seen a mob chase the collector and comptroller of his majesty's customs up the back streets of Boston, he had seen that mob transmute itself from an illegal riot, or at least an unlawful assembly,[30] into a lawful town meeting with which he was forced to deal. We may well imagine that both he and Hutchinson agreed with an observation that General Thomas Gage would soon make to Lord Hillsborough. Boston, he asserted, "has been under a kind of democratical despotism for a considerable time, and it had not been safe for people to act or speak contrary to the sentiments of the ruling demagogues."[31] If Gage, as Bernard and other imperial officials apparently thought, was describing the emerging form of government in British North America, we may well wonder what difference they expected the presence of regular troops to make.

11

In Great Danger

THE CREATION OF FACTS

The time has come to turn from the narrative to the analytical. The point of historical interest is not so much what occurred, as what individuals said occurred and what they hoped to establish with the facts they were creating. Governor Francis Bernard lost little time setting the theme for the imperial side. "[A] great riot happened in this town last evening, which had very bad consequences, tho' happily there were no lives lost," he wrote Lord Hillsborough the very next day. As noted before, Bernard was conceding nothing by mentioning the fact no one had been killed. The implication was that luck had prevented deaths, for the emphasis was on the adjective "great." It had, Bernard told the Massachusetts council, been "a great Riot . . . in which among other outrages the principal Custom House Officers were bruised and wounded and otherwise ill treated."[1]

Not so, Samuel Adams answered with perhaps as much truth. It had not been a "great riot," but a "little inconsiderable rising of the people." James Bowdoin agreed. The *Liberty* riot, he told former Governor Thomas Pownall, was "a trifling affair and was not in opposition to any act of Parliament, but sprung, as you have often heard, from the wickedness of a certain junto here."[2]

Adams and Bowdoin expressed these views in private communications. When speaking officially their fellow whigs made the same case: Bernard and the commissioners were wrong. "There was indeed on the 10th of June," the Massachusetts convention wrote the colony's political agent, "something that had rather more of the appearance of riot, but it was only of a few hours existence, and with very little mischief." "[I]t must be confessed," the Boston town meeting admitted, "there was a riot on that evening, which is by no means to be Justified. It was however far from

100

being so great a one as the Governor represents it to be. . . . It was not a numerous Mob; nor was it of long continuance, neither was there much mischief done."[3]

Thus each side sought its own advantage in facts, building up one case or tearing down the other. Even numbers became confusing, their precision lost in suppositions and factual glosses. What the town called "not a numerous Mob," Bernard put at "about 500 some say 1000." Surprisingly, the more moderate and certainly less alarmist Chief Justice Hutchinson reported a much larger and, therefore, more dangerous crowd than did the governor. He wrote an important member of parliament that sometime during the evening the crowd had "increased to 2 or 3000."[4]

Historians generally accept the imperialist perspective, writing of "a rabble some hundreds strong," threatening the customs men, perhaps even endangering their lives.[5] Yet the question never asked is *why* so vicious, so dangerous, and so large a mob never caught up with Joseph Harrison, Benjamin Hallowell, or the other individuals they so eagerly sought to hurt. Once the sailors and marines of *Romney* rowed away, there were only four customshouse representatives left behind to face what the lowest tory estimate put at 500 men. That would have made the affair roughly one hundred to one, not very favorable odds for middle-aged British officials confronted by members of the working class, probably much younger and generally merchant seamen.

There were gaps in the tale that had to be removed. Someone would ask how Harrison and Hallowell escaped. The two men had an answer. It was, they explained, due to nothing else but sheer good fortune. The riot had been so violent, London was told, they were lucky to be alive. Indeed, by a remarkable coincidence each of those attacked by the *Liberty* crowd survived due to a similar occurrence. Comptroller Hallowell swore that he "verily believes, that if some friendly people had not interposed, and rescued him from the fury of the mob, that he should have been murdered in the street." Each of the other men had a similar experience: Collector Harrison—"verily believes, that if a person had not pointed out to him a turning into another street, whilst the mob were surrounding a house, that the Deponent's life would have been in more imminent danger"; Harrison's son—"had he not taken refuge in a house by the assistance of some friendly people, the Deponent verily believes that he should have been murder'd in the street"; and Thomas Irving the inspector of imports and exports—"two men meanly dressed took compassion upon me, and with great difficulty pulling me from amongst the croud [crowd], got me conveyed through a house into a back yard, and from thence into another house, where I remained until the mob moved to some other part of the town."[6]

IN GREAT DANGER

A truly remarkable set of circumstances saved the revenue officers of George III from almost certain death. If we experience a tinge of suspicion, it would not do to think that London did as well. Lord Hillsborough may have read the depositions; surely his undersecretary did. Aside from these two, the statements most likely did not receive close scrutiny from officials. Along with other documents flowing across the Atlantic from Boston, they probably were summed up for the board of trade. It is unlikely anyone would be troubled by the odds favoring such a series of coincidences. Facts were not the probative consideration, impressions created by facts were.[7] The customs men had to persuade London their lives had been in peril. That no one had been killed was explained by four small miracles. Indeed, if London gave thought to specific facts there was one conclusion to be drawn. Imperial officials attacked by the *Liberty* rioters had survived due to a fortunate circumstance—a series of four anonymous rescues so unforeseen and inexplicable that it could not possibly be repeated the next time Boston's mob took to the streets. Troops would then be needed.

There is another aspect to be noted about these depositions. They were given in private and sent to London without being made public. It would be Boston's whigs, not the government's party, that printed them in America.

While some facts could be sworn to, others had to be demonstrated. To complete impressions, injuries were emphasized. Despite violent treatment and a brush with near death, both young Harrison and Inspector Irving seem to have escaped unscathed. The comptroller and collector were less fortunate. Both men took to their beds. They had been hurt, but it is difficult to say how seriously. One historian had Hallowell suffering from "wounds and bruises that at the time seemed fatal," but Thomas Hutchinson made nothing of these injuries, implying (though he would never have said so) agreement with whig newspapers that "none of them [were] much hurt." Harrison admitted that when he went to Hancock's wharf, "I was then so ill as to be just able to stir abroad," and that may be a reason why he was confined to his bed. One indication that the two men were not so badly injured as they represented was that both were well enough to give depositions the next day, a step the whigs did not think to duplicate for at least another week, and Hallowell was dispatched to Great Britain on the first ship sailing home, an eyewitness bearing testimony of Boston's violence, sent by the commissioners to press the case for troops.[8]

While revenue men were on the move Boston whigs remained inactive. Perhaps the course of events caught them by surprise. More likely, they hoped the *Liberty* affair would prove an unimportant incident, maybe even one they could ignore. After realizing what the commissioners were up to, whigs began to stir themselves. With Hallowell carrying tory depositions across the Atlantic, whigs swore out statements of their own. Facts asserted or even hinted by tories as damaging to the whig cause were refuted or balanced by counter facts.[9]

Daniel Malcom was the chief whig deponent. There is no need to quote from his statement or from those of the other men whom Harrison named as mob leaders. Better to look at the deposition of Benjamin Goodwin to judge how well whigs matched their opponents fact for fact. All we know about Goodwin is that he was a whig of at least strong enough convictions to lend his oath to the common cause. His purpose is clear: to create pro-whig facts. Truth was not the object, evidence was.

Goodwin had been lounging on Hancock's wharf when the customs men arrived and boarded *Liberty*. Curious, he got up to find out what was happening.

> I saw Captain Malcom talking to the Comptroller; and Capt. Malcom said, you better let the Vessel lay. Mr. Hallowel[l] said, she shou'd not; and ordered the Fast to be cut; with what he said one of the Marines fired off his Gun for Signal for another Barge, which was alongside in about two Minutes. Mr. Hallowel[l] said, cut the Fasts. the people that was there said, stop 'till the Owner comes. No Mr. Hallowel[l] said, damn you, cast her off. And the Master of the Romney said, damn you why don't you fire? I said, what Rascal is that, which dare tell them Marines to fire? I then spoke to the Collector, and said Mr. Harrison, you better let the vessel lay at the Wharf, until the Owner comes down, as he's sent for. He made answer, I will go with you to the owner. Then the Comptroller said, no, damn it, she shou'd go, and shew me the man that dare oppose it. I then askt the Collector, if he was not the Commanding Officer there? The Master of the Romney swore and made such a Noise I could not hear, what the Collector said. The Master swore, by God she shou'd go, and got some hatchetts out of the Barge, and cut away the Fasts, and swore, if any persons put their hands near, he'd cut them off, and called to the Marines several times, why don't you fire? They got Tow Ropes in the Barges, and the Master cut away the Fasts, and they tow'd her away in a piratical Manner.[10]

It would be a mistake to think this a masterpiece of hyperbole. Better to see Goodwin's deposition for what it was: a typical example of whig impression-making by arguing facts, by manipulating facts, or by fact creation, right down to that final tart analogy linking *Romney*'s seizure of *Liberty* to piracy. If we are not impressed it is because we do not understand the debate that was being conducted. Whigs were answering customs men in kind. They did not intend claiming that the riot did not occur. They intended claiming that the riot, a minor affair, was the fault of the men who seized *Liberty,* not the men who protested the seizure. To make their point they had to establish a few facts, facts creating the impression of arrogant behavior.

We must not make too much of competence. That Boston's whigs proved a match for those seeking British troops does not mean they had a chance to win. The initiative would never pass to the whigs. They could react, they could answer, but they could neither dominate the debate nor set its pattern. The initiative belonged to the commissioners of the American customs and they seized it by fleeing Boston.

Whether the commissioners were motivated by fear of the Boston crowd or seeking to create an unanswerable fact, their decision to flee the town established the basic event that dominated the debate. By fleeing Boston they created the most telling fact of all.

The commissioners had fled to H.M.S. *Romney* on 11 June, the day after *Liberty* was seized. While dining at Charles Paxton's house, in company with Governor Bernard, they "received a verbal message from the people, by a person of character," to the effect "that if the sloop that was seized was brought back to Mr. Hancock's wharf, upon his giving security to answer the Prosecution, the town might be kept quiet." This message, four of the five commissioners explained, "appeared to us to be a menace, we applied to Captain Corner to take us on board" *Romney.*[11]

It would not do to make much of the fact that the commissioners reacted to anonymous threats. We may have doubts about such warnings, but imperial officials and American tories thought them evidence of probative value. Three months later the judge of admiralty wrote Thomas Hutchinson that "I was informed by a gentleman of my acquaintance, who had his information from one intimate with and knowing to the internal purposes of the sons of liberty as they falsely stile themselves, that he verily believ'd, from the terrible threats and menaces by those catalines against you, that your life is greatly in danger." Again it is significant that Hutchinson, when he received this message, sent it to London as evidence of the state of affairs in Boston. The whigs, when they obtained a copy, published it for all the world to see.[12]

Whether spontaneous or staged, the flight of the four commissioners was one of the most carefully programmed and minutely recorded events that occurred during the entire prerevolutionary period. As soon as they were aboard *Romney,* a meeting was held at which their plight was documented in official papers prepared with an eye on the British cabinet. Pulling no punches to make the precise point they desired to get across, the factual danger was immediately and directly tied to the constitutional dilemma.

> The commissioners . . . finding no measures had been taken by the Governor and Council for securing the peace of the town, and the Governor having repeatedly told the commissioners that he could give them no protection, and that he would not apply to Gen. Gage for troops, unless the Council advised him to it, and at this time said there was no safety for them in this place, and they considering the temper of the people, and the appearance of further disturbances that night, tho't it most prudent to secure a retreat on board his Majesty's Ship . . . the Romney.[13]

Private letters to influential men back home also stressed the danger and the dilemma. The commissioners, it was said, had "met with every insult since their arrival at Boston," and now that they had been forced to flee, it did not "seem likely from the present Temper of the People that they will soon be permitted to return on Shore." In a matter of two days, that conjecture, first stated by Joseph Harrison, had for the commissioners become an absolute certainty. "Resolved," the customs board voted, "that from the outrageous behaviour of the people in the town of Boston, the commissioners cannot return there, but at the utmost hazard of their safety and the honor of the crown." This conclusion was reached on 14 June.[14]

On the same day, Harrison and Hallowell made an addition to the crescent records. They had just fled to *Romney* and, though now on the same warship and perhaps sitting in the same cabin with the commissioners, wrote them a letter telling why they had decided to come on board. Their explanation had no surprises. The story was as predictable as it was familiar. They had been forced to flee "from the fury of a distracted and enraged multitude."[15]

Soon there were "About fifty of us Refugees" aboard the man-of-war, and it was decided to transfer everyone to Castle William, the strongest fort guarding an American town, located on an island in Boston Harbor. From there the commissioners continued to call for help; the further they got from the people of Boston the greater the danger seemed to become.

> From their outrageous behaviour towards our officers, and their repeated threats of immediate violence to our persons, we found it absolutely necessary in order to save his Majesty's commission from further insult, and to preserve our lives, to take shelter on board his Majesty's Ship the Romney in Boston harbour, from whence we are removed into Castle William to carry on the busi-

ness of the Revenue, till we can receive such protection as will
enable us to act in safety at Boston.[16]

The pleas of the customs men brought sympathetic replies from army
officers stationed in North America. Lieutenant Colonel William Dalrymple at Halifax, "deeply affected" by news of their plight, was ready to
sail to their rescue as soon as he received orders from General Thomas
Gage. "My inclination," Gage told them, "would lead me to order troops
to march immediately for your protection; but you must be sensible that
it would be highly improper in me to order troops into a Province for the
purpose of quelling riots, unless application should be first made to that
end by the civil power." He was waiting to hear from the governor. Once
he did, troops would "move to his [Bernard's] assistance with as much
dispatch as it shall be possible for them to do." But until then, Gage's
hands were constitutionally tied.[17]

The navy was not bound by the same constitutional restraint. It had,
after all, been stationed in North American waters to support the revenue service, and although the original purpose had been to act against
smugglers, it was within the discretion of the commanding officer to give
assistance when customs men were threatened or prevented from performing their statutory duties. Commodore Samuel Hood had acted on
that authority when he sent *Romney* to Boston Harbor at the request of
the board. So had Captain Corner, not only when he honored Hallowell's
request that marines seize *Liberty*, but also when he provided shelter for
the commissioners and their subordinates aboard *Romney*. Now Hood
was able to respond again. "I have ordered the Beaver to return immediately," he informed the commissioners, "and if you think further Naval
Force essentially necessary for carrying on the King's business, I shall be
happy in sending it to the utmost of my Power on the first application."[18]

In less than a month, Commodore Hood's ships were anchored in Boston Harbor. While naval power was not what the customs officials had in
mind, the navy's presence created an additional fact to be argued, perhaps the final one necessary to prove their case. Actually, not one but
two new facts had been created: the presence of warships and the fact
that their presence made no difference in the political situation. The
commissioners created this second fact by remaining at the castle and
refusing to return to Boston. By standing pat they were arguing that the
army as well as the navy would have to be sent.

His Majesty's ship Romney, and sloops the Beaver and Senegal,
with two schooners, are now in this harbour; and this protection,
afforded us by Commodore Hood, has been most seasonable, as,

without them, we should not have considered ourselves in safety, nor his Majesty's Castle secured from falling into the hands of the people.[19]

With this argument the commissioners, stringing together the most egregious set of innuendos employed during the entire controversy, carried the creation of facts to new heights. It is important to appreciate what they were saying. The navy's presence was a reassuring comfort, but had proven to be not enough and that probative fact defined its only function. *Romney* and several sister vessels had kept a dangerous situation from becoming desperate and that was about all. The fact that these warships were in the harbor explained why the people had not stormed the castle. Left unsaid, for London to assume, were the additional facts that the people planned to storm the castle and that the local militia would not have defended the fort or the refugees inside. There was no need for the commissioners to suggest what would have become of themselves. After all, they had fled Boston because revenue laws could be enforced only at the "peril of their lives."[20] The factual case was now complete. On 11 July, one month and one day after the seizure of *Liberty*, the commissioners drew the legal conclusion. London had to occupy Boston with a military force or Great Britain's writ would cease to run in Massachusetts Bay.

> The inconveniences we are exposed to we bear with chearfulness, and beg leave to assure your Lordships, that no difficulties shall abate our zeal in the service: but it is impossible for us to set foot in Boston, until there are two or three regiments in the town, to restore and support Government: we further represent, that the Castle being situated on a small island in the Bay, about a league from the town, will render our situation, any longer than the summer months, insupportable. We therefore pray your Lordships, that orders may be given for our residence and protection before the winter.[21]

12

A Plausible Pretence

THE QUESTIONING OF FACTS

We must not make too much of logical progression. The impotency of the navy helped the commissioners of the American customs document the argument they were making to prove that British troops should be in Boston. They had not, in fact, needed a number of British vessels in the harbor to complete their case. The case had been completed by the *Liberty* riots themselves. Less than a week after *Liberty*'s seizure, long before H.M.S. *Beaver* arrived, the commissioners, pointing to the fact that they had been driven from the town despite *Romney*'s protection, drew the logical conclusion and made the ultimate demand. "We . . . beg leave to submit our opinion," they wrote the lords of trade, "that nothing but the immediate exertion of military power will prevent an open revolt of this town, which may probably spread throughout the provinces."[1]

The contention that a flame lit in Boston surely would spread throughout the colonies was a favorite theme with customs men. "[I]t is with deep concern," Collector Harrison and Comptroller Hallowell warned the commissioners, "that we acquaint your Honours, of what we hear repeatedly from all quarters, which is, that a general spirit of insurrection prevails, not only in the town, but throughout the whole provinces." Even tories who did not mention a "domino theory" agreed on one reality: if the remainder of America was not in revolt, Boston was on the verge, and it was not too late to bank the fire. "Unless we have immediately two or three regiments," Charles Paxton argued, " 'tis the opinion of all the friends to government, that Boston *will be in open rebellion*."[2]

Whigs were amazed. Was it possible London would take the commissioners seriously? The exodus of the customs men from town, the executive council told General Thomas Gage, should fool no one. They had "immured themselves in Castle-William," Samuel Adams wrote, "in order to draw troops to this quarter to support them in their unwarrantable proceedings." Their conduct was nothing but "a plausible pretence."[3]

There had been no need for any crown officer to flee Boston after the *Liberty* riot, the council contended. If there had been danger, it was "trifling in comparison with what . . . has been represented." Told by Governor Bernard that the commissioners had to seek protection from the navy, the councillors replied

> that the Commissioners were not obliged to quit the town; that there never had been any insult offered to them; that their quitting the town was a voluntary act of their own; that we do not apprehend there was any sufficient ground for their quitting it, and that when they had quitted it, and were at the Castle, there was no occasion for men of war to protect them.[4]

Whigs were on the defensive. By fleeing Boston the customs commissioners created a fact that had to be considered. It could be depreciated, it could be reassessed, it could be ridiculed, but, considering the issues at stake, it could not be ignored. The council took the expected, orthodox approach of questioning the probative value of the fact by casting doubt on both the sincerity and necessity of its creation. As previously noted, the people of Boston adopted a different technique. They heaped scorn on the fact that the customs men had fled, turning the fact into a conclusion of law: by leaving they had resigned their commissions. Boston, the town meeting voted, supposed that the commissioners of the customs had departed because they had relinquished their offices, "being convinced of the impropriety and injustice, of the appointment of a Board, with such enormous powers, and the inevitable destruction which would ensue from the exercise of their office."[5]

While the conclusion is questionable, it must not be passed over lightly. The technique of transmuting a harmful fact into a favorable conclusion of law was typical of whig argumentation. The purpose may not have been to convince their opponents or win over the doubtful. They were moving from the factual defensive to the legal offense, and trying— even if the contention was innocuous—to shift momentarily the burden of proof by making the other side answer them, turning attention away from their failure to provide a factual refutation to the original fact. Surprisingly, the technique often succeeded, especially with Francis Bernard. Instead of ignoring the town meeting's legal conclusion, or arguing that the commissioners had left town because they were unsafe, not because they had surrendered their commissions, Bernard treated the legal supposition seriously. He did not, the governor replied, understand that the commissioners had abandoned their posts or that their departure constituted resignation of public office. It was his duty as a servant of the crown to assist the commissioners, and he would do so until they actually resigned.[6]

By doubting the commissioners' stated reason for fleeing Boston, the whigs forced the imperial side both to question whig facts and defend tory facts. Whigs said there had been no need to flee. The revenue men replied that there had, and proved it by asking why Boston was still dangerous. The fact that the town was *now* dangerous helped prove the contention that it *then* had been dangerous. That Boston was now dangerous was proven by the fact the commissioners were still at the castle. As a result, the debate was expanded from questioning whether the *Liberty* affair had been a minor disturbance or a great riot, to whether the commissioners of the customs had cause to remain away from Boston.

It was a simple matter for the customs commissioners to shift the factual burden of proof onto the whigs. Had they returned to Boston they might have proven the town dangerous should a serious riot take place. There was risk, however. If the mob remained quiet, the commissioners might not have lost their case but it would have been weakened. By staying away they created a fact that supported, though it did not quite prove, their contention.

The commissioners had begun to document the facts of continual danger their first day aboard *Romney*. Informing Bernard that they had fled, they quoted him as saying that he "could give us no protection, and that Boston was no place of safety for us." They had been convinced he was right by that "verbal message from the people," previously noted, that they had interpreted as "a menace," purporting "further violence."[7]

The council might disagree with the commissioners, but not the governor. The situation was so perilous that Bernard gave thought of fleeing to the castle himself, or so he wrote Lord Hillsborough's undersecretary. "I carried my Expectations so far as to engage a Cabbin and fix upon a Day for embarking." Joseph Harrison's testimony that danger continued was more positive. Boston's "better Sort," he told the Marquis of Rockingham, "express much sorrow and Contrition for the cruel Treatment I have met with." He believed they would try to prevent a recurrence, but "so long as the Town continues to be governed by the Rabble, I shall be very cautious how I trust my self amongst them."[8]

Fear the mob might march from town, storm Castle William, and slay them in their beds, while sometimes implied by the commissioners, was not a genuine apprehension.[9] What troubled them can be summed up in two questions: who was in charge of Boston and who could guarantee order? The answer to both was the whigs. Though their most critical task was to convince London, the commissioners blunted their proof by resting it on anonymous gasconades and the most extreme statements that came to their ears. "The ferment amongst the people has greatly encreased," they contended five days after the seizure of *Liberty,*

> and [we] are persuaded, that their leaders will urge them to the most violent measures, even open revolt: for one of their demagogues in a town meeting yesterday, said, if they were called on to defend their liberties, and privileges, he hoped and believed they would one and all resist, even unto blood.[10]

If we think this tame evidence upon which to build a case of danger, we are missing some dimensions of eighteenth-century forensic science. The man to whom the commissioners sent the letter was Commodore Samuel Hood. He was not only convinced, he was moved to action. "The good people of Boston seem ready and ripe for open revolt," Hood wrote George Grenville, "and nothing, it is imagined, can prevent it but immediate armed force."[11]

The commissioners made a stronger case that Boston was in whig hands than that it was too dangerous for crown officials, somewhat surprising since they saw no distinction between the two facts, believing proof of the first established proof of the second. One reason may be that the assertion of whig control was demonstrably true while proof of the danger was challenged by counter proof from the whigs. Another was due to the manner adopted by customs officials when questioning pertinent facts: not only to argue but to manipulate them, hoping to convince the British government that they proved more than they did.

Joseph Harrison and Benjamin Hallowell used this technique when reporting John Hancock's effort to regain legal custody of *Liberty.* We may rely on their testimony. That it manipulates facts to reach a loaded question does not diminish but provides the significance to what they say. The conclusion they drew is what tells our story. From the tory perspective, their evidence proved that the whig crowd was in command of Boston.

The day after the seizure of *Liberty,* rumors of "a general insurrection or assembly" so alarmed some of Boston's "gentlemen" that they proposed a compromise. Fearing the "very terrible Consequences," Collector Harrison and Comptroller Hallowell concluded that the conditions of mob law made it necessary to reach an accommodation. And, of course, should they return *Liberty* to Hancock they would have a fact, whether created or unlooked for, implying they had been forced to do so to avoid violence: evidence that whig anarchy and not imperial law dictated the course of events.

Upon the whole we can only observe, that as the powers of government in this country, are in so weak and enervated a state, and the mob, by what we can learn, determined upon their point, we should consider it as a measure of policy, in the present dilemma, to take Mr. Hancock's security, and release the sloop for the preservation of the [customs] officers, and tranquility of the town, which we have reason to believe would otherwise be greatly endangered.[12]

Motivated by the highest considerations, the two men, who were supposedly so sick on that day that they had been confined to bed, made a deal with John Hancock. Unfortunately, accounts differ about what they hoped to accomplish.

Harrison and Hallowell said *Liberty* was to be returned to Hancock, who offered to post security that the sloop would be surrendered to customs if condemned at vice admiralty. The attorney general of England believed that "the Collector, seeing the Danger to which himself and the whole Town of Boston were exposed," told Hancock in writing that he was willing "to take his Word only as a Security for the Ship." Whigs were later told that no deal had been concluded because the commissioners demanded a "humble" petition from Hancock which, after the merchant "degraded" himself, they "cast upon the floor because it was not engrossed on gilt paper." Hancock himself left no record of what was negotiated. All we know is that he either did not conclude an agreement to take back *Liberty* or, after agreeing, changed his mind and repudiated the contract.[13]

Some historians believe that at a midnight meeting, Hancock was dissuaded by militant whigs such as James Otis and Samuel Adams. A better explanation is that lawyers advised him not to post security, as it could provide a color of legality to the seizure of *Liberty,* the constitutionality of which they intended to challenge. If, after the trial, the sloop was declared forfeited, Hancock would have acknowledged vice admiralty's jurisdiction, while obtaining nothing except temporary custody.[14]

The interesting question is not why Hancock repudiated the agreement, but how the customs men sought to turn the fact of repudiation into a fact proving Boston was controlled by the crowd. "The Sons of Liberty and Leaders of the Mob did not choose to let go their Hold of an affair so well adapted to keep up the Ferment," Collector Harrison rationalized. "Mr. Hancock was very earnest and desirous that this Proposal should take place, but was over awed by some of those Firebrands who have the chief Direction of the Mob and so the Treaty was broke off on Sunday Night."[15] In other words, the rabble that Hancock in the past had been accused of directing, now directed Hancock.

Tory dogma had long promulgated the premise that the crowd was controlled by a few whig leaders, a fact proven by the additional assumptions that the mob must be directed by someone and that it could be raised at will. If tories now envisioned new or different leaders calling the tune, the unanswered question is what purpose they could have had. On the surface, there appeared more to be gained by having Hancock complete the agreement than by stopping him. *Liberty* back at its berth would have helped keep the town quiet, weakening the tory contention that Boston was unsafe and damaging the commissioners' case for troops. If we think it possible that those unknown leaders would have encouraged riots in order to force the British hand, make Lord Hillsborough send troops, and attack the soldiers hoping to escalate the conflict, it should be kept in mind that not even Charles Paxton thought them so militant. Boston whigs, after all, had more to lose than gain by violence. They might not have been concerned about London, but they were troubled by unfavorable publicity in other colonies where reaction against pointless mob activities might leave Massachusetts isolated, without supporters or even sympathizers. Happily for Harrison, questions that occur to us could be ignored by him.

Joseph Harrison was not the only imperial official to manipulate these facts. Francis Bernard contributed his mite. Four months after they had first scurried aboard *Romney,* the commissioners asked if it was safe to come back. Seeing a chance to spring a trap, the governor put the question to the council. "This was very embarrassing," he wrote of the councillors' options. "If they answered Yea, they would be chargeable with advising the return of the Commissioners: If they said No, they would contradict all their assertions, that there was no occasion for troops to support the civil power."[16]

Obtaining a reply proved difficult. For over two hours the councillors resisted until Bernard wore them down. "At length I got an answer, twelve answering in the affirmative, five declining answering because they lived out of town, and two giving written answers, condemning the commissioners for going out of town, and therefore refusing advice about their return, but concluding that all persons would be safe."[17]

Although Bernard failed to trap the council, neither he nor the commissioners gave up. Evidence they could not wring from opponents might still be manufactured by friends. There was reason to believe that London would be as impressed by the second as by the first. Besides, the question was useful only if the right answer was obtained. As a right answer from tories was better than a wrong answer from whigs, Francis Bernard decided to answer the question himself.

Taking advantage of the certainty of creating a new and valuable fact, the commissioners redrafted the question and made the best of a good opportunity by expanding their single question into four. To answer the four questions, Bernard selected men whom Samuel Adams or James Otis would surely have put at the top of their list of biased witnesses: himself, Chief Justice Thomas Hutchinson, Provincial Secretary Andrew Oliver, and Admiralty Judge Robert Auchmuty. We need not consider the questions. The answers tell the story.

Yes, the four officials agreed, the commissioners "cou'd not have remained long in safety in the town of Boston after the Seizure of the Sloop *Liberty*." Had they not fled, they "wou'd have been in great danger of violence . . . from a Mob, which at that time, it was generally expected wou'd be raised for that purpose."[18] As the answer was in the guise of a private communication to be read in London only, there was no need to say who it was that "generally expected" a mob to be raised. Tories and whigs were advocates, not historians. They questioned only convenient facts: those facts supporting the contention they sought to prove.

Yes was also the answer to the second question. Experience had proven "that the authority of Government was insufficient to restrain, suppress, or punish, the several Mobs which had been assembled" since the stamp-act crisis first broke out. The commissioners had made the right decision retiring to the castle as no available force could have policed the crowd that took over Boston's streets following the seizure of *Liberty*.[19]

In reply to the third question the commissioners were again told they had acted prudently. They could "not have returned to town," nor could they have "executed" their "Commission with safety."[20]

The final answer was in the negative. "[W]e know of no better measure you cou'd have taken, than Your retiring to Castle William, there being no place within this Province, where Your persons wou'd have been equally safe."[21]

We may call these answers manufactured evidence, but it would not do to marvel at the audacity of men who so blatantly would manipulate a ploy to prove their case for constitutional reform. Much of the evidence supporting the argument that the British government had to send troops to Boston on its own initiative, and not wait for an application from the governor and council, had been, in some sense, manufactured. The case was not weakened by the probative quality of these answers, rather it was, most likely, strengthened if for no other reason than that London was not likely to weigh probativeness. The opinions of a group of men so respectable as these four enjoyed an independent weight of their own.

Before an impartial jury, the whigs might not have won an acquittal on the charge that Boston was too dangerous a place for customs men to linger, but they might have raised enough doubts to shift the onus of proof back on Bernard and the commissioners. There were facts that seemed to disprove the tory argument. The commissioners had fled and yet, as whigs several times pointed out, import duties continued to be paid to the imperial revenue service "with as much punctuality while they are at the Castle as if they were in the body of the Town."[22]

More telling was the fact that potentially explosive revenue business was conducted without mob interference or even a hint of trouble. Just twelve days after the seizure of *Liberty,* a suit was filed in admiralty to condemn the sloop. On 1 August, two months before British troops arrived in Boston and even more before the commissioners left the castle, *Liberty* was judged forfeited and the ship and cargo ordered confiscated.[23]

Surely this action was more provocative than the original seizure. John Hancock was now deprived of his property not just temporarily, but permanently. If there was any occasion for a crowd to gather, it would have been to prevent these proceedings. But neither Advocate General Jonathan Sewall, who filed the libel, nor Admiralty Judge Robert Auchmuty, who pronounced judgment, betrayed fear of the mob. Their conduct does not prove that they—compared to the revenue people—were brave men, nor is it possible to say they were without apprehension. It does, however, indicate that, unlike the commissioners, they did not expect a mob to materialize at the drop of James Otis's hat.

Even more damaging to the tory case was the fact that on 6 September—again before troops arrived and while the commissioners were still closeted in the castle—*Liberty* was sold to the imperial revenue service at a public auction of which prior notice was published. Joseph Harrison was the bidder. No mob rose that day.[24]

That Boston was generally quiet at a time when the commissioners were telling London it was too dangerous for their safety does not prove they were wrong. That the mob did not rise on such obvious occasions as the auction of *Liberty* may be evidence that the commissioners had been correct: that the Boston crowd followed orders of some mysterious leader and was waiting for them to return. Or it may be evidence that the rioters had not cared about the fate of *Liberty:* that they had been protesting *Romney*'s press gangs. Or it could have been evidence that the Boston crowd was a highly political phenomenon: the mob would protest constitutionally unprecedented events—the employment by the customs service of the navy within the harbor as a police force—but would not riot against legitimate judicial proceedings, even the "unconstitutional" vice-admiralty court which condemned the property of British citizens while denying them the right of trial by jury, a right that, in similar cases, was the privilege of Englishmen and Welsh.[25]

The point is not what general quiet in Boston might prove, but what it disproves. Unless refuted, it is evidence that, at the very least, tends to cast doubt on the commissioners' assertion that they could not return without the protection of one or two regiments of regular troops. The indisputable fact that Sewall, Auchmuty, and Harrison performed duties obnoxious to the whigs and not only were left unmolested, but acted as though they did not expect to be mobbed, creates a presumption of calm that should have shifted onto the commissioners the onus of explanation. Due to the dynamics of the argument and the predilections of those sitting in judgment, it was an onus they were not required to meet.

There was other evidence cited by the whigs to destroy the commissioners' case for troops. One was the fact that Commissioner John Temple saw no reason to join his four colleagues in the castle. For a while he did lodge there "to save appearances," but would not cooperate with what he later professed to believe a campaign to misrepresent American defiance of British authority.[26]

The whig list of other revenue officers who, like Temple, walked the streets of Boston at a time their superiors claimed it was unsafe, is remarkable for its length. Presenting it to the colonial public, the *Journal of the Times* reeked with sarcasm.

> It may not be unentertaining to remark, that when the four *fugitives,* fled to the Castle last summer, *as it is said,* for safety, the following gentlemen of the suit did not fall in with their plan, but resided *safely* in Boston, and went daily to the Castle to do business—the Hon. Mr. Temple, a Commissioner, Samuel Venner, Esq; Secretary, Charles Stuart, Esq; Receiver-General, John Williams, Esq; Inspector-General, William Wooten, Esq; Inspector-General, David Lytle [*sic*], Esq; Solicitor-General; Messrs. M'Donald and Lloyd, principal Clerks; to these may be added, the Collector and Comptroller of Halifax, then in Boston, the Collector of Falmouth, the Collector of Piscataqua, the officers of the port of Salem, occasionally in Boston, during the Board's residence at the Castle; the Searcher of Augustine, and all the officers of the port of Boston, at their respective duties, except the collector, who, ('tis said) was, by *positive* order, detained, to keep up the *farce* at the Castle, much against his will.[27]

That Harrison was forced against his will to live at the castle is a fact unsubstantiated by independent evidence and, when measured against other created facts, does not seem significant. More important—if true—was the whig charge that the commissioners suspended their secretary because he refused "to help *keep up the appearance* of their service being *obstructed* in the town of Boston" by "retiring with them . . . to the

Castle." If the man did refuse to move to the island, it was probably not due to hardships. There were even some who found life at Fort William both comfortable and gay. Tory society was so pleasant, one English lady wrote from the castle, that the refugees were "much happier in their exiled state than on the Land of Liberty."[28]

Then, too, there is the question of the commissioners' own movements. They may have avoided Boston, but they did not remain cooped up in the castle. "[T]hey frequently landed on the Main," the town meeting charged, "and made excursions into the Country; visiting the Lieu[tenant] Governor and other Gentlemen at their Seats, where it would have been easy to have seized them if any injury had been intended them." The Massachusetts council, in an official communiqué to General Gage, supported this assertion. The commissioners, the councillors claimed, could have been easily attacked and the fact that they were not "demonstrates the insincerity of their declarations, that they immuned themselves at the Castle for safety." Surely there could be no other conclusion than they were play acting, "an essential part of the concerted plan for procuring Troops to be quartered here."[29]

Two other facts are certain. There were whigs who both believed that the commissioners came ashore and acted upon that belief. At least twice, rumors that Commissioner John Robinson was on the mainland were sufficient to raise a mob. Once he was reported in Newport, Rhode Island, and "some Hundreds, not to say Thousands, assembled," but after an extensive search failed to locate him. On another occasion fifty or sixty Bostonians went out to Robinson's residence in Roxbury. Not finding him at home "they did nothing," Bernard reported to Hillsborough, "but plunder his fruit trees, and break off the branches thereof, and break down some of the fences, and trample down the garden." "This," the governor complained, "is called a frolick of a few boys to eat some cherries."[30]

Bernard exaggerated, but not by much. The whigs depreciated the factual damage that Robinson faced, but they did more besides. They asked whether such incidents were entitled to probative consideration. Had not the commissioners staged so many "attacks" in the past that it was impossible to separate reality from fantasy, the readers of London's *Public Advertiser* were asked just a few days after Bernard wrote of the "frolick" to pick Robinson's cherries. Before the *Liberty* riot occurred, Londoners were told, the commissioners of the American customs, while admittedly thoroughly despised by Bostonians, had never been insulted,

> yet either from a conscious guilt of being the immediate execu-
> tioners of what the people tho't Slavery, or at least temporary

Oppression, and therefore justly meriting the vengeance of the public, or perhaps to make themselves and services appear more important to their Patrons here and in England (and such artful methods are often practised by governors as well as other officers abroad) they had some considerable time before the present affair more than once arm'd themselves and their houses, under real or pretended apprehensions of losing their lives.[31]

Such stories were wasted on British readers. Even though the most exaggerated reports from America contained facts far milder than current English and Irish riots, it was easy to believe the worst. When the revenue officials attempted to seize *Liberty* "agreeable to the intention and direction of a late act of Parliament," other London newspapers reported, "the populace rose and drove the Commissioners out of the town, and damaged (some say destroyed) their houses."[32]

American whigs were seldom heard when they protested that tory tales about Boston riots were told "in so aggravated a light, as to incense to a high degree." Their supporters in parliament such as Colonel Isaac Barre were in the political opposition. "May not a little mob have been called a tumult, and a little insurrection a rebellion?" he asked the house of commons. "In being riotous, the colonies have mimicked the mother country."[33]

Even if Barre was understood, which is unlikely, it may well have been impossible for the open-minded members of parliament to have evaluated the opposing arguments, especially those whirling about the *Liberty* riots. By the time any debate could have occurred, the arguing and questioning of facts had been obscured if not displaced by the assertion of extreme conclusions that assumed facts had been proven and agreed upon. We need only recall that just a month to the day they fled town, the commissioners were telling the British administration that "it is impossible for us to set foot in Boston, until there are two or three regiments in the town, to restore and support Government." The whig defense was soon responding in kind. "In order to raise the jealousy of the [British] nation," the Massachusetts convention protested, "the most trifling incidents have been wrought up to the highest pitch of aggravation, by persons who still find means to gain a credit there"[34]

It would appear that both sides assumed minds were already made up, and, since no one was likely to be converted, that arguments might as well be pitched to extreme assertions if not to win proselytes, at least to retain partisans. More likely, however, the commissioners set the tone because it served their ends. There was little purpose arguing about the degree of danger or the probativeness of specific facts. The *Liberty* riots were useful only to obtain troops. Halfway measures did not interest them. They had nothing to lose by clouding the merits of the debate with the ultimate demand, for the ultimate demand was the only reason they were playing the game.

The tone of the debate set by the participants explains why the *Liberty* affair cannot be satisfactorily reconstructed and why historians have provided such contrary interpretations. The contending sides were interested in forensic facts, not historical facts, yet what they said has been accorded the authority of evidence, not weighed as argument. We should, therefore, not be puzzled that today's historians of the tory persuasion accept the tory account as readily as yesterday's historians accepted the whig account. One consequence is that it may now be impossible to estimate how much danger the commissioners would in reality have faced had they returned to Boston.

John Temple is said to have declared they would have been safe,[35] and while his testimony is impressive, his fellow commissioners objected that he was not an impartial witness. They themselves furnished rather convincing evidence by coming ashore to dine with friends and conduct business. They never admitted they did so, of course, and our proof is that whigs were so certain that they did, at least sixty took the trouble of going out to Roxbury to flush one of them out. Thus the best evidence that the commissioners knew they were not in danger helps to prove that they may, in fact, have been—a mob looking for Commissioner John Robinson.

Impartial witnesses are impossible to find. Thomas Hutchinson was not one, yet he was fairer than Bernard or the revenue men and his opinion should carry some weight. "I own I was in pain for them," he wrote of the commissioners after the *Liberty* riots. "I do not believe if the mob had seized them, there was any authority able and willing to have rescued them."[36]

General Thomas Gage was most likely more objective, perhaps the only man to offer testimony who had no bone to pick. Married to an American woman, he was the one person to undertake an investigation of the incident who was neither a Bostonian nor a member of the Massachusetts government. After considering the factual evidence, Gage was unable to support the imperial side although he did not say the whigs had been right. The commissioners, Gage concluded, had not been attacked personally, "yet the assault upon some of their officers, and the threats daily thrown out against themselves was certainly a sufficient reason to make them apprehensive of danger to their own persons. Whether any harm would have actually happened to them, had they remained in town, it is not possible to judge."[37]

While we can give Gage credit for reaching an objective, though imprecise, factual conclusion, we must not overlook the tory premises upon which he based that conclusion. Unable to measure the degree of danger, he nevertheless accepted the assertion that danger existed. The commissioners may not have been in immediate peril, Gage was saying to Lord Hillsborough, but there had been "threats daily thrown out against themselves." The general never told London who made the threats or gave him testimony. Again facts were stated and in the stating itself, not in independent evidence, is found the presumption of validity.

In fairness to Gage it must be acknowledged that he was more interested in the solution than in the problem. Actual danger did not have to be proven to establish the principal contention. "From what has been said," Thomas Gage concluded, it was evident that "there is no government in Boston; in truth there is very little at present, and the constitution of this province leans so much to the side of democracy, that the Governor has not the power to remedy the disorders that happen in it."[38]

We should not be surprised that General Gage and the highest ranking naval officer in North America accepted as proven facts whatever stories the commissioners told them. The military mind is prepared for the worst, and both men were convinced that nothing would do but to flood Boston with imperial land and sea forces.[39] What might have surprised us, did we not realize what was going on, was the reaction of England's attorney general. Summing up the *Liberty* riots in an official opinion, Charles de Grey argued that Harrison and Hallowell had been roughed up by "about 4 or 500 Persons." The two crown officials "were so much beat and wounded by them, that it was with the greatest Difficulty they Escaped with their Lives, nor did the Fury of the Mob stop here, Every Officer of the Customs they could meet with felt their Resentment, and narrowly escaped being murthered."[40]

As attorney general of England, de Grey was a member of the British administration, but the views he expressed were not political, they were legal. He was writing an opinion of law. Facts, accurate facts, were his only tools for reaching a correct decision. If de Grey, a common lawyer trained and experienced at shifting, questioning, weighing, and arguing facts, could conclude that the Boston mob planned to murder "Every Officer of the Customs," surely the Earl of Hillsborough, a politician, not an attorney, could not be expected to heed whig cries that Boston was being misrepresented by servants of the crown.

13

A Quiet Reception

THE TRIUMPH OF FACTS

The heaviest cross Francis Bernard had to bear was the executive council. During the stamp-act crisis the governor of Massachusetts Bay had even argued that, for all intents and purposes, he was without a council. Some whigs would have been surprised to read his words. Just three weeks before the *Liberty* riots, Boston's most influential whig newspaper printed criticism of the councillors. "Search the council records for these seven years," an anonymous correspondent wrote, "and see if you can find it produce a single resolution in favour of the people!" The *Liberty* affair produced many such votes.[1]

As soon as he was able to assemble the councillors following the *Liberty* riots, Bernard pressed them for cooperation. They paid him no heed. When he expressed alarm that the sons of liberty had called a meeting to "promote the peace, good order and security of the town," the council saw no reason for concern. What Bernard called "a most violent and virulent paper," the councillors said was neither dangerous nor improper. If the sons of liberty wanted to keep the town quiet, it did not trouble them that an organized citizenry did a task the king's men could not perform. Finally Bernard asked if a member would move that he be advised to request imperial troops. "I added, that though I was well assured, that if I put this question, every gentleman would answer in the negative, yet I doubted not but every one would be glad to see the peace of the town restored by this method, if it should appear to be the only one left. No answer was given."[2]

For a month and a half the Massachusetts executive remained locked in stalemate. For six weeks and three days Bernard pressed the council and the councillors refused to put the question to a vote. The whigs understood the constitutional issue at stake and what the governor sought to accomplish. He did not expect them to advise troops, but wanted their negative "to form a complaint to the Ministry that they were negligent of their duty in not advising to proper measures for the Protection of the Commissioners; and from thence to enforce a necessity of military force to restore and support Government in Boston."[3]

Bernard, himself, "kept quite clear of applying or sending for Troops," although he was hopeful that someone, Gage or London, had issued marching orders to the regiments stationed at Halifax. "I have publickly declared in Council that I have not and I will not make any such Application unless they advise it."[4]

General Gage forced the issue. Hearing of the *Liberty* riots and getting pleas from the beleaguered commissioners, he had ordered the commander at Halifax to be prepared to march to Boston as soon as a request was received from the governor. Now Gage wrote asking for a decision.

For a final time Bernard put the question to the councillors: "Whether they would advise, that the Governor should, according to General Gage's offer, require troops from Halifax to support the execution of the civil power, and preserve the peace of the town."[5]

There were no dissents. Tories and future loyalists joined whigs making the council's reply unanimous. "The Board answer, the civil power does not need the support of Troops; and that it is not for his Majesty's Service nor the Peace of this Province that any Troops be required, or that any come into the Province, and therefore they unanimously advise, That the Governor do not require any Troops."[6]

With that vote, Governor Bernard completed the factual elements needed to prove his constitutional case. Saying that the commissioners were not in danger, the Massachusetts council had refused to advise and consent to a request for imperial troops. If he could persuade London that the vote was not limited to this one occasion or due to a sincere disagreement about necessity, but to incontrovertible evidence that the council would never consent to an application for British soldiers either to maintain order in the town of Boston or to enforce imperial revenue law, he might complete his legal case as well. Should the Earl of Hillsborough become convinced that Massachusetts Bay was a lawless province and Boston governed by a rebellious mob, the council's refusal to advise and consent a requisition for troops would wrap into one convenient argument the constitutional dilemma and the necessity for constitutional reform.

"I shall have frequent occasion to observe," the governor wrote Hillsborough two months after the council's decision, "how impossible it will be for me to execute his Majesty's commands, according to his expectation, until I have a Council more dependent upon the King than the present is." Elected by the general court, the councillors made "the humouring [of] the people their chief object," and "will never join with the Governor in censuring *the overflowings of liberty*." Probably the most persuasive argument of all was Bernard's contention that "the Council of this province is as much out of the controul of the King as the House of Representatives is." The comparison was as timely as it was true. Recent events had made Hillsborough keenly aware of American legislative independence; he had been frustrated and defied by the rebellious spirit of Massachusetts' lower house.[7]

In the midst of the *Liberty* crisis—only twenty days after the seizure of Hancock's sloop—one of the most momentous constitutional decisions of the prerevolutionry era had been made by the Massachusetts house of representatives. Four and one half months earlier, on 11 February to be exact, the house sent a circular letter to other assemblies on the continent, urging that they "harmonize" opposition to the Townshend duties. It was the extreme defiance and Lord Hillsborough answered with the extreme demand. The audacity "of writing to the other Colonies on the Subject of their intended Representations against some late Acts of Parliament," he informed Governor Bernard, was "a Measure of so inflamatory a Nature," he had no alternative but to order the letter recalled. Bernard laid the royal command before the lower house, urging on the members "the expediency of your giving his Majesty this testimonial of your duty and submission." On 30 June the house notified the governor that it would not rescind the offensive letter. The vote had been ninety-two to seventeen, and the legislators who refused to obey Hillsborough's command became known in Massachusetts as "the Glorious Ninety-two." If the vote was an insult to the crown, its size was a shock to Francis Bernard. "[A]mong the majority," he observed, "were many members who were scarce ever known, upon any other occassion, to vote against the government-side of a question; so greatly has infatuation and intimidation gained ground."[8]

This event, the first critical test of whig strength in the Bay colony, was on Bernard's mind when he warned Hillsborough that the council was "as much out of the controul of the King as the House of Representatives." The governor was urging London to promulgate two constitutional reforms. The first that the colonial secretary order troops to Boston and, second, that the council be appointed by the king, not elected by the general court. It was to effect these two changes in the colonial constitution that he, the customs commissioners, and their colleagues in the imperial civil service had created, manipulated, questioned, and argued the facts of the *Liberty* riots.

Some may think it an exercise in futility. There had been no need for

Governor Francis Bernard and the customs officials to build their case, and the whig defense was never heard. The issue had been resolved before the *Liberty* controversy began. The earl of Hillsborough, secretary of state for the American colonies, had already decided to order troops to Massachusetts Bay. A plea by the commissioners as early as 12 February, before they and Bernard had the March riots about which to complain, persuaded him that the situation in Boston was desperate.[9] Measured against all the evidence collected, argued, and eventually sent across the Atlantic in an unrivaled flood of words, it is remarkable how quickly Hillsborough was convinced. The commissioners won their case less than three months after first setting foot on Massachusetts soil. Whigs can hardly be blamed for complaining it was not enough time for London to evaluate that case or know if there was substance in its proof.

Lord Hillsborough may not have received the commissioners' memorial until 7 May, two days before *Liberty* sailed into Boston Harbor. The moment could hardly have been more unfavorable for the whig cause. London was recovering from the fright of mob rule. During April, four or five regiments of foot had been ordered into the city to put down the John Wilkes riots. "[N]othing but a strong military force will be able to prevent the mob from rescuing him," a London newspaper had reported. Lord Hillsborough's own carriage had been attacked by the crowd. "This capital," Benjamin Franklin wrote from London, "is now a daily scene of lawless riot and confusion." That same day Lord Hillsborough wrote a letter to Governor Francis Bernard reporting his decision. The commissioners had convinced him "that their Officers meet with great Obstructions, and are deterred from exerting themselves in the Execution of their Duty." Soldiers were needed and soldiers would be sent.[10]

General Thomas Gage did not receive his orders until early September or possibly late August, long after he and London were aware of the *Liberty* riots. It is small wonder then that not only many whigs, but even Gage, believed he had been told to occupy Boston because of what had occurred on Hancock's wharf. Asked by loyalist lawyer George Chalmers what had been "the true object," Gage said it was *Liberty*. "A vessel having been seized by the officers of the customs at Boston, the people rose and forced the Commissioners of the customs to fly to Castle William, then garrisoned by a Provincial company of soldiers, and committed other outrages. This was the cause of sending out General [Alexander] Mackay, with two regiments, and supposed to have been done to show a resolution in Government to protect the crown officers." The commissioners' case not only motivated crown policy, it became official history.[11]

There appears to be a discrepancy, but there is none. Several regiments were ordered to Boston, not one, and as Gage believed, the *Liberty* affair probably played a role in that decision. Hillsborough, in his original dispatch, had suggested that one regiment might be enough. The number multiplied after news of the revenue officials' flight reached Great Britain. At least such was the understanding of Governor Bernard. He told the council that "the Halifax Regiments were ordered hither in consequence of the Riots in March last, and the two Irish Regiments in consequence of that of the 10th of June last."[12]

Bernard had his regiments, but his words helped strengthen a new whig argument. They gave fresh conviction to what otherwise might have been familiar, shopworn accusations. The whigs were now saying that misrepresentations had prevailed: because of false stories "a standing army is to be sent." The councillors, whom Bernard had attempted to depict as secretly favoring troops while too fearful to advise them, lashed out at the governor. "[T]hey are fully persuaded," the council resolved, "his Majesty's ministers could never have judged it either necessary or expedient to go into such extraordinary Measures, as those of sending Troops hither, unless in the Representations made from hence by some ill-minded Persons, the said Riots had been greatly magnified and exaggerated."[13]

Once the troops arrived in Boston the propaganda continued, with the whigs on the offensive, the revenue officers wondering if the prize had been worth the quest. "We have now the appearance before this Town of 13 or 14 Ships of War, and two Regiments in the Common with a Train of Artillery," the *Evening-Post* exclaimed, "and all this mighty and expensive Parade, is, as his E[xcellenc]y had told the C[ounci]l, in consequence of the Disorders on the 18th of March last, which were nothing more than a few disorderly Boys hallooing before Mr. Inspector William's Door."[14]

[W]e now behold Boston surrounded at a time of profound peace, with about 14 ships of war, with springs on their cables, and their boardsides to the town! . . . this mighty armament has no other rebellion to subdue than what existed in the brain or letter of the inveterate G[overno]r B[ernar]d and the detested Comm[is]s[ione]rs of the Board of C[ustom]s.[15]

During the entire controversy over troops truer words were seldom spoken. The army found no insurrection to suppress. "There is not the smallest Intention of any Revolt," the commander of the military garrison wrote General Thomas Gage after his soldiers had been in Boston for over half a year. Whigs did not have to read army dispatches to know many officers believed that Lord Hillsborough had been duped. "It is observed," the *Evening-Post* noted, "that the Enemies to this Town and Province are much chagrin'd to perceive this Town in that Peace and good Order which has astonished the Gentlemen of the Military, who by the Representations made to them might have expected to have found us in a State of Disorder and Rebellion."[16]

14

A Loaded Word

CONCLUSION

Facts misled Lord Hillsborough and they misled us. We note that after British regiments landed in Boston there was a long period of civic calm, and we conclude that the presence of the soldiers explains the calm. Certain effect, however, does not always arise from obvious cause. British regulars had been sent to Boston to police the town, but they had no constitutional role to play. Lord Hillsborough had given no thought to the law, assuming that where troops were stationed troops could act. In truth, they could not. Local constitutional law and whig control of the magistracy rendered them politically impotent. When the Boston mob rose again, it would be as unimpeded as before. Indeed, the leisurely process of tar and feathers was not introduced until the beginning of military occupation. While evidence may be direct and uncomplicated, conclusions from that evidence must be drawn with care.[1]

There are issues that cannot be resolved. We will never be certain what happened at Hancock's wharf on 10 June 1768 or at any of the other crowd events in prerevolutionary New England that imperial officials called riots and American whigs depreciated. When we realize that the people gathered around Daniel Malcom's house may have been waiting to see if Sheriff Stephen Greenleaf dared open the front gate and risk a lawsuit, we begin to doubt those historians of the tory persuasion who explain Greenleaf's retreat by saying the threat of physical violence deterred him. Yet we cannot be certain we understand what was on his mind. We know he felt intimidated, but are left to wonder if he feared the mob as well as the law of *trespass*.

Our problem is not whether Governor Francis Bernard and the commissioners of the American customs misled the Earl of Hillsborough. Our problem is whether they still mislead us. "When we consider the lawless condition of Boston," a loyalist historian has argued, "there cannot be any question that Governor Bernard was fully authorized to seek the presence of troops."[2] If now we doubt the writer's accuracy, it must be asked what is doubted. The facts upon which he relied when saying Boston was "lawless" is the obvious answer. Easily overlooked is his use of the word "lawless."

Definitions are not our undoing. Our undoing is the tendency to accept words about law without thinking to define them. We read that Boston was "lawless" and agree with the assertion, not because facts are unquestioned but because the word "lawless" is. We cannot escape from inbred predilections about legality or from the notion that "law" is the sovereign's command. When we think of the Boston mob, our thoughts are shaped by a perspective more akin to that of Lord Hillsborough than Samuel Adams. We are all latent tories, judging prerevolutionary crowds by the principles of imperial law and the standards of British order. The definitions of Thomas Hutchinson and Francis Bernard are our definitions. Every instance of crowd force is a riot and every riot is unlawful.[3]

We may never escape our legal prenotions, but we can revise our factual assumptions. When it is realized that much of the evidence of prerevolutionary mobs comes from manufactured probative facts, the traditional picture should be modified. If not altered in detail, it has become less sharp in focus and therefore more accurate or, at least, less misleading. For too long forensic facts have been weighed as historical facts. We may cling to our definitions of "lawful" and "lawless," while no longer assuming that self-help is usually violent and violence is always lawless.

It would not do to draw the wrong conclusion. To realize that most facts upon which we have relied are not furnished by balanced reports evaluating a political situation, but were manipulated by advocates arguing a constitutional case, does little more than enlighten us as to probativeness. It must be acknowleged that there is less evidence upon which to reconstruct the story than had been thought. The question that remains is not so much the truth as whether the truth can be uncovered.

Returning to Boston from the castle, a tory lady wrote home to Great Britain that "our safety & quiet depends on the Army & Navy being here." While doubting her judgment, we may be certain she was sincere. Just as certain is the fact that the voters of Boston were not sincere when they complained of words attributed to George III. He was reported to have said that even before the *Liberty* riots their town "had been in a state of disorder and confusion." Bostonians asserted that they could not believe any fair-minded person would make such a charge. "[W]e were struck with astonishment as well as grief," they told the king.[4]

It would be a mistake to wonder where Boston whigs found the brass.

CONCLUSION

They knew what they were doing. Their words were intended for New York and Maryland, not for George III. Our confusion arises from forgetting that law and history mix badly. Forensic facts are of even less value as evidence than facts argued in a political debate. Histories of the prerevolutionary era are colored by our failure to caliper degrees of probativeness. Differences are seldom reconciled. Historians of tory leanings accept the imperial definition of law. Those of whig predilections quote from whig depositions as if they were historical rather then legal evidence, while others merely state the puzzle and leave the truth unresolved.[5] We may never be able to reconcile differences though we can be certain that many statements seemingly exaggerated to us were sincerely made. Imperial officials all over the continent, not merely in Boston, struggled to convince London they needed troops, and were motivated by reasons that to them were convincing. Apparent danger could be actual danger if one was unable to control its growth. The eighteenth century, it must be remembered, was a time when men of the class that staffed Britain's civil service equated freedom with anarchy. A press that did not respect authority made the future unstable, and responsible officials of the whig persuasion had an unnerving habit of stating in public their contempt for individual imperial placemen. What could not be ignored was the fact that on some occasions the colonial crowd caused serious injuries to those who felt its wrath.[6]

If tories were sincere, so were whigs. They believed that imperialists of the school of Hutchinson and Bernard were flooding the ministry with "a budget of little malicious stories, of inflammatory details, and gross misrepresentations." In London on business for John Hancock during 1771, William Palfrey met former Commissioner John Temple. "Mr. Temple tells me," Palfrey wrote Hancock, "that it would amaze any person to be informed of the misrepresentations, which have been made for four or five years past to the ministry, by persons on your side of the Atlantic." Palfrey, a correspondent of John Wilkes and militant whig, had once sought to expose "misrepresentations" by the pro-imperialist *Boston Chronicle* charging local merchants with violations of the intercolonial nonimportation agreement. That as late as 1771, such a man might think John Hancock could be "amazed" at tory "misrepresentations" surely is impressive evidence that whigs were genuinely concerned about what London was being told. That they were surprised should cause surprise for us.[7]

It is not enough to acknowledge sincerity. The historical problem must also be acknowledged. We may be impartial, but we cannot impartially reconstruct events on partial evidence. Our inability to gauge probativeness is a handicap more easily conceded than overcome. If it is asked who was telling the truth about the *Liberty* affair, the answer must be that both sides were arguing a case, not reporting facts or explaining motivations. Bernard wanted to reform the imperial constitution. Whigs knew what he was about. They were not so much interested in disproving his facts as negating his legal conclusion.[8]

We are left to wonder how to weigh the unweighable; what probative value can be given the nonprobative. On one hand we have the imperially appointed governor of Massachusetts Bay telling us that he had reason to fear the Boston crowd. On the other hand we have the council, chosen by the popularly elected house of representatives, telling us that Boston's famous mob was not a mob. We should not yearn to reconcile the discrepancy. We should be wary of answering the unanswerable. Surely historians need not despair. They may still debate in confidence where lawyers fear to tread. Common-law standards of probativeness do not bind historians. Questions can still be asked. We need only acknowledge that we use evidence that is tainted to draw conclusions that are inconclusive.

Notes

1
Introduction

1. History as precedent: Charles A. Miller, *The Supreme Court and the Uses of History* (1969). Bernard: Governor Francis Bernard to Board of Trade, 8 November 1765, quoted in Thomas, *British Politics,* at 150.

2. Lieutenant Governor Thomas Hutchinson to Richard Jackson, 5 May 1765, Gray, "Appendix," at 440; Lieutenant Governor Thomas Hutchinson to Former Governor Thomas Pownall, 8 March 1766, ibid. at 445.

3. Whig law: *In a Defiant Stance,* at 118–34; "In a Defensive Rage," at 1087–91. Bernard: Letter of 28 February 1766, Bernard, *Select Letters,* at 43.

4. Hutchinson: Lieutenant Governor Thomas Hutchinson to Former Governor Thomas Pownall, March 1766, quoted in Bailyn, *Ordeal,* at 73. Authority: The Declaratory Act of 18 March 1766, Jensen, *Documents,* at 695–96. Tax: Channing, "Board," at 479.

5. Proclamation by Governor Francis Bernard, 15 March 1766, *Evening-Post,* 17 March 1766, p. 2, col. 1; Postscript, Hutchinson to Governor Thomas Pownall, March 1765, Gray, "Appendix," at 445.

6. Governor Francis Bernard to Lords of Trade, 17 March 1766, Gray, "Appendix," at 445.

7. Proclamation by Governor Francis Bernard, 18 August 1766, *Boston Gazette,* 25 August 1766, p. 2, col. 1.

8. Governor Francis Bernard to Lords of Trade, 18 August 1766, Gray, "Appendix," at 446.

9. North Carolina: *Evening-Post,* 24 March 1766, p. 2, col. 2–3. Rhode Island: Proclamation by Surveyor-General John Temple, 31 January 1764, *Post-Boy,* 6 February 1764, p. 2, col. 3. New York: Lieutenant Governor Cadwallader Colden to Earl of Shelburne, 26 December 1766, 2 *Colden Papers,* at 124. Pennsylvania: Martin, "Customs," at 214–15. Connecticut: *Massachusetts Gazette,* 6 March 1766, p. 1, col. 2; *Evening-Post,* 13 July 1767, p. 3, col. 2. Naval captain: Captain Durell to Commissioners of Customs, 14 August 1766, Wolkins, "Malcom," at 63.

10. Bernard: Governor Francis Bernard to Lords of Trade, 18 August 1766, Gray, "Appendix," at 446. Usages: "In Accordance With Usage," at 335–68.

2

The American Board

1. Customs board: Clark, "Board," at 802; Barrow, *Trade*, at 218–24. Mob: the crowd was celebrating "Pope's Day," the anniversary of the Gunpowder Plot and the annual occasion in colonial Boston for mass rowdyism. Longley, "Mob," 101–3; Bridenbaugh, *Cities*, at 114; Anderson, "Mackintosh," at 26; Cunningham, "Diary," at 290–91; Forbes, *Revere*, at 94.

2. Letter of 17 December 1767, Hulton, *Letters*, at 8; Clark, "Board," at 785.

3. Born: Stark, *Loyalists*, at 318. Riot: Gordon, *Revolution*, at 123; Anderson, "Mackintosh," at 35.

4. Appointment: *Boston Gazette*, 27 April 1767, p. 3, col. 2; *South-Carolina Gazette*, 15 June 1767, p. 2, col. 1. Adams: 1 Adams, *Writings*, at 261.

5. For reasons why the board was located in Boston see Barrow, *Trade*, at 222–23; Dickerson, *Acts*, at 198–99. But see Stout, *Royal Navy*, at 112–13.

6. Obedience: see e.g., *Boston Gazette*, 4 May 1767, p. 3, col. 1, and 27 April 1767, p. 1, col. 1. Hutchinson: Lieutenant Governor Thomas Hutchinson to Thomas Whately, August 1768, Hutchinson, *Letters*, at 5. Violence: "In a Defensive Rage," at 1062–67. Otis: Governor Francis Bernard to Board of Trade, 22 December 1766, 51 *Shelburne Abstracts*, at 509, and Gray, "Appendix," at 446; *Evening-Post*, 23 November 1767, p. 2, col. 3; Gordon, *Revolution*, at 148–49; Hosmer, *Adams*, at 91.

7. *Evening-Post*, 30 November 1767, p. 1, col. 2.

8. *Evening-Post*, 23 November 1767, p. 2, col. 3.

9. Hulton, *Account*, 17–18, 28–29.

10. Letter of 6 April 1769, Brown, "Hulton," at 14–15; Hulton, *Account*, at 86; Letter of 11 May 1770, Brown, "Hulton," at 21. Consider one of Hulton's descriptions of the American character: "As the family encreases, the young men go back into the woods, & do as they fathers did before them, there seems no prospect of advancement, or chance of opulence for them, & as their principles being on a level, they feel no oppression from anyone above them, & see nothing to excite envy, or raise admiration, but leave us without emulation, or desire of distinction, & what is human nature?" Letter of 3 August 1771, ibid., at 24.

11. Governor Francis Bernard to Earl of Shelburne, 22 December 1766, Gray, "Appendix," at 446.

3

The Malcom Affair

1. "Malcom's affair" was well enough known to be mentioned without further identification by newspapers far from Boston. See *South-Carolina Gazette*, 22 June 1767, p. 1, col. 1.

2. Malcom: Stark, *Loyalists*, at 320. Officials: Martin, "Customs," at 202; Barrow, *Trade*, at 186.

3. John Temple to Commissioners of the Customs, n.d., Wolkins, "Malcom," at 64.

4. Force: *Boston Gazette*, 13 April 1767, p. 3, col. 2. Malcom: Declaration of Daniel Malcom, 21 October 1766, Wolkins, "Malcom," at 39 [hereinafter Declaration].

5. Declaration of William Sheaffe and Benjamin Hallowell, 24 September 1766, Wolkins, "Malcom," at 26 [hereinafter Declaration]; Benjamin Hallowell to Commissioners of the Customs, 14 November 1766, ibid., at 77 [hereinafter Letter].

6. Threat: Declaration, *supra* note 5, at 26–27. Malcom: Declaration, *supra* note 4, at 40.

7. Law: Wolkins, "Malcom," at 17. Boston: Town of Boston to Dennys de Berdt, 22 October 1766, 1 Adams, *Writings,* at 94.

8. Suspicion: Anderson, "Mackintosh," at 40. Threat: Deposition of Vincent and Turner, 14 November 1766, Wolkins, "Malcolm," at 82.

9. Declaration of William Mackay, 20 October 1766, Wolkins, "Malcom," at 44.

10. Deputy: Wolkins, "Malcom," at 18–19. Malcom: Declaration, *supra* note 4, at 40.

11. Offer: Letter, *supra* note 5, at 79. Malcom: Zobel, *Massacre,* at 52.

12. Council Records, 24 September 1766, quoted Gray, "Appendix," at 447.

13. Declaration, *supra* note 5, at 27–28.

14. Warrant: ibid., at 28. Ruling: opinion of Chief Justice Thomas Hutchinson and Attorney General Edmund Trowbridge, 31 July 1765, Gray, "Appendix," at 440.

15. Declaration, *supra* note 5, at 28.

16. Declaration of John Ruddock, 25 September 1766, Wolkins, "Malcom," at 30 [hereinafter Declaration].

17. Declaration of Stephen Greenleaf, 1 October 1766, Wolkins, "Malcom," at 37 [hereinafter Declaration].

18. Reply: ibid. Weight: Zobel, *Massacre,* at 52. Fisticuffs: *Journal of the Times,* 6 March 1769, pp. 74–75.

19. Declaration, *supra* note 16, at 29. Of the many refusals by magistrates to assist customsmen, perhaps the one most pertinent to our tale involved John Robinson, collector of Newport and destined to be one of the five commissioners appointed in 1767. Robinson seized a sloop in a Massachusetts port. The sloop was rescued. Robinson applied to the local magistrates, one of whom was Speaker of the Massachusetts House, for assistance in searching private buildings where he thought the rescued cargo had been hidden. The magistrates not only refused but one drew a writ for the owner of the sloop, seeking 3000 pounds damages against Robinson for seizing both ship and cargo. A warrant was sworn out, Robinson was arrested, jailed for one night, and the council voted that "the Justices were justified in doing as they did." Gray, "Appendix," at 439–40; Morgan & Morgan, *Crisis,* at 66; Nelson, "Restraint," at 31.

20. Declaration, *supra* note 17, at 37.

21. Bridenbaugh, *Cities,* at 307; Anderson, "Mackintosh," at 41; *Evening-Post* (Supplement), 30 December 1765, p. 2, col. 3.

22. Greenleaf: Declaration, *supra* note 17, at 38. Man's answer: First Deposition of Nathaniel Barber, 25 September 1766, Wolkins, "Malcom," at 33.

23. Deposition of John Pigeon, 20 October 1766, Wolkins, "Malcom," at 54.

24. Declaration of Benjamin Goodwin, 20 October 1766, Wolkins, "Malcom," at 47.

25. Hutchinson, *History (1828),* at 125–26.

26. One minor figure believed to have taken part in the Boston Tea Party was arrested during 1776 but not tried.

27. Declaration, *supra* note 17, at 38.

28. Ibid., at 39.

29. Wolkins, "Malcom," at 20.

4

The Uses of Law

1. Zobel, *Massacre,* at 51–53.

2. Temple: John Temple to Commissioners of the Customs, n.d., Wolkins, "Mal-

com," at 64. Boston: Town of Boston to Dennys de Berdt, 22 October 1766, 1 Adams, *Writings,* at 94.

3. Qualification: Declaration of Benjamin Goodwin, 20 October 1766, Wolkins, "Malcom," at 47 [hereinafter Declaration].

4. Declaration of Enoch Rust, 20 October 1766, Wolkins, "Malcom," at 48 [hereinafter Declaration].

5. Deposition of John Pigeon, 20 October 1766, Wolkins, "Malcom," at 55 [hereinafter Deposition].

6. Declaration of Daniel Malcom, 21 October 1766, Wolkins, "Malcom," at 41–42 [hereinafter Declaration].

7. Deposition, *supra* note 5, at 55; Declaration of William Mackay, 20 October 1766, Wolkins, "Malcom," at 45. See also Deposition of Caleb Hopkins, 20 October 1766, ibid., at 51.

8. Malcom: Declaration, *supra* note 6, at 41. Witnesses: Declaration, *supra* note 4, at 48; Declaration of William Mackay . . . , *supra* note 7, at 43. Hallowell: Benjamin Hallowell to Commissioners of the Customs 14 December 1766, Wolkins, "Malcom," at 77. Tidewaiters: Deposition of Vincent and Turner, 14 November 1766, Wolkins, "Malcom," at 81 [hereinafter Deposition].

9. Gray, "Appendix," at 447.

10. Deposition, *supra* note 8, at 81; Declaration of Sheaffe and Hallowell, 24 September 1766, Wolkins, "Malcom," at 27 [hereinafter Declaration].

11. There was no restraint on a lawyer preventing him from arguing such a point to the jury and even contending that Malcom's fear gave him a legal justification to resist the officers with force. To have done so would have been to argue incorrect law, but the court did not have authority to rule the argument invalid or grant a motion for a new trial.

12. Suggestion: Wolkins, "Malcom," at 6. Secret: The advantage was that "a writ, or warrant, to be issued only in cases where special information was given upon oath, would rarely, if ever, be applied for, as no informer would expose himself to the rage of the people." Hutchinson, *History (1828),* at 94. Delays: The advantage to the officer is that "if he is obliged, every Time he knows, or has received information of prohibited or uncustomed Goods being cancealed, to apply to the Supreme Court of Judicature for a Writ of Assistants [*sic*], such concealed Goods may be conveyed away before the Writ can be obtained." Opinion of Attorney General William de Grey, 20 August 1768, Gray, "Appendix," at 453 [hereinafter Opinion].

13. Attorney General: Opinion, *supra* note 12, at 453. Hutchinson: Thomas Hutchinson to Sheriff William Tyng of Cumberland County, 11 February 1770, Gray, "Appendix," at 465.

14. Dickerson, "Writs," at 40; Gray, "Appendix," at 401–11 & 421n5; Knollenberg, *Origin,* at 68; Wolkins, "Malcom," at 11; and especially Dickerson, *Acts,* at 251.

15. Hutchinson: Hutchinson, *History (1828),* at 94. Bollan: Bowdoin, "Notes," at 5n; Wolkins, "Writs," at 415; Barrow, *Trade,* at 153–56, 167. Prestige: Shipton, "Hutchinson," at 167; Governor Francis Bernard to Lords of Trade, 30 November 1765, Gray, "Appendix," at 416. Information: William Bollan to Duke of Newcastle, 12 April 1766, Wolkins, "Writs," at 420–21.

16. Other colonies: Dickerson, *Acts,* at 250; Dickerson, "Writs," at 75. Connecticut: Collector and Comptroller of New London to Commissioners of the Customs, 14 May 1766, Wolkins, "Malcom," at 61.

17. Exchequer: "An act to prevent frauds," 12 Charles II, cap. 19 (1660), 7 *Statutes at Large,* at 460. Extension: "An act for preventing frauds," 13 & 14 Charles II, cap. 11, sec. 5 (1662); 8 *Statutes at Large,* at 81. "Like assistance:" "An act for . . . regulating abuses," 7 & 8 William III, cap. 22, sec. 6 (1696), 9 *Statutes at Large,* at 431.

NOTES

18. Gridley: 2 Adams, *Legal Papers*, at 137–38. Statute: "An Act for Establishing a Superiour Court... , " Chap. 3, 1st Sess., Province Laws of 1699–1700, 1 *Acts and Resolves*, at 370–71; 2 Adams, *Legal Papers*, at 132.

19. Writ granted to Charles Paxton, December 1761, 2 Adams, *Legal Papers*, at 145–46, and Gray, "Appendix," at 420.

20. See e.g., whig argument based on the fact that parliament always referred to the writ as "*a Writ of Assistance under the Exchequer seal.*" *Evening-Post,* 9 December 1765, p. 1, col. 1.

21. Opinion: Opinion of Attorney General William de Grey, 17 October 1766, Wolkins, "Malcom," at 73 [hereinafter Opinion]. Reconsider: Barrow, *Trade,* at 203.

22. De Grey: Gordon Goodwin, "William de Grey," 23 *Dictionary of National Biography* 216 (1890); 8 Edward Foss, *The Judges of England* 264–66 (1864). Baffled: Wolkins, "Malcom," at 22. The documents related to the Massachusetts convention of 1768. 4 George Bancroft, *History,* at 116.

23. Query: Grey Cooper to Thomas Nuthall, 14 February 1767, Wolkins, "Malcom," at 74. Answer: Treasury Minutes, 6 February 1767, Wolkins, "Malcom," at 73; Barrow, *Trade,* at 203.

24. Correction: "An act for granting certain duties," 7 George III, cap. 46, sec. 10 (1766), 27 *Statutes at Large,* at 512. Reason: Opinion, *supra* note 12, at 453. Use of writ: 2 Adams, *Legal Papers,* at 179n21.

25. Instructions of the Commissioners of the Customs to subordinate officers, 28 February 1769, Gray, "Appendix," at 450. Note, however, that the commission given to the American commissioners of the customs authorized them not only to enter such buildings but to search and even break open trunks, boxes, and packs, without any mention of needing a writ of assistance. Moreover, they were empowered to call for assistance of all "our Officers and subjects," a power seemingly not qualified by having to display the writ. Commission of the Commissioners of the Customs, 14 September 1767, *Evening-Post,* 26 September 1768, p. 1, cols. 2–3.

26. Letter dated 26 May 1768 but marked "not sent." Gray, "Appendix," at 451–52.

27. *In a Defiant Stance,* at 160–73.

28. "Probable Cause": Nelson, "Restraint," at 9. Juries: "Civil Law as a Criminal Sanction," at 211–47.

29. Sanction: *In a Defiant Stance,* at 27–40. Legality: Nelson, "Restraint," at 9.

30. Malcom: Declaration, *supra* note 6, at 42. Defendant's reply: The defendant, of course, could also plea further special matter, such as that the plaintiff used force preventing him from producing the writ, or that the plaintiff refused to look at the writ, or that the mob (as in the Maine case discussed in chapter 1) had destroyed the writ. But such special matter would not have solved the defendant's dilemma, as it would have been factual, raising a question of fact that the court had to submit to the jury.

31. *In a Defiant Stance,* at 27–40.

32. The most memorable instance was the *Lydia* affair as it may be assumed that the same lawyer, James Otis, who advised Malcom advised John Hancock. When Hancock's ship *Lydia* docked in Boston two years later, a tidewaiter was put on board. The customs man insisted on the right of inspecting the hold, and Hancock undertook to test that claim at law. He confronted the official, the men accompanying him were unarmed. Hancock demanded to see the official's papers. Finding they were not dated he professed to find them technically defective. Hancock asked the customs man to leave the hold and backed up his demand by the application of physical force. That force, which consisted of seizing the tidewaiter under the arms, was, under the circumstances, reasonable and therefore lawful if the tidewaiter was, as Hancock insisted, a trespasser and not an officer privileged to enter the hold. The only threat voiced came, interestingly enough, from Daniel

Malcom. He was a member of Hancock's party, and when the tidewaiter was being pushed up the companionway, he is said to have shouted "damn him hand him up, if it was my vessel I would knock him down." Once the men were above deck and the hatch had been fastened, Hancock stated his legal position for the record. "Do you want to search the vessel?" he asked. The tidewaiter answered no. "You may search the vessel," Hancock announced, "but shall not tarry below." Surely he had his witnesses on hand to hear that particular statement. When the customshouse sought prosecution, the attorney general ruled that Hancock had acted within his legal rights in every respect. Sewall, "Opinion," at 501–4 (1947). The inescapable conclusion is that Hancock had been coached by a lawyer and acted as that lawyer told him to act. Indeed, the tory attorney general said as much. "Mr. Hancock," he explained, "may not have conducted [himself] so prudently or courteously as might be wished, yet from what appears it is probable his Intention was to keep within the boundaries of the Law." Ibid., at 504; Baxter, *Hancock,* at 262. Perhaps the best documented instance of such law knowledge in a noncustoms case involved the attempt of the army to acquire the manufactory house in Boston as barracks for the troops. The whigs rented the building to a man named Brown. Using the same tactics as had Malcom, Brown turned back an army officer, Sheriff Stephen Greenleaf, and finally Chief Justice Hutchinson himself. He closed all the windows, bolted the doors, detained "some persons to serve as evidences of the transactions," stated his reasons for retaining exclusive possession clearly and correctly, and told Hutchinson (who tried to persuade Brown his law was invalid) "that his council [*sic*] were of the ablest in the province, and he shou'd adhere to their advice be the consequences what they would." *Evening-Post,* 24 October 1768, p. 3, col. 1.

33. Historians: e.g., Zobel, *Massacre,* at 53–54; Hersey, "Daniel Malcolm," at 218. No bar: See Erving v. Cradock, *Quincy Reports* 553–58 (1761); "Civil Law as a Criminal Sanction," at 230–34.

34. "An Act for granting certain duties," 4 George III, cap. 15, sec. 46 (1764), 26 *Statutes at Large,* at 51 [hereinafter "An Act"].

35. Collusion: 1 Adams, *Legal Papers,* at xlvi. Statute: "An Act," *supra* note 34, at 51.

36. "Ordeal by Law," at 605–12.

37. Judgments: In South Carolina, Henry Laurens collected a judgment of £1,400 local money. Barrow, *Trade,* at 234. In Rhode Island, Lieutenant Dudingston had three judgments returned against him in civil court. The plaintiffs asked for and the jury granted damages of £295, £5 short of the amount that would have permitted the defendant to appeal the verdict to London. Channing, "Board," at 486–87. Inspecting goods: Martin, "Customs," at 204. Personal injury: e.g., Barrow, *Trade,* at 245–46. Hulton: Hulton, *Account,* at 57.

38. "An act for preventing frauds," 13 & 14 Charles II, cap. 11, sec. 16 (1662), 8 *Statutes at Large,* at 88 [hereinafter "An act"].

39. Verdicts: Wertenbaker, *Puritan,* at 326. Pattern: For 1720s see Barrow, *Trade,* at 87–101. Hutchinson: *In a Defiant Stance,* at 31. Naval officer: Johnson & Syrett, "Customs Law," at 439–40; *Boston Gazette,* 17 November 1766, p. 3, col. 2.

40. "An act to prevent frauds," 12 Charles II, cap. 19, sec. 4 (1660), 7 *Statutes at Large,* at 461.

41. The Townshend acts, one of which created the board of American customs commissioners, also included another attempt to make customs officers judgment proof in colonial common-law courts, a sure indication that the provisions of the sugar act (*supra,* at 32) had been reported to London as ineffective. Under this imperial statute, defendants (that is, revenue agents sued for damages arising from enforcement of British customs laws) were not only permitted to plea the general issue and move for dismissal, but were to recover treble costs when the plaintiff was nonsuited. "An act for granting certain duties," 7 George III, cap. 46,

sec. 11 (1766), 27 *Statutes at Large,* at 512. It may be doubted if this provision was any more successful than earlier acts. What did deter further civil suits seeking criminal-law-type sanctions was the decision of the customs board to pay judgments obtained against revenue men. Thus James Otis decided not to sue Commissioner John Robinson for libel. "Should I recover ever so high damages at law," Otis explained, "I know of nothing to restrain them [the board] from paying them out of the public Chest, which money, extorted as it is, I desire not to touch." The real reason was probably that a private suit would no longer "punish" Robinson. *Boston Gazette,* 11 September 1769, p. 2, col. 3.

5

The Development of Facts

1. *Evening-Post,* 23 November 1767, p. 2, col. 3.

2. Whig understanding: "In a Defensive Rage." Sovereignty: Bailyn, *Pamphlets,* at 121–23.

3. Arbitrary: "In Legitimate Stirps," at 454–99. Resistance: "In a Defensive Rage," at 1067–69. Ingersoll: Jared Ingersoll to Good People of Connecticut, 24 August 1765, *Prior Documents,* at 12. Resolution: *Boston Gazette,* 23 November 1767, p. 3, col. 3.

4. *Boston Gazette,* 23 November 1767, p. 3, col. 3.

5. Nonimportation: See *Evening-Post,* 7 September 1767, p. 2, col. 1, and 12 October 1767, p. 1, col. 1. Slogan: *Boston Gazette,* 9 November 1767, p. 3, col. 1. Statement: Notice from the Selectmen of Boston, 25 November 1767, *Post-Boy,* 30 November 1767, p. 1, col. 1 [hereinafter Notice].

6. *Boston Gazette,* 23 November 1767, p. 3, col. 3.

7. Notice, *supra* note 5, p. 1, col. 1.

8. Letter of 21 November 1767, quoted in Harlow, *Adams,* at 106; Governor Francis Bernard to Earl of Shelburne, 19 March 1768, quoted in *Report of October 1769,* at 303.

9. Charles Paxton to Viscount Townshend, 24 February 1768, Wolkins, "Paxton," at 348 [hereinafter Letter].

10. Hulton: Hulton, *Account,* at 102, 122; Letter of 11 May 1770, Brown, "Hulton," at 21. Although Hulton wrote these words after both the *Liberty* riot and Boston Massacre, it is evident that he held such views for some time. See the thoughts of his sister written a few days after arriving in Boston, reflecting ideas she must have heard him speak. Letter of 30 June 1768, Hulton, *Letters,* at 13.

11. Report from the American Customs Commissioners to Lords of the Treasury, 12 February 1768, Wolkins, "Liberty," at 264–65 [hereinafter Report].

12. Paxton: Letter, *supra* note 9, at 348. Newspapers: Report, *supra* note 11, at 264; Members of parliament: Letter of 30 June 1768, Hulton, *Letters,* at 13; Report, *supra* note 11, at 265. The attitude of the ministry toward the opposition in parliament may be judged by George Grenville's assertion during the debate over the repeal of the stamp act: "The seditious spirit of the colonies owes its birth to the factions in the house." *Prior Documents,* at 60. See also Governor Francis Bernard to Lord Barrington, 28 January 1768, Bernard & Barrington, *Correspondence,* at 250.

13. Letter, *supra* note 9, at 350.

14. Abington Resolves, 19 March 1770, *Boston Gazette,* 2 April 1770, p. 3, col. 1.

15. Report, *supra* note 11, at 267.

16. Ibid., at 265.

17. Vote of Newport Town Meeting, 4 December 1767, *Boston Gazette,* 14 December 1767, p. 3, col. 2. The offer of reward was publicized in the colonies. See e.g., *South-Carolina Gazette,* 11 January 1768, p. 2, col. 3. For whig suspicions

that London withheld the funds for coercive and political purposes, see Governor Samuel Ward to Earl of Shelburne, 6 November 1766, *Prior Documents,* at 119. When the king's warehouse at Newport was broken into, the governor offered a reward for the arrest of the person responsible. *Massachusetts Gazette,* 15 August 1768, p. 1, col. 2.

18. Other towns: An example is Philadelphia charging the *Liberty* riot was provoked. Philadelphia Committee of Merchants to Merchants' Committee in London, 25 November 1769, Gordon, *Revolution,* at 179. Report: *Report of October 1769,* at 304.

19. For charges made before the commissioners arrived, see Samuel Adams to Dennys de Berdt, 2 December 1766, 1 Adams, *Writings,* at 104–5; *Boston Gazette,* 28 September 1767, p. 2, col. 1. Bernard was called a man who "will misrepresent and vilify them [the people] to their Sovereign." *Evening-Post* (Supplement), 1 December 1766, p. 1, col. 1.

20. Shelburne: Earl of Shelburne to Governor Francis Bernard, 13 September 1766, *Evening-Post,* 17 November 1766, p. 2, col. 2; also Secretary of State Henry Seymour Conway to Governor Francis Bernard, 31 March 1766, *Boston Gazette,* 9 June 1766, p. 2. col. 1. House: house of representatives to Governor Francis Bernard, 2 June 1767, *Speeches,* at 110; same to same, 18 February 1768, ibid., at 114–15. Clergyman: Letter of 18 February 1769, Cooper, "Letters," at 303–4.

21. *Report of October 1769,* at 304.

22. Francis Bernard to Earl of Hillsborough, 19 March 1768, Jensen, *Documents,* at 736.

23. *Report of October 1769,* at 304–5.

24. House of representatives to Earl of Hillsborough, 30 June 1768, *Speeches,* at 152. "And as every offensive thing done in America is charged upon all, and every province though unconcerned in it, suffers in its interests through the general disgust given and the little distinction here [i.e., London] made." Benjamin Franklin to Thomas Wharton, 20 February 1768, 5 Franklin, *Writings,* at 106.

25. *Report of October 1769,* at 313–14. For a discussion of using an event in one town to indict the entire province, see "Determinatus" [Samuel Adams], *Boston Gazette,* 8 August 1768, p. 2, col. 2; 1 Adams, *Writings,* at 239.

26. *Report of October 1769,* at 323–24. "[Bernard] envinced too great an inclination to make the worst of every thing; and at times hearkened to and transmitted the strangest rumours." Gordon, *Revolution,* at 183.

27. Beacon: Colbourne, *Lamp,* at 20, 25, 31–36, 50–53, 63–69; Bailyn, *Pamphlets,* at 43–44, 52–53, 103; Miller, *Origins,* at 472. Post: *Evening-Post,* 3 February 1766, p. 1, col. 1. Middlesex Petition: Petition of the Freeholders of the County of Middlesex to the King, May 1769, *Evening-Post,* 31 July 1769, p. 2, col. 1. *North Briton: North Briton* (108), 20 May 1769, quoted in *Evening-Post,* 7 August 1769, p. 1, col. 2.

28. Benjamin Franklin to Massachusetts Committee of Correspondence, 15 May 1771, 5 Franklin, *Writings,* at 317–18. For a similar view published in London's *Chronicle,* 9 April 1767, see *Franklin's Letters to the Press,* at 82.

29. Resolutions such as the one by Boston's inhabitants which used these words. *Supra,* note 3.

6

The Argument of Facts

1. Inhabitants of Boston to Agent Dennys de Berdt, October 1766, *Town Records,* at 194 [hereinafter Letter]; 1 Adams, *Writings,* at 95.

2. Hutchinson, *History (1828),* at 262.

3. Ibid., at 263 footnote.

NOTES

4. See for example, Morgan & Morgan, *Crisis,* at 133.

5. Law abiding: *Boston Gazette,* 16 November 1767, p. 3, col. 2; Letter, *supra* note 1, at 193. Massachusetts Council: Report of the Council, 29 November 1773, quoted in Franklin, "True State," at 510.

6. Boston: Bridenbaugh, *Cities,* at 6, 116. Shirley: Governor William Shirley to Lords of Trade, 1 December 1747, 1 Shirley, *Correspondence,* at 418. Bostonians: "Determinatus" [Samuel Adams], *Boston Gazette,* 8 August 1768, p. 2, col. 2.

7. Bernard: House of representatives to Governor Francis Bernard, 17 January 1766, *Evening-Post,* 20 January 1766, p. 2, col. 1. Meeting: Samuel Adams to John Smith, 20 December 1765, 1 Adams, *Writings,* at 60. Vote: Meetings of 27 August 1765, *Town Records,* at 152. House: House of Representatives to Governor Francis Bernard, 3 June 1766, *Speeches,* at 78.

8. Instructions: Meetings of 22 October 1766, *Town Records,* at 190. Emphasis: Letter, *supra* note 1, at 192. Boston vote: Boston Town Meeting, 8 October 1766, *Boston Gazette,* 13 October 1766, p. 1, col. 1.

9. A test not always adhered to as, for example, the burning of Hallowell's boat during the *Liberty* riot discussed below. It is, however, significant that unlike the looting of Thomas Hutchinson's house that act of destruction was not condemned. The special circumstances of the occasion made it less objectionable. The hated tory newspaper publisher John Mein, who was chased by a whig crowd, never had his printing press or bookstore damaged

10. Portsmouth: *Evening-Post,* 11 November 1765, p. 1, col. 2. New London: *Evening-Post,* 2 September 1765, p. 2, col. 2. Newburyport: *Evening-Post,* 10 March 1766, p. 3, col. 1. Similarly, it was boasted there was no violence in North Carolina when a crowd of about 1000 forced the collector of a port and a naval officer to agree to disregard the stamp act. *Evening-Post,* 24 March 1766, p. 2, cols. 2–3.

11. New Jersey: *Evening-Post,* 27 January 1766, p. 1, col. 1. Men of Property: *Prior Documents,* at 12. Virginia: Governor Francis Fauquier to Board of Trade, 3 November 1765, Knollenberg, *Origin,* at 215. New Hampshire: *Evening-Post,* 20 January 1766, p. 3, col. 1. Oliver: *Evening-Post,* 23 December 1765, p. 1, col. 2.

12. *Evening-Post,* 6 October 1766, p. 3, col. 1.

13. Fears: *Massachusetts Gazette,* 7 November 1765, p. 1, col. 3. Reports of Pope's Day: *Evening-Post,* 11 November 1765, p. 1, col. 3; *Massachusetts Gazette,* 7 November 1765, p. 1, col. 3. The same was true for Pope's Day the next year. "To convince the Inhabitants that no Disorder or ill Usage were intended, the Front of their Lanthorns were inscribed to Liberty, underneath which was wrote, *Love and Unity.*" *Evening-Post,* 10 November 1766, p. 3, col. 1.

14. Warning: *Evening-Post,* 19 May 1766, p. 3, col. 1. Town meeting: Meeting of 21 April 1766, *Boston Gazette,* 28 April 1766, p. 4, col. 2; *Town Records,* at 175–76. Boast: *Boston Gazette,* 26 May 1766, p. 2, col. 2.

15. *Boston Gazette,* 27 October 1766, p. 3, col. 2.

16. Town alarm: Town of Boston to Agent Dennys de Berdt, 22 October 1766, 1 Adams, *Writings,* at 95, 94. Bernard: *Boston Gazette,* 24 November 1766, p. 3, col. 2. Bowdoin: James Bowdoin to Former Governor Thomas Pownall, 10 May 1769, *Bowdoin Papers,* at 143. See also Samuel Adams as "Vindex," in *Boston Gazette,* 26 December 1768, p. 1, cols. 1–3; 1 Adams, *Writings,* at 277.

17. *Boston Gazette,* 13 October 1766, p. 1, col. 1.

18. "Partial account": Letter, *supra* note 1, at 193. "Endeavour": "Freeborn American," *Boston Gazette,* 27 April 1767, p. 4, col. 1. See also "Philalethes," *Boston Gazette,* 11 May 1767, p. 1, col. 2.

19. "Esquire": William Palfrey to John Wilkes, 5 March 1770, Elsey, "Palfrey," at 416. "Weight": Letter, *supra* note 1, at 194; Committee: *Boston Gazette,* 27 October 1766, p. 3, col. 2. The "friend" was the colony's agent, Dennys de Berdt.

20. Second Deposition of William Nickells, 20 October 1766, Wolkins, "Malcom," at 57.

21. Asked in council if he told Greenleaf the bell would ring and the streets fill, he said he had for he had been told that the people expected the informer to ring it so he could make his escape. First Declaration of William Wimble, 25 September 1766. Wolkins, "Malcom," at 32 [hereinafter Wimble].

22. Second Deposition of William Wimble, 17 October 1766, Wolkins, "Malcom," at 57.

23. Hallowell: Declaration of Sheaffe and Hallowell, 24 September 1766, Wolkins, "Malcom," at 28 [hereinafter Sheaffe & Hallowell]. Tidewaiters: Declaration of Vincent and Turner, 14 November 1766, Wolkins, "Malcom," at 83 [hereinafter Tidewaiters]. Tudor: Declaration of John Tudor, 25 September 1766, Wolkins, "Malcom," at 31 [hereinafter Tudor]. Malcom: Declaration of Daniel Malcom, 21 October 1766, Wolkins, "Malcom," at 42 [hereinafter Malcom]. Rust: Declaration of Enoch Rust, 20 October 1766, Wolkins, "Malcom," at 49, 48 [hereinafter Rust]. Member of crowd: Second Deposition of Nathaniel Barber, 20 October 1766, Wolkins, "Malcom," at 56 [hereinafter Barber]. Second member: Declaration of Benjamin Goodwin, 20 October 1766, Wolkins, "Malcom," at 47 [hereinafter Goodwin].

24. Reverend Samuel Peters of Connecticut. Morris, *Reconsidered,* at 66.

25. Sheaffe & Hallowell, *supra* note 23, at 28–29; Sworn Testimony in Council of William Sheaffe, 25 September 1766, Wolkins, "Malcom," at 29.

26. Tidewaiters, *supra* note 23, at 83.

27. Declaration of Sheriff Stephen Greenleaf, 1 October 1766, Wolkins, "Malcom," at 38.

28. Tudor, *supra* note 23, at 31.

29. A fact that may explain why he was not examined by Otis's committee. While his estimate of the crowd was high, that evidence was not damaging since he also termed it peaceful.

30. Revere: Deposition of Paul Rivere [Revere], 20 October 1766, Wolkins, "Malcom," at 52 [hereinafter Revere]. Hopkins: Deposition of Caleb Hopkins, 20 October 1766, Wolkins, "Malcom," at 51. Barber: Barber, *supra* note 23, at 56. Two witnesses: Deposition of Samuel Harris and Samuel Aves, 20 October 1766, Wolkins, "Malcom," at 53.

31. "Church": Wimble, *supra* note 21, at 32. See also First Deposition of William Nichols, 25 September 1766, Wolkins, "Malcom," at 31. "[A]s for the good People, who were *curious spectators,* they behav'd as orderly, to use the words of some of the Deponents, as if they were at Church." *Boston Gazette,* 27 October 1766, p. 3, col. 2. "Funeral": Goodwin, *supra* note 23, at 46. Recurring description: Deposition of John Ballard, 20 October 1766, Wolkins, "Malcom," at 50 [hereinafter Ballard]; Deposition of Edward Jarvis, 20 October 1766, Wolkins, "Malcom," at 49–50 [hereinafter Jarvis]. Bernard's depositions: First Deposition of Nathaniel Barber, 25 September 1766, Wolkins, "Malcom," at 32. See also Deposition of John Baker, 25 September 1766, Wolkins, "Malcom," at 33. "Good order and sober": Rust, *supra* note 23, at 49. "Decency and good order": Barber, *supra* note 23, at 56; Revere, *supra* note 30, at 52; Deposition of John Matchet, 20 October 1766, Wolkins, "Malcom," at 50 [hereinafter Matchet]; Deposition of Moses Tyler, 20 October 1766, Wolkins, "Malcom," at 49. See also Deposition of Benjamin Harrod, 20 October 1766, Wolkins, "Malcom," at 53 [hereinafter Harrod]; Deposition of Benjamin Burt, 20 October 1766, Wolkins, "Malcom," at 55; Deposition of Thomas Kimble, 20 October 1766, Wolkins, "Malcom," at 52 [hereinafter Kimble].

32. Neighbor: Kimble, *supra* note 31, at 52. Other witnesses: Revere, *supra* note 30, at 52; Ballard, *supra* note 31, at 50; Jarvis, *supra* note 31, at 50; Harrod, *supra* note 31, at 53; Matchet, *supra* note 31, at 50. Malcom: Malcom, *supra* note 23, at 41–42.

33. Rust, *supra* note 23, at 48; Malcom, *supra* note 23, at 42.

34. "An Act for Preventing and Suppressing of Riots, Routs and Unlawful Assemblies." *Province Laws,* chapter 17, section 1, p. 545 (14 February 1750/51).

NOTES

35. If the people-proclaimed rioters failed to "disperse themselves within one hour," Greenleaf was authorized to call on "other persons" to arrest them. Ibid.

36. Revere, *supra* note 30, at 52. Sullen: but see Zobel, *Massacre,* at 53.

37. See Lord Mansfield's explanation of the law. *Chronicle,* 23 March 1769, p. 93, col. 1.

38. Commissioners of American Customs to Lords of the Treasury, 12 February 1768, Wolkins, "Liberty," at 264; Hulton, *Account,* at 65–66.

39. A Gentleman in London to his Friend in Boston, 14 February 1767, *Evening-Post,* 27 April 1767, p. 2, col. 3.

40. *Evening-Post,* 4 May 1767, p. 1, col. 1. Massachusetts would hear echoes of the Malcom affair for some time. Hutchinson began to warn grand juries of the danger to society of perjury. Chief Justice Thomas Hutchinson's Charge to the Grand Jury, March Term, *Quincy Reports* 261 (1768); Chief Justice Thomas Hutchinson's Charge to the Grand Jury, March Term, ibid., at 310. Governor Bernard asserted that the Malcom affair was designed to make "an example of a Governor who dared to stand in the Gap, and support the Royalty of Government." Letter From Governor Francis Bernard to the Earl of Shelburne, 22 December 1766, Wolkins, "Malcom," at 15. And when the house of representatives petitioned the king to remove Bernard from office, it cited the depositions as one of his offenses. "He has practiced the sending over depositions to the ministry, privately taken, against gentlemen of character here, without giving the persons accused, the least notice of his purposes and proceedings." Petition of the house of representatives to the King, 27 June 1769, *Speeches,* at 189.

7

The Uses of Fact

1. Philadelphia: Philadelphia Committee of Merchants to London Merchants' Committee, 25 November 1769, Gordon, *Revolution,* at 179. Massachusetts house: House to Dennys de Berdt, 12 January 1768, 1 Adams, *Writings,* at 149 [hereinafter Letter].

2. Placemen: *London Chronicle,* 9 April 1767, *Franklin's Letters to the Press,* at 82. Ministers: *Evening-Post* (Supplement), 18 July 1768, p. 2, col. 1. Bowdoin: James Bowdoin to Former Governor Thomas Pownall, 10 May 1769, quoted in Bailyn, *Ordeal,* at 232.

3. Governor Francis Bernard to Lord Barrington, 23 November 1765, Bernard & Barrington, *Correspondence,* at 98–100.

4. Warning: *Evening-Post,* 3 March 1766, p. 1, col. 1. Merchants: Principal Merchants of London to John Hancock, et al., 18 March 1766, *Evening-Post,* 16 June 1766, p. 2, col. 1. Bostonians: Town of Boston to Agent Dennys de Berdt, 22 October 1766, 1 Adams, *Writings,* at 93.

5. Bernard: Governor Francis Bernard to General Thomas Gage, 27 August 1765, Anderson, "Mackintosh," at 35. Tory: James Murray quoted in Bridenbaugh, *Cities,* at 307. Gage: General Thomas Gage to Secretary of State Henry Seymour Conway, 23 September 1765, 1 Gage, *Correspondence,* at 67.

6. Boston: Resolution of Boston, 4 October 1769, *Evening-Post,* 30 October 1769, p. 1, col. 2. (this resolution refers to Gage's reports about Boston following the *Liberty* riot). House of Lords: Agent Richard Jackson to Governor Francis Bernard, 15 March 1766, *Speeches,* at 73.

7. Newspapers: e.g., *Boston Gazette,* 28 April 1766 and (Supplement) 9 June 1766; *Evening-Post* (Supplement), 9 June 1766 and 16 June 1766. Gage: General Thomas Gage to Secretary of State Henry Seymour Conway, 7 November 1765, quoted in Protest of Dissentient Lords to the Repeal of the Stamp Act, 10 March 1766, *Protests,* at 277 [hereinafter, First Protest].

NOTES

8. First Protest, *supra* note 7, at 273, 278–79.

9. Ibid., at 279–81.

10. Testimony: Ibid., at 280. Letters: Second Protest of the Dissentient Lords to the Repeal of the Stamp Act, 17 March 1766, *Protests*, at 293.

11. Bloodshed: First Protest, *supra* note 7, at 280. Pattern: Benjamin Franklin to Massachusetts Committee of Correspondence, 5 Franklin, *Writings,* at 318.

12. Warned: *Boston Gazette,* 27 October 1766, p. 3, col. 1. Tories: Longley, "Mob," at 110. Bernard: Letter of 28 October 1765, Bernard, *Select Letters,* at 27.

13. Helplessness: Governor Francis Bernard to General Thomas Gage, 27 August 1765, Anderson, "Mackintosh," at 35. Expects troops: same to same, 13 September 1765, *Gage Papers.*

14. Rumors: See e.g., *Evening-Post,* 17 February 1766, p. 4, col. 2. Threat: Maier, *Resistance,* at 154. Mackay: Declaration of William Mackay, 20 October 1766, Wolkins, "Malcom," at 44–45. Continued rumors: See e.g., *Evening-Post* (Supplement), 20 April 1767, p. 2, col. 3. But see *Evening-Post,* 27 April 1767, p. 2, col. 3.

15. Commissioners: English Customs Commissioners to Lords of the Treasury, 31 October 1766, Wolkins, "Malcom," at 65. Parliament: Agent Dennys de Berdt to Massachusetts House, 10 January 1767, *Boston Gazette,* 13 April 1767, p. 3, col. 1. See also Hulton, *Account,* at 66. Paxton: Gordon, *Revolution,* at 160. Hutchinson: Lieutenant Governor Thomas Hutchinson to Former Governor Thomas Pownall, 11 May 1766, Gray, "Appendix," at 445. Need for troops: Commissioners of American Customs to the Lords of the Treasury, 12 February 1768, Wolkins, "Liberty," at 266–67.

16. *The London Chronicle,* 22 April 1769, quoted in Maier, *Resistance,* at 155n65.

17. Benjamin Franklin to William Strahan, 29 November 1769, 5 Franklin, *Writings,* at 242–43; Benjamin Franklin to *The Publick Ledger* (1774), 6 Franklin, *Writings,* at 217 [hereinafter Letter].

18. Often ignored: Maier, *Resistance,* at 213–14. Massachusetts house: Letter, *supra* note 1, at 144.

19. London mobs: *Boston Gazette,* 8 August 1768, p. 2, col. 2; 1 Adams, *Writings,* at 237. Irish riots: *Boston Gazette* (Supplement), 1 August 1768, p. 2, col. 3. Scotland and England: *Evening-Post* (Supplement), 1 August 1768, p. 2, cols. 2–3; Longley, "Mob," at 99–100, 105–7. Bristol: *Evening-Post,* 8 December 1766, p. 2, col. 2. Noblemen: *Connecticut Courant,* 2 October 1769, p. 1, col. 2; *Evening-Post,* 6 June 1768, p. 2, col. 2 and 16 October 1769, p. 1, col. 2. Magistrates: *Evening-Post,* 27 November 1769, p. 1, col. 3. Wilkes: *Boston Gazette,* 1 August 1768, p. 1, col. 3; Benjamin Franklin to John Ross, 14 May 1768, 5 Franklin, *Writings,* at 133 (this letter was printed in several colonial newspapers including *Evening-Post,* 5 September 1768, p. 2, col. 2); *Evening-Post,* 30 May 1768, p. 2, col. 1 and 13 June 1768, p. 1, col. 1. English mobs of 1766: *Evening-Post,* 29 December 1766, p. 2, col. 3.

20. Board of Trade to George III, 10 October 1765, *Prior Documents,* at 45.

21. "No violence": Letter from Boston, 26 August 1765, *Prior Documents,* at 10. "Justified": Samuel Adams to John Smith, 20 December 1765, 1 Adams, *Writings,* at 60. Annual celebration: *Evening-Post,* 21 August 1769, p. 2, col. 1. "Villainous Proceedings": Toast offered at the first annual celebration of 14 August riot, *Boston Gazette,* 18 August 1766, p. 2, col. 3. "Shocking": *Evening-Post,* 2 September 1765, p. 3, col. 1. Distinguishable: Thus the thirteenth toast of the 1766 celebration was "Detestation to the villainous Proceedings of the 26th of August last." The fourteenth toast: "May the everlasting Remembrance of the 14th of August, serve to revive the dying Sparks of Liberty, whenever America shall be in Danger of Slavery." *Evening-Post,* 18 August 1766, p. 3, col. 1. For similar toasts see *Evening-Post,* 17 August 1767, p. 3, col. 1. And a Boston clergyman wrote, "The good people of Boston are very careful to distinguish between the 14th and the 26th of

NOTES

August. The attack on Secretary [Andrew] Oliver, our S[tam]p M[aste]r—, it is supposed was under the direction of some persons of character. It is certain, people in general were not displeased. The 26th of August was under a very different direction. It was a scene of riot, drunkeness, profaneness, and robbery." Reverend Andrew Eliot to Thomas Hollis, 27 August 1767, Eliot, "Letters," at 406–7. Patrols: Vote of Boston Town Meeting, 27 August 1765, *Town Records,* at 152; *Evening-Post,* 2 September 1765, p. 1, col.2.

22. Controlled: 2 Higgins, *Bernard,* at 178. Armed power: *In a Defiant Stance,* at 170–71.

23. Hulton: Letter of 30 June 1768, Hulton, *Letters,* at 11. Franklin: Benjamin Franklin to Governor William Franklin, 16 April 1768, 5 Franklin, *Writings,* at 121.

24. George Rudé, *The Crowd in History: A Study of Popular Disturbances in France and England 1730–1848,* 66, 255 (1964); George Rudé, *Wilkes and Liberty: A Social Study of 1763 to 1774,* 13–14 (1962); Walter James Shelton, *English Hunger & Industrial Disorders: A Study of Social Conflict During the First Decade of George III's Reign* (1973).

25. Smyth, "The Life of Benjamin Franklin," in 10 Franklin, *Writings,* at 239 [hereinafter, "Life"].

26. Benjamin Franklin to John Ross, 14 May 1768, 5 Franklin, *Writings,* at 133 (see *supra* note 19); Letter, *supra* note 17, at 218.

27. "Life," *supra* note 24, at 239. Samuel Adams entertained Bostonians with a remarkably similar description: "It is certainly a grievous hardship that we should be so grossly misrepresented; and if these falsehoods make such impressions on the minds of persons so near to us as Halifax, it cannot be wondered at, if the mother-country at the distance of a thousand leagues, should think that we are in a state of confusion, equal to what we hear from the orderly and very polite cities of London and Westminster. There, we are told, is the Weavers mob, the Seamens mob, the Taylors mob, the Coal miners mob, and some say, the Clergys mob." *Boston Gazette,* 8 August 1768, p. 2, col. 2; 1 Adams, *Writings,* at 237. For a similar account see, *Evening-Post,* 5 September 1768, p. 2, col. 2.

28. Benjamin Franklin to Joseph Galloway, 14 May 1768, 5 Franklin, *Writings,* at 134; Earl of Hillsborough to Governor Francis Bernard, 14 May 1768, *Boston Gazette,* 10 October 1768, p. 3, col. 2.

29. Risk lives: Benjamin Franklin, "On Smuggling," 5 Franklin, *Writings,* at 60–65. Burn vessels: Letter, *supra* note 17, at 218. Kill: *Evening-Post,* 21 November 1768, p. 4, col. 2; Longley, "Mob," at 107. Bernard: e.g., Proclamation of 13 August 1768, *Evening-Post,* 5 September 1768, p. 1, col. 3. Attitudes: *Boston Gazette,* 5 September 1768, p. 1, col. 1; mob: p. 2, col. 3.

8
The Constitutional Dilemma

1. Edward Sidgwick quoted in, Clark, "Board," at 785n38.

2. Hulton: Brown, "Hulton," at 13. Ostracism: Reverend Andrew Eliot to Thomas Hollis, 28 June 1770, Eliot, "Letters," at 452. Harrison: Harrison, "Letter to Rockingham," at 594–95.

3. Paxton: Charles Paxton to Viscount Townshend, 24 February 1768, Wolkins, "Paxton," at 348. Bernard: See e.g., Letter of 28 January 1768, Bernard, *Select Letters,* at 53–54. Hopeless: Commissioners of American Customs to Lords of the Treasury, 12 February 1768, Wolkins "Liberty," at 267 [hereinafter Memorial]. Hood: Commissioners to Commodore Samuel Hood, 12 February 1768, Wolkins, "Liberty," at 278.

4. Commissioners of American Customs to Lords of the Treasury, 28 March 1768, Wolkins, "Liberty," at 268 [hereinafter Memorial].

NOTES

5. See Commission of the Commissioners, 14 September 1767, *Evening-Post,* 26 September 1768, p. 2, col. 1.

6. Commissioners: Memorial, *supra* note 4, at 268. Bernard: Governor Francis Bernard to John Pownall, 14 March 1768, Wolkins, "Liberty," at 245 [hereinafter Bernard]. A whig historian believed Malcom ran sixty pipes of wine ashore. Gordon, *Revolution,* at 149. See also Barrow, *Trade,* at 228.

7. Governor Francis Bernard to Earl of Hillsborough, 21 March 1768, *Evening-Post,* 21 August 1769, p. 3, col. 1; Governor Bernard to Earl of Shelburne, 21 March 1768, Bernard & Gage, *Letters,* at 24.

8. Memorial, *supra* note 3, at 265–66. See also Memorial, *supra* note 4, at 268–69.

9. Bernard: Bernard *supra* note 6, at 245. The commissioners also reported that event. "For several Evenings in the beginning of March a number of people armed with Clubs assembled about the Houses of some of the Members of the Board, blowing Horns, beating Drums, and making hideous Noises, so that the Familys quitted their Houses expecting they would proceed to Violence." Commissioners to Lords of the Treasury, 28 March 1768, Wolkins, "Liberty," at 269 [hereinafter Commissioners].

10. Commissioners, *supra* note 9, at 269.

11. *Boston Gazette,* 23 March 1767, p. 3, col. 2; *Massachusetts Gazette,* 20 March 1766, p. 3, col. 2; Pierce, "Rowe," at 45; Governor Francis Bernard to Earl of Hillsborough, 19 March 1768, Jensen, *Documents,* at 737 [hereinafter Bernard], and Bernard & Gage, *Letters,* at 16–18.

12. Effigies: Bernard, *supra* note 11, at 737; Commissioners, *supra* note 9, at 270; Clark, "Board," at 787n49. Removal: Entry for 18 March 1768, Rowe, "Diary," at 66. Commissioners: Commissioners, *supra* note 9, at 270. Governor: Bernard, *supra* note 11, at 737.

13. Council to Governor Francis Bernard, 26 September 1768, *Bowdoin Papers,* at 108 [hereinafter Council].

14. Bernard, *supra* note 11, at 737–38.

15. Whigs: Massachusetts convention of 1768 to Dennys de Berdt, 27 September 1768, *Evening-Post,* 10 October 1768, p. 2, col. 2. Rowe: Entry for 18 March 1768, Rowe, "Diary," at 66. Whig leaders: Massachusetts convention to Dennys de Berdt, 27 September 1768, 1 Adams, *Writings,* at 244 [hereinafter Convention].

16. Gage: General Thomas Gage to Earl of Hillsborough, 31 October 1768, *Letters to Hillsborough,* at 40. Council: Council, *supra* note 13, at 108; Convention, *supra* note 15, at 244. Argument continued: *Evening-Post* (Supplement), 26 September 1768, p. 2, col. 2.

17. Commissioners, *supra* note 9, at 270.

18. Commissioners: Ibid., at 270–71. Bernard: Bernard, *supra* note 11, at 739. It is worth noting how closely the accounts of imperial officials echoed each other. Just as Bernard drew the same inference from nonviolence that the commissioners drew, so the commissioners, unable to report physical attacks on their persons, were reduced, like the governor, to stressing the frightfulness of the sound. "[T]hey paraded through the Streets making hideous Cries and Noises at the Houses of the Governor and some of the Commissioners." Commissioners, *supra* note 9, at 270.

19. Lord Barrington to Governor Francis Bernard, 13 December 1766, Bernard & Barrington, *Correspondence,* at 119.

20. Bernard, *supra* 11, at 738.

21. Bernard: Ibid. London: Secretary of State Henry Seymour Conway, 24 October 1765, *Prior Documents,* at 42. Seeks council's consent: Governor Francis Bernard to General Thomas Gage, 29 August 1765, Bernard & Barrington, *Correspondence,* at 229 [hereinafter Letter]. See also General Gage to Secretary Conway, 23 September 1765, 1 Gage, *Correspondence,* at 68; Bernard, *supra* note 11,

at 738. Refusal: Zobel, *Massacre,* at 85; Carter, "Commander in Chief," at 207. Governors in other colonies encountered the same problem, for example, New York. Lieutenant Governor Cadwallader Colden to General Gage, 10 September 1765, *Gage Papers.*

22. Governor Francis Bernard to Lord Barrington, 4 March 1768, Bernard & Barrington, *Correspondence,* at 148 [hereinafter Bernard].

23. *Evening-Post,* 15 January 1770, p. 2, col. 1 (quoting Junius Americanus).

24. George III: Letter dated 15 October 1776, quoted in G. F. Russell Barker, "Wills Hill," 26 *Dictionary of National Biography* 427, 428 (1891) [hereinafter Barker]. Historian: Wright, *Freedom,* at 29.

25. Barker, *supra* note 24, at 428.

26. Bernard, *supra* note 22, at 148; Governor Francis Bernard to Lord Barrington, 2 July 1768, Bernard & Barrington, *Correspondence,* at 169.

27. Bernard, *supra* note 11, at 738; Governor Francis Bernard to Earl of Hillsborough, 30 June 1768, Bernard & Gage, *Letters,* at 46–47.

28. See e.g., series of articles by Samuel Adams in the *Boston Gazette.* December 1768; 1 Adams, *Writings,* at 255–78.

9
The Docking of *Liberty*

1. Governor Francis Bernard to Earl of Shelburne, 19 March 1768, Bernard & Gage, *Letters,* at 19; Bernard to Lord Barrington, 20 April 1768, Bernard & Barrington, *Correspondence,* at 153.

2. Commissioners of the Customs to Lords of the Treasury, 28 March 1768, Wolkins, "Liberty," at 270.

3. For example, parliament's Address to the King, 9 February 1769, Jensen, *Documents,* at 720; Governor Francis Bernard to Lord Barrington, 18 March 1769, Bernard & Barrington, *Correspondence,* at 197.

4. Commodore Samuel Hood to George Grenville, 15 October 1768, 4 *Grenville Papers,* at 377; *In a Defiant Stance,* at 79–81.

5. Commodore Samuel Hood to Captain John Corner, 2 May 1768, Wolkins, "Liberty," at 271.

6. Ibid., at 271–72.

7. Disappointed: Wolkins, "Liberty," at 249. Belief: "Information" filed in case of Sewall v. Hancock, 2 Adams, *Legal Papers,* at 194; Gray, "Appendix," at 458.

8. Charles Paxton to Viscount Townshend, 18 May 1768, in Wolkins, "Paxton," at 349.

9. Bernard: Letter of Francis Bernard, 12 May 1768, quoted in Harlow, *Adams,* 121. Warren: 1 Warren, *Revolution,* at 60.

10
The *Liberty* Riots

1. Time: Gordon, *Revolution,* at 157. Hulton: Wolkins, "Liberty," at 252. Harrison: Harrison, "Letter to Rockingham," at 590. Tide: 2 Adams, *Legal Papers,* at 175.

2. Hulton, *Account,* at 87.

3. Zobel, *Massacre,* at 72; Deposition of Benjamin Hallowell, 11 June 1768, *Evening-Post,* 18 September 1769, p. 4, col. 1.

4. Gordon, *Revolution,* at 157; *Evening-Post,* 20 June 1768, p. 2, col. 1.

5. Affidavit of Daniel Malcom, 17 June 1768, *Chronicle,* 9 January 1769, p. 1, col. 1 [hereinafter Malcom].

6. Deposition of Benjamin Hallowell, 11 June 1768, Bernard & Gage, *Letters,* at 124 [hereinafter Hallowell].

7. Malcom: Malcom, *supra* note 5, at 1, col. 1. Biographer: Hersey, "Daniel Malcom," at 219.

8. Harrison, "Letter to Rockingham," at 590.

9. *Evening-Post,* 20 June 1768, p. 2, col. 1; Lemisch, "Jack Tar," at 371 *passim;* Lemisch, "Bottom Up," at 23–24; Waters, *Otis Family,* at 89–90; Bridenbaugh, *Cities,* at 26, 114–16, 308–10.

10. "Combustible": Gordon, *Revolution,* 157. Hutchinson: Lieutenant Governor Thomas Hutchinson to Richard Jackson, 16 June 1768, Wolkins, "Liberty," at 281. Harrison: Harrison, "Letter to Rockingham," at 589, 590.

11. Harrison's son: *Chronicle,* 13 June 1768, p. 247, col. 2. Harrison: Harrison, "Letter to Rockingham," at 590–91.

12. Ibid., at 591; *Evening-Post,* 20 June 1768, p. 2, col. 1.

13. The actual sequence of events is confused. The leading tory newspaper in Boston reported them exactly the reverse of Governor Bernard's account. First the mob went to the home of Inspector General Williams and

broke some of the windows of his house; as also of the houses of the Collector and Comptroller, but were prevented doing further damage by some gentlemen of the town.—After which, they burned a pleasure boat belonging to the Collector in the Common.—Mr. Irvine, Inspector of Exports and Imports, was also attacked the same night; he had his sword broke, and with some difficulty made his escape with the assistance of some of the people present.

Chronicle, 13 June 1768, p. 247, col. 2. If this account is compared to that of Bernard and others, it becomes apparent that few on the imperial side of the controversy thought it necessary to check their facts or strive for accuracy. They were satisfied with general descriptions, as they were well aware that the main purpose of their reports was not so much to describe conditions as to argue that conditions had deteriorated to a point where British troops were needed to restore order.

14. Governor Francis Bernard to Earl of Hillsborough, 11 & 13 June 1768, Bernard & Gage, *Letters* at 26–27 [hereinafter Bernard].

15. Ibid., at 27.

16. Pride: Harrison, "Letter to Rockingham," at 591–92. Bernard: Bernard, *supra* note 14, at 27. Tory: Letter of 30 June 1768, Hulton, *Letters,* at 12.

17. Bernard, *supra* note 14, at 28; *Boston Gazette,* 20 June 1768, p. 1, col. 3.

18. Governor Francis Bernard to Earl of Hillsborough, 16 June 1768, in Bernard & Gage, *Letters,* at 33 [hereinafter Bernard]; Minutes of the Commissioners of the Customs, 14 June 1768, *Evening-Post,* 18 September 1769, p. 1, col. 2; *Evening-Post,* 20 June 1768, p. 2, col. 2; Hutchinson, *History (1828),* at 191.

19. Bernard, *supra* note 18, at 33.

20. Ibid.; *Chronicle,* 20 June 1768, p. 253, col. 1; *Chronicle,* 27 June 1768, p. 263, col. 2; Bernard, *supra* note 18, at 33.

21. *Boston Gazette,* 20 June 1768, p. 1, col. 3; *Chronicle,* 20 June 1768, p. 253, col. 1; Samuel Adams to Arthur Lee, 31 December 1773, 3 Adams, *Writings,* at 74.

22. Harrison, "Letter to Rockingham," at 593; Bernard, *supra* note 18, at 34.

23. Entry of 14 June 1768, Rowe, "Diary," at 67; Petition of Boston Town Meeting to Governor Francis Bernard, 14 June 1768, *Boston Gazette,* 20 June 1768, p. 2, col. 1 [hereinafter Petition].

24. Petition, *supra* note 23, at 2, col. 1.

25. *Chronicle,* 20 June 1768, p. 253, col. 3; *Boston Gazette,* 20 June 1768, p. 2, cols. 1–2.

26. *Boston Gazette,* 20 June 1768, p. 3, col. 1; *Chronicle,* 20 June 1768, p. 254, col. 1.

27. Instructions of the Town of Boston to their Representatives, 17 June 1768, 3 Adams, *Works,* at 501–2.

28. Ibid., at 502.

29. Hutchinson, *History (1828),* at 193.

30. In tory eyes, at least, it was on Monday morning a "riot" because it had gathered to oppose the exercise of parliamentary statutes.

31. General Thomas Gage to Earl of Hillsborough, 31 October 1768, *Letters to Hillsborough,* at 42.

11

The Creation of Facts

1. Governor Francis Bernard to Earl of Hillsborough, 11 June 1768, Bernard & Gage, *Letters,* at 26; Proceedings of the Council, 27 July 1768, *Evening-Post* (Supplement), 10 October 1768, p. 1, col. 1.

2. "Determinatus" [Samuel Adams], *Boston Gazette,* 8 August 1768, p. 2, col. 2 1 Adams, *Writings,* at 238; James Bowdoin to Former Governor Thomas Pownall, 10 May 1769, *Bowdoin Papers,* at 141.

3. Massachusetts convention of 1768 to Agent Dennys de Berdt, 27 September 1768, 1 Adams, *Writings,* at 245; *Report of October 1769,* at 308.

4. Bernard: Wolkins, "Liberty," at 254. Hutchinson: Lieutenant Governor Thomas Hutchinson to Richard Jackson, 16 June 1768, Wolkins, "Liberty," at 281.

5. See e.g., Baxter, *Hancock,* at 265.

6. Deposition of Benjamin Hallowell, 11 June 1768, Bernard & Gage, *Letters,* at 124; Deposition of Joseph Harrison, 11 June 1768, ibid., at 123; Deposition of Richard Acklom Harrison, 11 June 1768, ibid., at 125; Deposition of Thomas Irving, 11 June 1768, *Evening-Post,* 18 September 1769, p. 4, col. 2. For a slightly garbled text of Irving's testimony, see Bernard & Gage, *Letters,* at 126.

7. Harrison did not even take the trouble to tell the same tale each time he wrote about the *Liberty* riot. Compare the quotation from his deposition in the last paragraph to Harrison, "Letter to Rockingham," at 590–91, quoted in Chapter 10, text to note 11.

8. Historian: Stark, *Loyalists,* at 281. Hutchinson: Hutchinson, *History (1828),* at 190–91. Newspapers: *Evening-Post,* 20 June 1768, p. 2, col. 1; *Boston Gazette,* 20 June 1768, p. 1, col. 3. Harrison: Harrison, "Letter to Rockingham," at 589–90. Reason for confinement: Gordon, *Revolution,* at 157; Stark, *Loyalists,* at 320. Hallowell: Commissioner Charles Paxton to Thomas Whately, 20 June 1768, Hutchinson, *Letters,* at 37.

9. Ignore: The 13 June issue of the *Boston Gazette* did not mention the riot. It was not noticed until the next week. *Boston Gazette,* 20 June 1768, p. 1, col. 3. Refuted: for example, the tory *Boston Chronicle* inferred that Harrison's boat was burned in front of Hancock's house. The Massachusetts convention answered:

> The truth is, the barge was burnt on a common, surrounded with gentlemens seats; and the scene could not be said to be before Mr. Hancock's door, any more than before the doors of divers other gentlemen in the neighbourhood. The mean insinuation that it was done under the influence of Mr. Hancock, is so far from the least shadow of truth, that it is notorious here, that the tumult was finally disper'd principally by his exertions, animated by his known regard to peace and good order.

Letter from the Massachusetts convention to Dennys de Berdt, 27 September

1768, *Boston Gazette,* 10 October 1768, p. 1, col. 2. It is interesting that years later Mercy Otis Warren would repeat the story that the boat was burned in front of Hancock's door. It is quite likely that it was burned there and deliberately. 1 Warren, *Revolution,* at 61.

10. Deposition of Benjamin Goodwin, 16 June 1768, Baxter, *Hancock,* at 265.

11. Commissioners of the Customs to Governor Francis Bernard, 12 June 1768, Bernard & Gage, *Letters,* at 128. Commissioner John Temple did not sign.

12. Admiralty Judge Robert Auchmuty to Chief Justice Thomas Hutchinson, 14 September 1768, Hutchinson, *Letters,* at 13. Writing that "there has been continued danger of mobs," Hutchinson said: "I have not been without some apprehensions for myself, but my friends have had more for me, and I have had repeated and frequent notices from them from different quarters, *one of the last I will enclose to you.* In this state of things there is no security but quitting my posts, which nothing but the last extremity would justify." Lieutenant Governor Thomas Hutchinson to Thomas Whately, 4 October 1768, ibid., at 10.

13. Minutes of the Commissioners of the Customs, 11 June 1768, *Evening-Post,* 18 September 1769, p. 1, col. 2.

14. Insult: Charles Paxton to Thomas Whately, 20 June 1768, Hutchinson, *Letters,* at 37. "Permitted to return": Harrison, "Letter to Rockingham," at 592. Resolution: Minutes of the Commissioners of the Customs, 14 June 1768, *Evening-Post,* 18 September 1769, p. 1, col. 3.

15. Collector Joseph Harrison and Comptroller Benjamin Hallowell to Commissioners of the Customs, 14 June 1768, *Evening-Post,* 25 September 1769, p. 1, col. 3 and p. 4, col. 1.

16. Refugees: Letter of 30 June 1768, Hulton, *Letters,* at 12. Commissioners: Memorial of Commissioners of the Customs to Lords of Trade, 16 June 1768, *Evening-Post,* 18 September 1769, p. 1, col. 1.

17. Dalrymple: Lieutenant Colonel William Dalrymple to Commissioners of the Customs, 23 June 1768, Bernard & Gage, *Letters,* at 145–46. Gage: General Thomas Gage to Commissioners of the Customs, 21 June 1768, ibid., at 144.

18. Commodore Samuel Hood to Commissioners of the Customs, n.d., Bernard & Gage, *Letters,* at 145.

19. Memorial of the Commissioners of the Customs to Lords Commissioners of the Treasury, 11 July 1768, ibid., at 142 [hereinafter Memorial]. On this date there were five warships in Boston Harbor.

20. Hulton, *Account,* at 89.

21. Memorial, *supra* note 19, at 143.

12

The Questioning of Facts

1. Memorial from the Commissioners of the Customs to Lords of Trade, 16 June 1768, *Evening-Post,* 18 September 1769, p. 1, col. 1.

2. Harrison and Hallowell: Joseph Harrison and Benjamin Hallowell to Commissioners of the Customs, 14 June 1768, Bernard & Gage, *Letters,* at 136; *Evening-Post,* 25 September 1769, p. 4, col. 1. Paxton: Charles Paxton to Thomas Whately, 20 June 1768, Hutchinson, *Letters,* at 37.

3. Council: Council to General Thomas Gage, 28 October 1768, *Chronicle,* 31 October 1768, p. 523, col. 3. Adams: "T.Z.," in *Boston Gazette,* 9 January 1769; "Candidus," *Evening-Post,* 12 December 1768; 1 Adams, *Writings,* at 291, 262. "Plausible pretence": Samuel Adams to Dennys de Berdt, 3 October 1768, in 1 Adams, *Writings,* at 248.

4. Council to Earl of Hillsborough, 15 April 1769, *Chronicle,* 31 July 1769, p.

243, col. 1; Council to Governor Francis Bernard, 29 July 1768, *Letters to Hillsborough* at 117; *Boston Gazette,* 10 October 1768, p. 2, col. 3.

5. Town of Boston to Governor Francis Bernard, 14 June 1768, *Chronicle,* 20 June 1768, p. 253, col. 2.

6. Governor Francis Bernard to Boston Town Meeting, 15 June 1768, *Boston Gazette,* 20 June 1768, p. 2, col. 2.

7. Chapter 11, text to note 11.

8. Bernard: Governor Francis Bernard to John Pownall, 20 September 1768, quoted in Wolkins, "Liberty," at 258. Harrington: Harrington, "Letter to Rockingham," at 594.

9. Perhaps the most extreme accusations of the type were made by Henry Hulton's sister writing to a friend in Great Britain. The commissioners, she contended,

> are prohibit[ed] setting foot on Shore again at their peril, & in case any of them does, the Sexton of each Church has orders to give Notice by tolling a Bell, when all the Bells are to ring as for Fire to alarm the Inhabitants & raise the Mob to tear [th]em to pieces. They likewise threaten to drive Us hence saying this Castle belongs to the province & not to the King, But have not yet taken this step to an Open Rebellion tho from good intelligence we know they have been plotting to surprize us in the Night. Sh[ould] they make this desperate attempt, they might mas[s]acre Us.

Letter of 30 June 1768, Hulton, *Letters,* at 14.

10. Commissioners of the Customs to Commodore Samuel Hood, 15 June 1768, *Evening-Post,* 25 September 1769, p. 4, col. 1.

11. Commodore Samuel Hood to George Grenville, 11 July 1768, 4 *Grenville Papers,* at 306 [hereinafter Hood].

12. Compromise: Joseph Harrison and Benjamin Hallowell to John Robinson, 12 June 1768, *Evening-Post,* 25 September 1769, p. 1, col. 2 [hereinafter Harrison and Hallowell]. "Terrible Consequences": Opinion of Attorney General Charles de Grey, 25 July 1768, Wolkins, "Liberty," at 275 [hereinafter Opinion]. Necessity of accommodation: Joseph Harrison and Benjamin Hallowell to Commissioners of the Customs, 12 June 1768, Bernard & Gage, *Letters,* at 131.

13. Security: Harrison and Hallowell, *supra* note 12, at 1, col. 2. Attorney general: Opinion, *supra* note 12, at 275. "Humble" petition: "Detector" to "Chronus," *Evening-Post,* 6 January 1772, p. 2, col. 1.

14. Historians: See e.g., Baxter, *Hancock,* at 266. Lawyers: These issues were raised at a collateral trial arising out of the condemnation of *Liberty.* 2 Adams, *Legal Papers,* at 195–209.

15. Harrison, "Letter to Rockingham," at 592.

16. Governor Francis Bernard to Earl of Hillsborough, 5 November 1768, *Letters to Hillsborough,* at 13.

17. Ibid., at 14.

18. Governor Francis Bernard, Lieutenant Governor Thomas Hutchinson, Secretary Andrew Oliver, and Admiralty Judge Robert Auchmuty to Commissioners of the Customs, 22 December 1768, Wolkins, "Liberty," at 280.

19. Ibid.

20. Ibid.

21. Ibid.

22. *Boston Gazette,* 3 October 1768, p. 2, col. 2.

23. 2 Adams, *Legal Papers,* at 177–80; Watson, "Harrison," at 586.

24. *Massachusetts Gazette,* 1 September 1768, p. 1, col. 2. *Liberty* was sold at public auction on 6 September, "and was struck off to the Collector of his Majesty's

Customs for this Port, and its said is now to be improved as a Cruiser for the Protection of Trade." *Evening-Post,* 12 September 1768, p. 3, col. 1.

25. "In a Defensive Rage"; *In a Defiant Stance,* at 65–73.

26. Letter of 12 July 1768, Hulton, *Letters,* at 15; Akers, "Temple," at 86.

27. *Journal of the Times,* 25 January 1769, at 54–55. Falmouth is now Portland, Maine. Piscataqua was the shipping name for Portsmouth, New Hampshire.

28. Harrison: The Collector seems at first to have acted voluntarily. See Harrison, "Letter to Rockingham," at 592. Secretary: *Journal of the Times,* 25 January 1769, p. 54, col. 2. English lady: Letter of 12 July 1768, Hulton, *Letters,* at 16.

29. Town Meeting: *Report of October 1769,* at 316. Councillors: Council to General Thomas Gage, 27 October 1768, *Boston Gazette,* 31 October 1768, p. 2, col. 2.

30. Newport: *Boston Gazette,* 5 September 1768, p. 2, col. 3. Roxbury: Governor Francis Bernard to Earl of Hillsborough, 9 July 1768, Bernard & Gage, *Letters,* at 51.

31. "Meanwell," London *Public Advertiser,* 28 July 1768, reprinted in *Evening-Post,* 26 September 1768, p. 2, col. 2.

32. *Boston Gazette,* 19 September 1768, p. 3, col. 2; *Evening-Post,* 19 September 1768, p. 2, col. 2.

33. "Aggravated light": Massachusetts convention of 1768 to Agent Dennys de Berdt, 27 September 1768, 1 Adams, *Writings,* at 246. Barre: Quoted in Gray, "Appendix," at 463.

34. Commissioners: Commissioners of the Customs to Lords Commissioners of the Treasury, 11 July 1768, Bernard & Gage, *Letters,* at 143. Convention: Massachusetts convention of 1768 to Agent Dennys de Berdt, 27 September 1768, *Evening-Post,* 10 October 1768, p. 2, cols. 1–2.

35. Channing, "Board," at 482.

36. Lieutenant Governor Thomas Hutchinson to Thomas Whately, August 1768, Hutchinson, *Letters,* at 6. In his next two sentences, Hutchinson made a statement that can be regarded as true only if one shares all his tory predilections: "After they [commissioners] had withdrawn the town signified to the governor by a message that it was expected or desired they should not return. It was then the general voice that it would not be safe for them to return."

37. General Thomas Gage to Earl of Hillsborough, 31 October 1768, *Chronicle,* 4 May 1769, p. 141, col. 3.

38. General Thomas Gage to Earl of Hillsborough, 31 October 1768, quoted in a Resolution of the Massachusetts house of representatives, *Chronicle,* 6 July 1769, p. 216, col. 2.

39. General Thomas Gage to Commissioners of the Customs, 21 June 1768, and Commodore Samuel Hood to Commissioners, n.d., Bernard & Gage, *Letters,* at 144, 145; Hood, *supra* note 11, at 306–7.

40. Opinion, *supra* note 12, at 274–75.

13

The Triumph of Facts

1. Bernard: 2 Higgins, *Bernard,* at 21. Whig: "A NORTH AMERICAN," *Boston Gazette,* 23 May 1768, p. 2, col. 2.

2. Governor Francis Bernard to Earl of Hillsborough, 14 June 1768, Bernard & Gage, *Letters,* at 30–32.

3. *Report of October 1769,* at 310.

4. Governor Francis Bernard to Richard Jackson, 11 July 1768, Wolkins, "Liberty," at 258n3.

5. Proceedings of the Governor and Council of Massachusetts Bay, 27 July 1768, *Letters to Hillsborough,* at 110.

NOTES

6. Council to Governor Francis Bernard, 29 July 1768, *Boston Gazette,* 10 October 1768, p. 3, col. 1; *Letters to Hillsborough,* at 119.

7. Governor Francis Bernard to the Earl of Hillsborough, 23 September 1768, Bernard & Gage, *Letters,* at 82, and 14 November 1768, *Letters to Hillsborough,* at 22, 25, 24.

8. "Harmonize": Circular letter from Massachusetts house to Speakers of houses of representatives and Burgesses "on this Continent," 11 February 1768, *Speeches,* at 134. Hillsborough: Earl of Hillsborough to Governor Francis Bernard, 22 April 1768, *Glorious Ninety-Two,* at 25. Bernard: Governor Francis Bernard to house of representatives, 21 June 1768, *Speeches,* at 146. House: house of representatives to Governor Francis Bernard, 30 June 1768, *Speeches,* at 147–50. Bernard on majority: Governor Francis Bernard to Earl of Hillsborough, 1 July 1768, Bernard & Gage, *Letters,* at 43.

9. Wolkins, "Liberty," at 247.

10. *Liberty:* ibid. London newspaper: *Boston Gazette,* 13 June 1768, p. 1, col. 1. Hillsborough's carriage: *Evening-Post,* 6 June 1768, p. 2, col. 2. Franklin: Letter from London to Philadelphia, 14 May 1768, *Evening-Post,* 5 September 1768, p. 2, col. 2. Decision: Earl of Hillsborough to Governor Francis Bernard, 14 May 1768, *Boston Gazette,* 10 October 1768, p. 3, col. 2.

11. Orders: Wolkins, "Liberty," at 247. Gage: 4 (4th Series) *Collections Mass. Hist. Soc.* 367, 370 (1858).

12. Massachusetts Council to Governor Francis Bernard, 26 September 1768, *Letters to Hillsborough,* at 122 [hereinafter Answer]; *Bowdoin Papers,* at 107–8; *Evening-Post* (Supplement Extraordinary), 26 September 1768, p. 2, col. 1.

13. Whigs: Petition of Massachusetts convention to Governor Bernard, 22 September 1768, *Evening-Post* (Supplement), 26 September 1768, p 1, col. 1. Council: Answer, *supra* note 12, at 123; Walett, "Bernard," at 218.

14. *Evening-Post,* 3 October 1768, p. 3, col. 2.

15. *Journal of the Times,* 30 September 1768, p. 1, col. 2.

16. General Alexander Mackay to General Thomas Gage, 5 July 1769, quoted in Waters, *Otis Family,* at 174; *Evening-Post,* 3 October 1768, p. 3, col. 2.

14

Conclusion

1. "In a Constitutional Void," at 3–19.

2. Stark, *Loyalists,* at 42.

3. See e.g., Brown, "Violence," at 81 *passim.*

4. Letter of 10 April 1769, Hulton, *Letters,* at 17; Town of Boston to George III, March 1769, *Evening-Post,* 24 July 1769, p. 2, col. 1.

5. Consider for example the following: "Gage, fearing to lose a good man, ordered [Jonathan] Sewall into Boston, so on September 1, 1774, he rode in . . . That night the mob appeared at the Sewall mansion. According to the Whig versions, they did no damage when they found that he was not at home. According to Loyalist versions, the mob smashed windows and did other damage but was driven off by the brave defence put up by the young gentlemen of the family." Shipton, "Sewall," at 314–15.

6. Need for troops: Maier, *Resistance,* at 141–42. Serious injuries: Most notably, the searcher of the port of Philadelphia less than a year after the *Liberty* affair. Frese, "Board," at 24.

7. Whig beliefs: *Journal of the Times,* 1 August 1769, p. 123, col. 1. Palfrey: Letter of February 1771, quoted in Akers, "Temple," at 89. Wilkes: See Elsey, "Palfrey." Violations: *Chronicle,* 28 August 1769, p. 273, col. 1.

8. It may be objected that private impressions, written to friends, would tell us

more than official reports, but the probativeness of the evidence Hillsborough actually read and weighed is our only concern. There is, however, one piece of personal testimony that indicates true fear on the part of the revenue men or their families. Following the Boston massacre and removal of British troops in 1770, the commissioners again fled Boston and again created facts proving "dangerousness." A crowd traveled out to Roxbury and besieged the house of Henry Hulton. In a letter written to a friend in England, Hulton's sister makes it clear that the family experienced genuine fright and believed the crowd intended to kill her brother. Yet the man was not touched though far outnumbered. Whigs ridiculed the assertion of danger, pointing out that the commissioners could easily be injured by anyone who wished to harm them, that the despised Commissioner John Robinson would have been a far more likely target than hapless Hulton, and what probably happened was that the customshouse hired some boys to smash Hulton's windows to give the appearance of a riot. Letter of 25 July 1770, Hulton, *Letters,* at 22–24; *Boston Gazette,* 25 June 1770, p. 2, cols. 1–2; Speaker James Bowdoin to Commodore Samuel Hood, 7 July 1770, *Bowdoin Papers,* at 195.

Short Titles

Acts and Resolves.   The Acts and Resolves, Public and Private, of the Province of Massachusetts Bay (1869), vol. 1.

Adams, Legal Papers.   Legal Papers of John Adams (L. Kinvin Wroth & Hiller B. Zobel, editors, 1965), vols. 1 & 2.

Adams, Works.   The Works of John Adams, Second President of the United States (Charles Francis Adams, editor, 1851), vol 3.

Adams, Writings   The Writings of Samuel Adams (Harry Alonzo Cushing, editor, 1904), vol. 1.

Akers, "Temple."   Charles W. Akers, "New Hampshire's 'Honorary' Lieutenant Governor: John Temple and the American Revolution," 30 Hist. New Hampshire 79–99 (1975).

"A Lawyer Acquitted."   John Phillip Reid, "A Lawyer Acquitted: John Adams and the Boston Massacre Trials," 18 American Journal of Legal History 189–207 (1974).

Anderson, "Mackintosh"   George P. Anderson, "Ebenezer Mackintosh: Stamp Act Rioter and Patriot," 26 Publications of the Colonial Society of Massachusetts 15–64 (1924).

Anderson, "Note"   George P. Anderson, "A Note on Ebenezer Mackintosh," 26 Publications of the Colonial Society of Massachusetts 348–61 (1926).

Bailyn, Ordeal   Bernard Bailyn, The Ordeal of Thomas Hutchinson (1974).

Bailyn, Pamphlets   Pamphlets of the American Revolution, 1750–1776 (Bernard Bailyn, editor, 1965), vol. 1.

Bancroft, History   George Bancroft, History of the United States of America from the Discovery of the Continent (revised edition, 1879), vol. 4.

Barrow, Trade   Thomas C. Barrow, Trade and Empire: The British Customs in Colonial America 1660–1775 (1967).

Baxter, Hancock   W. T. Baxter, The House of Hancock: Business in Boston 1724–1775 (1965 edition).

Bernard, *Select Letters*   *Select Letters on the Trade and Government of America; and the Principles of Law and Polity, Applied to the American Colonies. Written by Governor Bernard at Boston* (1774).

Bernard & Barrington, *Correspondence*   *The Barrington-Bernard Correspondence and Illustrative Matter 1760–1770* (Edward Channing & Archibald Cary Coolidge, editors, 1912).

Bernard & Gage, *Letters*   *Letters to the Ministry From Governor Bernard, General Gage, and Commodore Hood. And Also, Memorials to the Lords of the Treasury From the Commissioners of the Customs, With Sundry Letters and Papers Annexed to the Said Memorials* (1769).

Boston Gazette   *The Boston Gazette and Country Journal*

Bowen, *Adams*   Catherine Drinker Bowen, *John Adams and the American Revolution* (1950).

Bowdoin, "Notes"   "Notes" to the *Bowdoin Papers*

Bowdoin Papers   *The Bowdoin and Temple Papers: Collections of the Massachusetts Historical Society* (Sixth Series, vol. 9, 1897).

Bridenbaugh, *Cities*   Carl Bridenbaugh, *Cities in Revolt: Urban Life in America, 1743–1776* (1971 edition).

Brown, "Hulton"   Wallace Brown, "An Englishman Views the American Revolution: The Letters of Henry Hulton, 1769–1776," 36 *Huntington Library Quarterly* 1–26 & 139–51 (Nov. 1972 & Feb. 1973).

Brown, "Violence"   Richard Maxwell Brown, "Violence and the American Revolution," in *Essays on the American Revolution* 81–120 (Stephen G. Kurtz & James H. Hutson, editors, 1973).

Carter, "Commander in Chief"   Clarence E. Carter, "The Office of Commander in Chief: A Phase of Imperial Unity on the Eve of the Revolution," in *The Era of the American Revolution* 170–213 (Richard B. Morris, editor, Harper Torchbook Edition, 1965).

Channing, "Board"   Edward Channing, "The American Board of Commissioners of the Customs," 43 *Massachusetts Historical Society Proceedings* 477–90 (1910).

Chronicle   *The Boston Chronicle*

"Civil Law as a Criminal Sanction"   "Civil Law as a Criminal Sanction: The Use of the Jury in the Coming of the American Revolution," in *Studies in Comparative Criminal Law* 211–63 (Edward M. Wise & G. O. W. Mueller, editors, 1975).

Clark, "Board"   Dora M. Clark, "The American Board of Customs, 1767–1783," 45 *American Historical Review* 777–806 (1940).

Colbourn, *Lamp*   H. Trevor Colbourn, *The Lamp of Experience: Whig History and the Intellectual Origins of the American Revolution* (1965).

Colden Papers   *The Colden Letter Books, Vol. II 1765–1775* (10 *Collections of the New-York Historical Society for the Year 1877,* 1878).

Cooper, "Letters"   Frederick Tuckerman, "Letters of Samuel Cooper to Thomas Pownall, 1769–1777," 8 *American Historical Review* 301–30 (1903).

Cunningham, "Diary"   Henry W. Cunningham, "Diary of the Rev. Samuel Checkley, 1735," 12 *Publications of the Colonial Society of Massachusetts* 270–306 (1909).

Dickerson, *Acts*   Oliver M. Dickerson, *The Navigation Acts and the American Revolution* (1951).

Dickerson, "Writs"   O. M. Dickerson, "Writs of Assistance as a Cause of the Revolution," in *The Era of the American Revolution* 40–75 (Richard B. Morris, editor, Harper Torchbook Edition, 1965).

Eliot, "Letters"   "Letters from Andrew Eliot to Thomas Hollis," 4 *Collections of the Massachusetts Historical Society* 398–461 (1858).

Elsey, "Palfrey"   George M. Elsey, "John Wilkes and William Palfrey," 34 *Publications of the Colonial Society of Massachusetts* 411–28 (1941).

Evening-Post   The Boston *Evening-Post*

Forbes, *Revere*   Esther Forbes, *Paul Revere & the World He Lived In* (1942).

Franklin's Letters to the Press   Benjamin *Franklin's Letters to the Press 1758–1775* (Verner W. Crane, editor, 1950).

Franklin, "True State"   [Arthur Lee], "A True State of the Proceedings in the Parliament of Great Britain and in the Province of Massachusetts Bay, Relative to the Giving and Granting the Money of the People of that Province, and all America, in the House of Commons in which they are not Represented," in 4 *The Works of Benjamin Franklin* 466–515 (Jared Sparks, editor, 1837).

Franklin, *Writings*   The *Writings of Benjamin Franklin 1767–1772* (Albert Henry Smyth, editor, 1906), vols. 5, 6, 10.

Frese, "Board"   Joseph R. Frese, "Some Observations on the American Board of Customs Commissioners," 81 *Proceedings of the Massachusetts Historical Society* 3–30 (1969).

Gage, *Correspondence*   The *Correspondence of General Thomas Gage With the Secretaries of State 1763–1775* (Clarence Edwin Carter, editor, 1931), vol. 1.

Gage, *Correspondence*   The *Correspondence of General Thomas Gage with the Secretaries of State, and with the War Office and the Treasury 1763–1775* (Clarence Edwin Carter, editor, 1933), vol. 2.

Gage Papers   Military Papers of General Thomas Gage (ms.), The Clements Library, Ann Arbor, Michigan.

Glorious Ninety-Two   The *Glorious Ninety-Two Members of the House of Representatives—Selections from Journals of the Honourable House of Representatives, of His Majesty's Province of the Massachusetts-Bay in New England: Begun and held at Boston, in the County of Suffolk, December 30, 1767 and May 25, 1768* (1949).

Gordon, *Revolution*   William Gordon, *The History of the Rise, Progress, and Establishment of the Independence of the United States of America* (3d American edition, 1801), vol. 1.

Gray, "Appendix"   Horace Gray, "Appendix I," in *Quincy Massachusetts Reports* 395–540 (1865).

Grenville Papers   The *Grenville Papers: Being the Correspondence of Richard Grenville Earl Temple, K.G., and the Right Hon: George Grenville, their Friends and Contemporaries* (William James Smith, editor, 1853), vol. 4.

Harlow, *Adams*   Ralph Volney Harlow, *Samuel Adams Promoter of the American Revolution: A Study in Psychology and Politics* (1923).

Harrison, "Letter to Rockingham"   "Letter from Joseph Harrison to the Marquis of Rockingham, 17 June 1768," 20 *William & Mary Quarterly* 587–95 (1963).

Hersey, "Daniel Malcolm"   Frank W. C. Hersey, "Daniel Malcolm," 12 *Dictionary of American Biography* 218 (1933).

Higgins, *Bernard*   Mrs. Napier Higgins, *The Bernards of Abington and Nether Winchendon: A Family History* (1903), vols 1 & 2.

H. M. & C. M. T., "Introduction"   H. M. & C. M. T., "Introduction," in *Letters of a Loyalist Lady* [herein cited as Hulton, *Letters*].

Hosmer, *Adams*   James K. Hosmer, *Samuel Adams* (1899).

Hulton, *Account*   Henry Hulton, *Some Account of the proceedings of the People in New England from the Establishment of a Board of Customs in America, to the breaking out of the Rebellion in 1775* (ms.), Princeton University Library.

Hulton, *Letters*   *Letters of a Loyalist Lady: Being the Letters of Anne Hulton, sister of Henry Hulton, Commissioner of the Customs at Boston, 1767–1776* (1927).

Hutchinson, *History (1828)*   Thomas Hutchinson, *The History of the Province of Massachusetts Bay, From 1749 to 1774, Comprising a Detailed Narrative of the Origin and Early Stages of the American Revolution (1828)*.

Hutchinson, *Letters*   *Copy of Letters Sent to Great-Britain, By His Excellency Thomas Hutchinson, the Hon. Andrew Oliver, and Several Other Persons, Born and Educated Among Us* (1773).

Impartial History   Anonymous, *An Impartial History of the War in America Between Great Britain and Her Colonies* (1780).

"In Accordance With Usage"   John Phillip Reid, "In Accordance With Usage: The Authority of Custom, the Stamp Act Debate, and the Coming of the American Revolution," 45 *Fordham Law Review* 335–68 (1976).

"In a Constitutional Void"   John Phillip Reid, "In a Constitutional Void: The Enforcement of Imperial Law, the Role of the British Army, and the Coming of the American Revolution," 22 *Wayne Law Review* 1–37 (1975).

"In a Defensive Rage"   John Phillip Reid, "In a Defensive Rage: The Uses of the Mob, the Justification in Law, and the Coming of the American Revolution," 49 *New York University Law Review* 1043–91 (1974).

In a Defiant Stance   John Phillip Reid, *In a Defiant Stance: the Conditions of Law in Massachusetts Bay, the Irish Comparison, and the Coming of the American Revolution* (1977).

"In Legitimate Stirps"   John Phillip Reid, "In Legitimate Stirps: The Concept of "Arbitrary," the Supremacy of Parliament, and the Coming of the American Revolution," 5 *Hofstra Law Review* 459–499 (1977).

Jensen, *Documents*   Merrill Jensen (editor), 9 *English Historical Documents: American Colonial Documents to 1776* (1955).

Johnson & Syrett, "Customs Law"   Herbert A. Johnson & David Syrett, "Some Nice Sharp Quillets of the Customs Law: The New York Affair, 1763–1767," 25 *William & Mary Quarterly* 432–51 (1968).

Journal of the Times   "Journal of the Times," in *Boston Under Military Rule 1768–1769 as Revealed in A Journal of the Times* (Oliver Morton Dickerson, compiler, 1970 reprint).

Knollenberg, *Origin*   Bernhard Knollenberg, *Origin of the American Revolution 1759–1766* (revised edition, 1965).

Lemisch, "Bottom Up"   Jesse Lemisch, "The American Revolution Seen From the Bottom Up," in *Towards a New Past: Dissenting Essays in American History* 3–45 (Barton J. Bernstein, editor, 1968).

Lemisch, "Jack Tar"   Jesse Lemisch, "Jack Tar in the Streets: Merchant Seamen in the Politics of Revolutionary America," 25 *William & Mary Quarterly* 371–407 (1968).

Letters to Hillsborough   *Letters to the Right Honourable the Earl of Hillsborough, From Governor Bernard, General Gage, and the Honourable His Majesty's Council for the Province of Massachusetts-Bay* (1769).

Longley, "Mob"   R. S. Longley, "Mob Activities in Revolutionary Massachusetts," 6 *New England Quarterly* 98–130 (1933).

Maier, *Resistance*   Paulene Maier, *From Resistance to Revolution: Colonial Radicals and the Development of American Opposition to Britain, 1765–1776* (1972).

Martin, "Customs"   Alfred S. Martin, "The King's Customs: Philadelphia, 1763–1774," 5 *William & Mary Quarterly* 201–16 (1948).

Massachusetts Gazette   *The Massachusetts Gazette*

Miller, *Origins*   John Chester Miller, *Origins of the American Revolution* (1943).

Morgan & Morgan, *Crisis*   Edmund S. Morgan & Helen M. Morgan, *The Stamp Act Crisis: Prologue to Revolution* (1953).

Morris, *Reconsidered*   Richard B. Morris, *The American Revolution Reconsidered* (1967).

Nelson, "Restraint"   William E. Nelson, "The Legal Restraint of Power in Pre-Revolutionary America: Massachusetts as a Case Study, 1760–1775," 18 *American Journal of Legal History* 1–32 (1974).

News-Letter   *The Massachusetts Gazette and Boston News-Letter*.

"Ordeal by Law"   "The Ordeal by Law of Thomas Hutchinson," 49 *New York University Law Review* 593–613 (1974).

Pierce, "Rowe"   Edward L. Pierce, "Introduction," to Rowe, "Diary."

Pitkin, *Civil History*   Timothy Pitkin, *A Political and Civil History of the United States of America From the Year 1763* (1828), vol. 1.

Post-Boy   *The Boston Post-Boy & Advertiser.*

Prior Documents   [John Almon], *A Collection of Interesting, Authentic Papers, Relative to the Dispute Between Great Britain and America; Shewing the Causes and Progress of that Misunderstanding From 1764 to 1775* (1777).

Protests   *A Complete Collection of the Lords' Protests, from the First Upon Record, in the Reign of Henry the Third, to the Present Time* (1767), vol. 2.

Protests of the Lords   *A Complete Collection of the Protests of the Lords With Historical Introductions 1741–1825* (James E. Thorold, editor, 1875), vol. 2.

Report of October 1769 "Report of the Committee appointed to vindicate the Town of Boston from the many false and malicious Asper-
sions contained in certain Letters and Memorials, written by Governor Bernard, General Gage, Commodore Hood, the Commissioners of
the American Board of Customs, and Others . . . , " 18 October 1769,
in *Town Records,* at 303–25.

Rowe, "Diary"   "Diary of John Rowe," 10 *Proceedings of the Massachusetts Historical Society* 11–108 (1895).

Sewall, "Opinion"   "Opinion of Attorney General Jonathan Sewall in
the Case of the Lydia, Given to the Commissioners of Customs at
Boston, April 23, 1768," 4 *William & Mary Quarterly* 501–4 (1947).

Shelburne Abstracts   Abstracts of Colonial Dispatches to the Earl of
Shelburne, *Shelburne Papers,* vols. 51 and 52 (ms.), The Clements
Library, Ann Arbor, Michigan.

Shipton, "Hutchinson"   Clifford K. Shipton, "Thomas Hutchinson," 8
Sibley's Harvard Graduates 1726–1730 149–217 (1951).

Shipton, "Sewall"   Clifford K. Shipton, "Jonathan Sewall," 12 *Sibley's
Harvard Graduates* 306–24 (1962).

Shirley, *Correspondence   Correspondence of William Shirley Governor
of Massachusetts and Military Commander in America 1731–1760*
(Charles Henry Lincoln, editor, 1912), vol. 1.

*Speeches   Speeches of the Governors of Massachusetts From 1765 to
1775; And the Answers of the House of Representatives to the Same;
with their Resolutions and Addresses for the Period* (1818).

Stark, *Loyalists*   James H. Stark, *The Loyalists of Massachusetts and
the Other Side of the American Revolution* (1910).

Stout, *Royal Navy*   Neil R. Stout, *The Royal Navy in America, 1760–
1775: A Study of Enforcement of British Colonial Policy in the Era of
the American Revolution* (1973).

Thomas, *British Politics*   P. D. G. Thomas, *British Politics and the
Stamp Act Crisis: The first phase of the American Revolution 1763–
1767* (1975).

*Town Records   A Report of the Record Commissioners of the City of
Boston Containing the Boston Town Records, 1758 to 1769* (Report
16, 1886).

Walett, "Bernard"   Francis G. Walett, "Governor Bernard's Undoing:
An Earlier Hutchinson Letter Affair," 38 *New England Quarterly*
217–26 (1965).

Warren, *Revolution*   Mercy Warren, *History of the Rise, Progress and
Termination of the American Revolution* (1805), vol. 1.

Waters, *Otis Family*   John J. Waters, Jr., *The Otis Family in Provincial and Revolutionary Massachusetts* (Norton Library edition, 1975).

Watson, "Harrison"   D. H. Watson, "Joseph Harrison and the *Liberty*
Incident," 20 *William & Mary Quarterly* 585–87 (1963).

Wertenbaker, *Puritan*   Thomas Jefferson Wertenbaker, *The Puritan
Oligarchy: The Founding of American Civilization* (1947).

Williamson, "Destruction"   "Destruction of the Tea in the Harbor of
Boston, December 16, 1773," 4 *Collections Massachusetts Historical
Society* 373–86 (1858).

Wolkins, "Liberty"   George G. Wolkins, "The Seizure of John Hancock's Sloop 'Liberty,' " 55 *Massachusetts Historical Society Proceedings* 239–84 (1922).

Wolkins, "Malcom"   George G. Wolkins, "Daniel Malcom and Writs of Assistance," 58 *Massachusetts Historical Society Proceedings* 5–87 (1924).

Wolkins, "Paxton"   George G. Wolkins, "Letters of Charles Paxton," 56 *Massachusetts Historical Society Proceedings* 343–52 (1923).

Wolkins, "Writs"   George G. Wolkins, "Bollan on Writs of Assistance," 59 *Massachusetts Historical Society Proceedings* 414–19 (1926).

Wood, "Mobs"   Gordon S. Wood, "A Note on Mobs in the American Revolution," 23 *William & Mary Quarterly* 635–42 (1966).

Wright, *Freedom*   Esmond Wright, *Fabric of Freedom 1763–1800* (1961).

Zobel, *Massacre*   Hiller B. Zobel, *The Boston Massacre* (1970).

Acknowledgments

This study is the second I have written for The Pennsylvania State University Press on the subject of the conditions of law during the prerevolutionary era. The first volume was entitled *In a Defiant Stance: The Conditions of Law in Massachusetts Bay, the Irish Comparison, and the Coming of the American Revolution.* As with the first book, much is owed to the many friends and associates who aided the research and execution of this publication. It was Jane Gordon Walsh of Atherton, California, who, during a trip to Salinas, persuasively demonstrated the validity of Franklin Pierce's interpretation of the Malcom affair. Debts of gratitude are also due to Wendy Van Bellingham, Lisa G. Zimmermann, and Mary W. Smith. Irvin Brum checked all citations for accuracy of both quotations and substantive arguments. It goes without saying that the responsibility for correctness is his alone. This book was published sooner than it otherwise would have been thanks to the generosity of Dean Norman Redlich and the trustees of the Law Center Foundation of New York University School of Law. Finally, mention must be made of Professor William E. Nelson of Yale Law School. As usual, Professor Nelson succeeded in cutting the original manuscript almost in half. As he says, the work is now more "tight" and the theme more manageable, but lamentably at the cost of consigning many gems of history to the waste basket.

Vanderbilt Hall
Washington Square
1 January 1978

JOHN PHILLIP REID

Index

TE DU